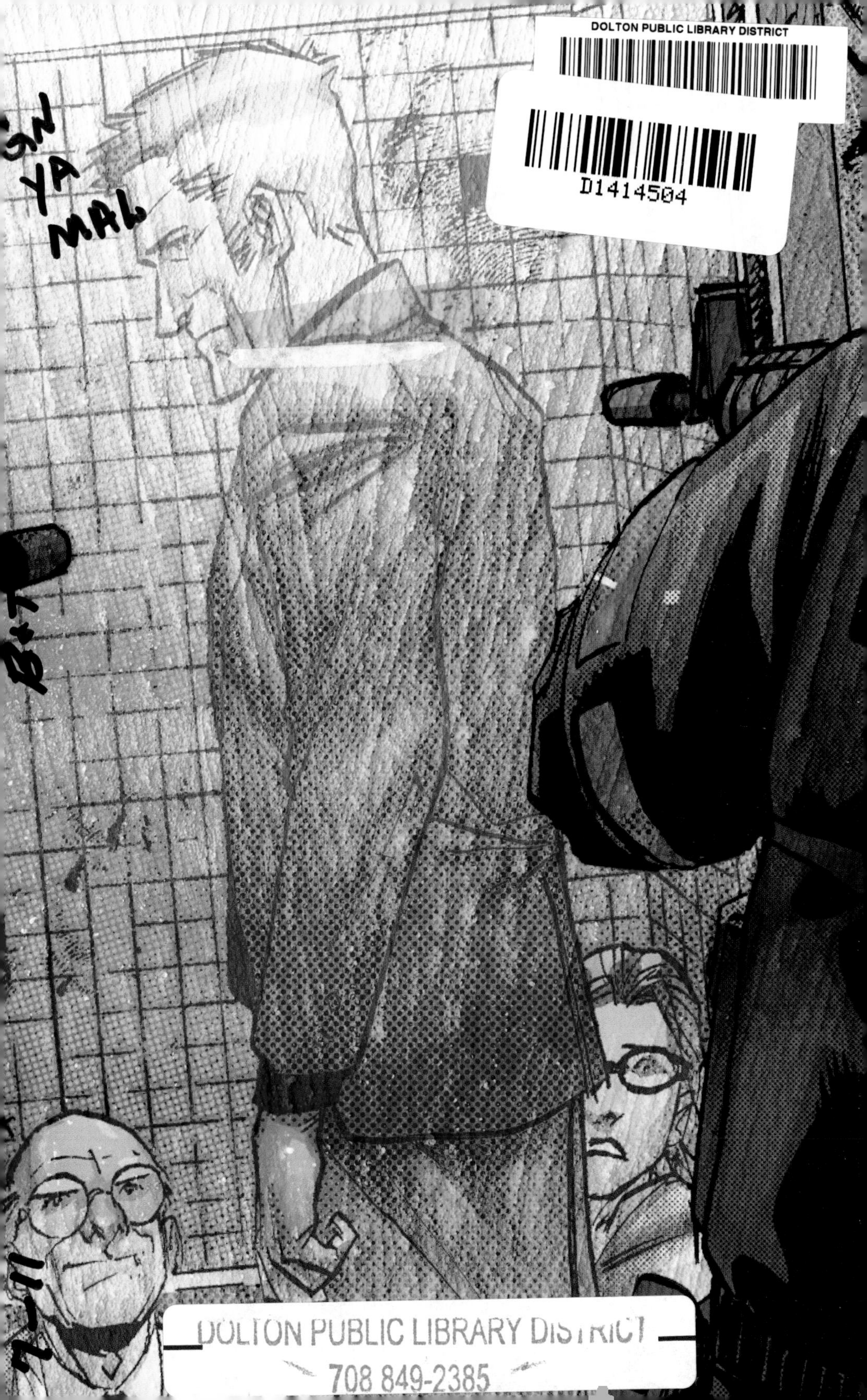

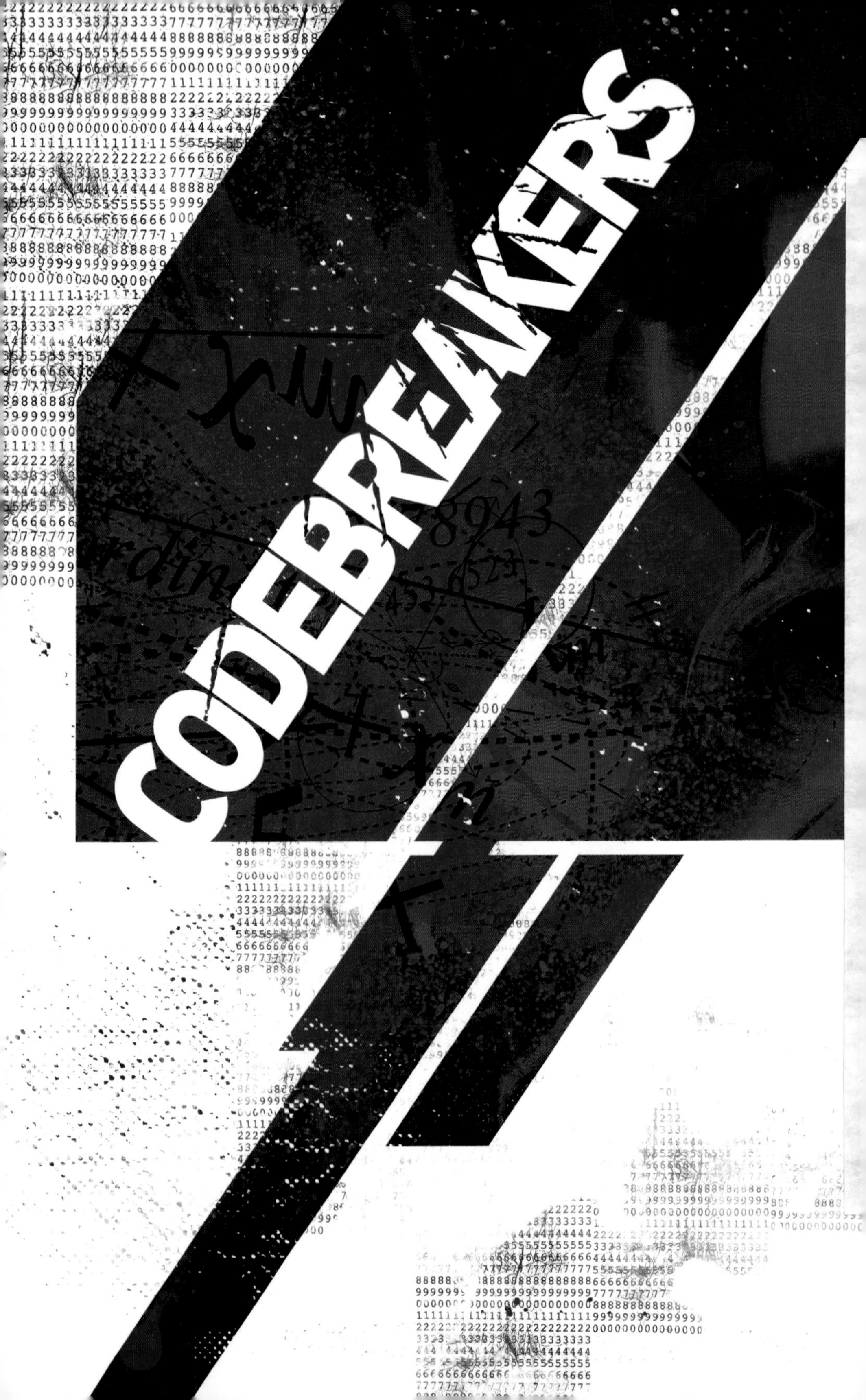
CODEBREAKERS

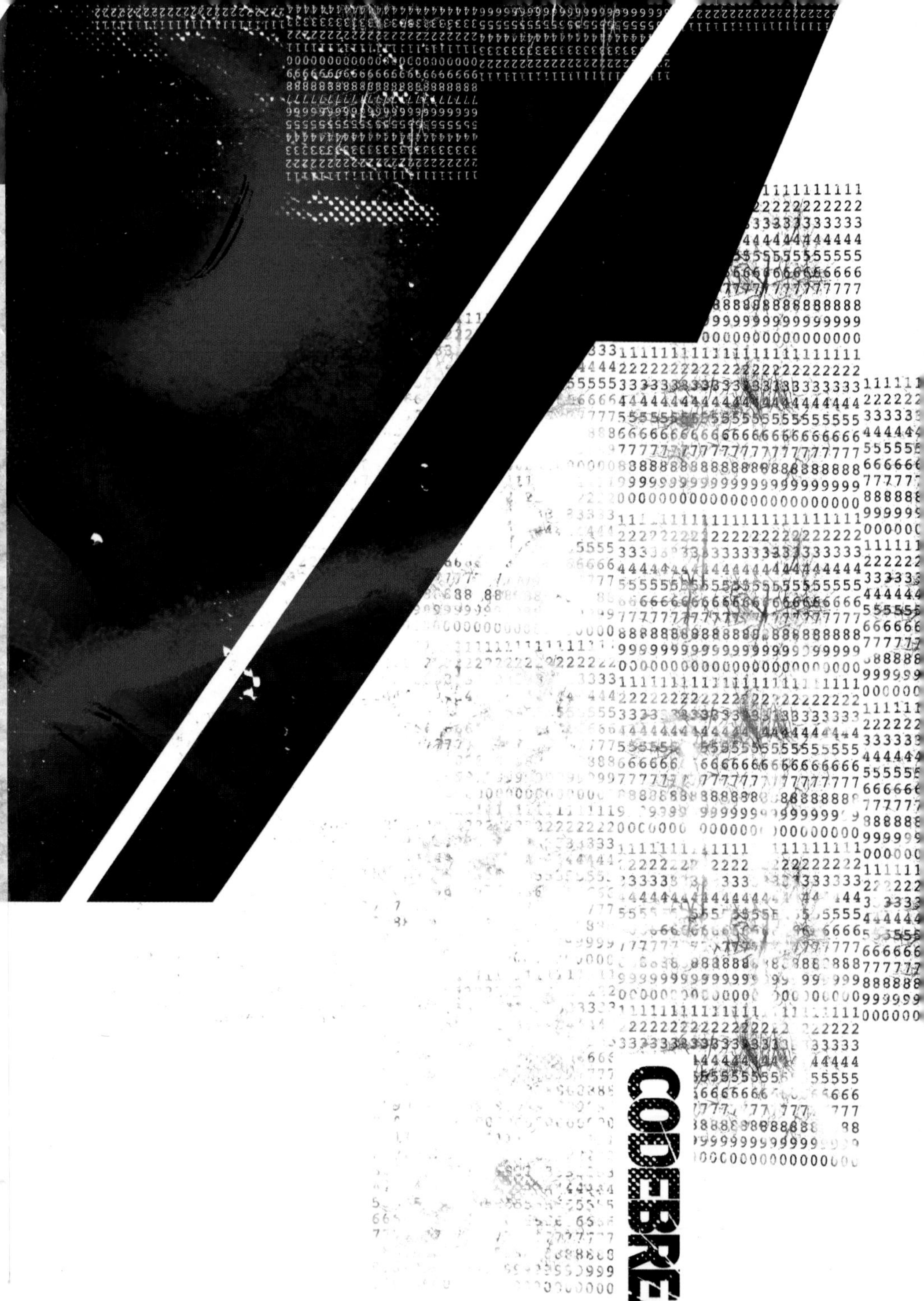

CODEBREAKERS

CREATED BY:
ROSS RICHIE

WRITTEN BY:
CAREY MALLOY

ARTIST:
SCOTT GODLEWSKI

COLORIST: STEPHEN DOWNER
LETTERER: JOHNNY LOWE
COVER: JULIAN TOTINO TEDESCO

EDITOR: DAFNA PLEBAN
TRADE DESIGN: BRIAN LATIMER

BOOM! STUDIOS

Ross Richie - Chief Executive Officer
Mark Waid - Chief Creative Officer
Matt Gagnon - Editor-in-Chief
Adam Fortier - VP-New Business
Wes Harris - VP-Publishing
Lance Kreiter - VP-Licensing & Merchandising
Chip Mosher - Marketing Director

Ian Brill - Editor
Bryce Carlson - Editor
Dafna Pleban - Editor
Christopher Meyer - Editor
Shannon Watters - Assistant Editor
Christopher Burns - Assistant Editor
Jason Long - Assistant Editor

Neil Loughrie - Publishing Coordinator
Travis Beatty - Traffic Coordinator
Ivan Salazar - Marketing Assistant
Kate Hayden - Executive Assistant
Brian Latimer - Graphic Designer
Erika Terriquez - Graphic Designer

A catalog record for this book is available from OCLC and on our website www.boom-studios.com on the Librarians page.

First Edition: August 2010
10 9 8 7 6 5 4 3 2 1
Printed in Canada

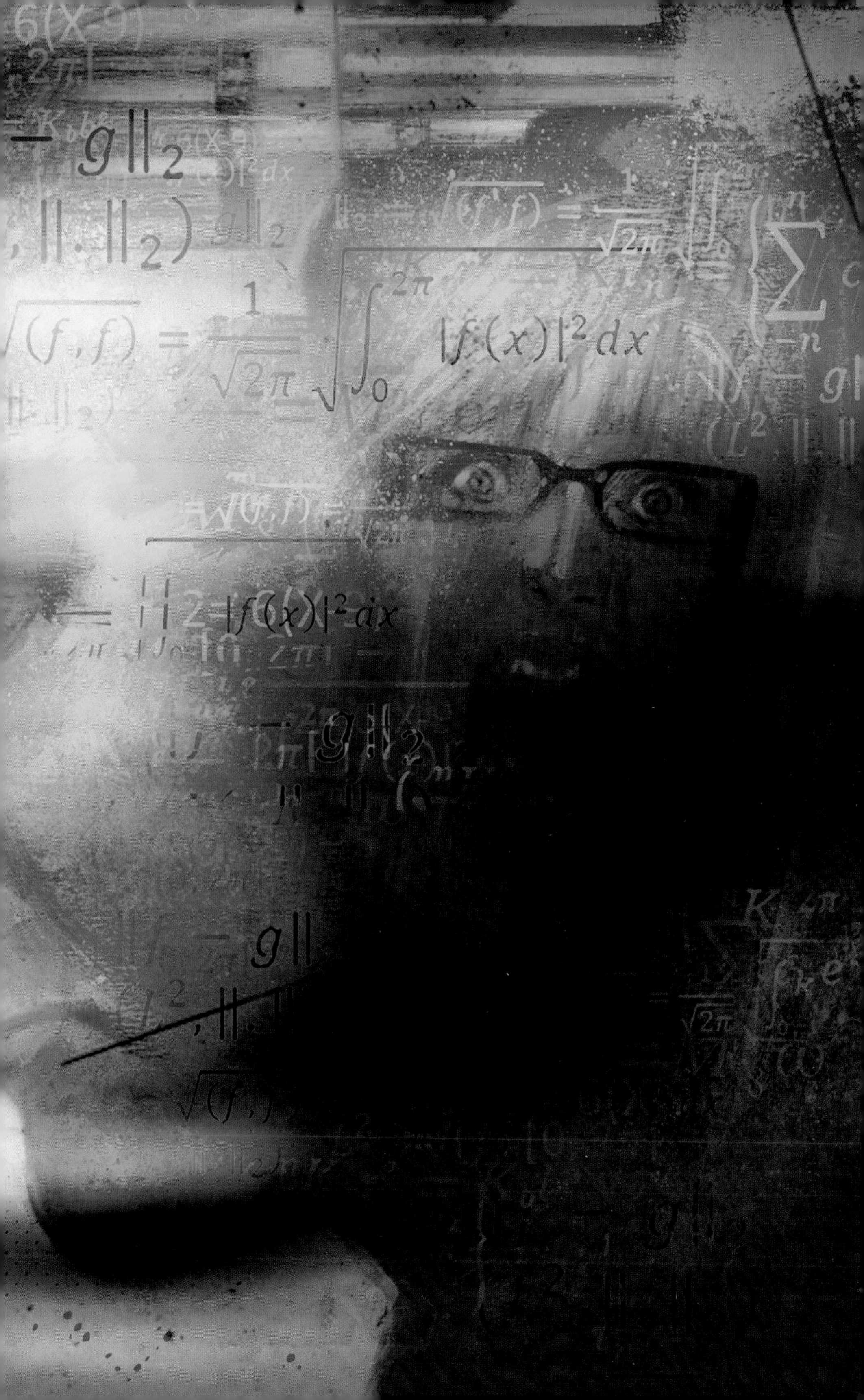
$\sqrt{(f,f)} = \frac{1}{\sqrt{2\pi}} \sqrt{\int_0^{2\pi} |f(x)|^2 dx}$

CHAPTER: ONE

CODE BREAKERS

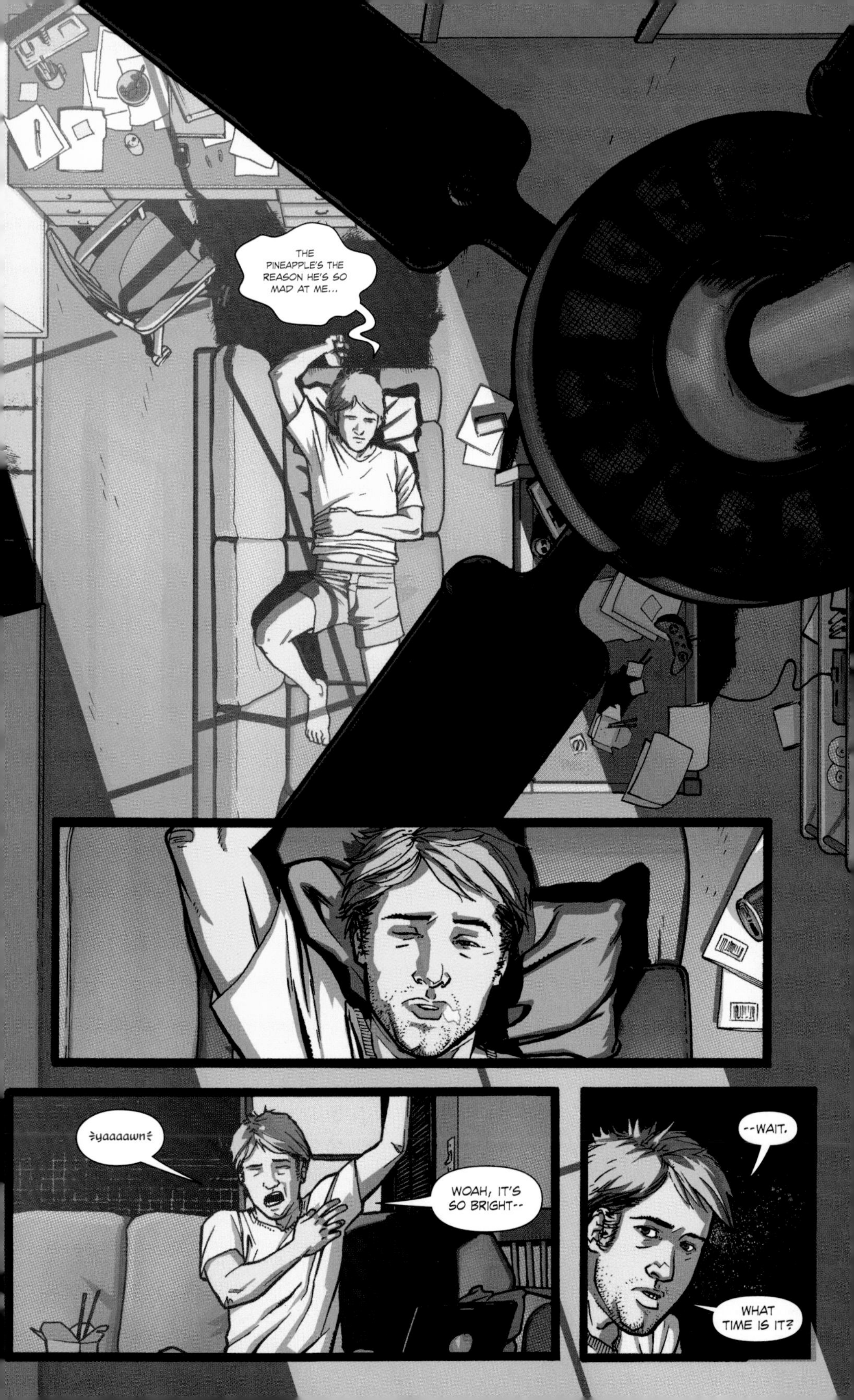
THE PINEAPPLE'S THE REASON HE'S SO MAD AT ME...
yaaaawn
WOAH, IT'S SO BRIGHT--
--WAIT.
WHAT TIME IS IT?

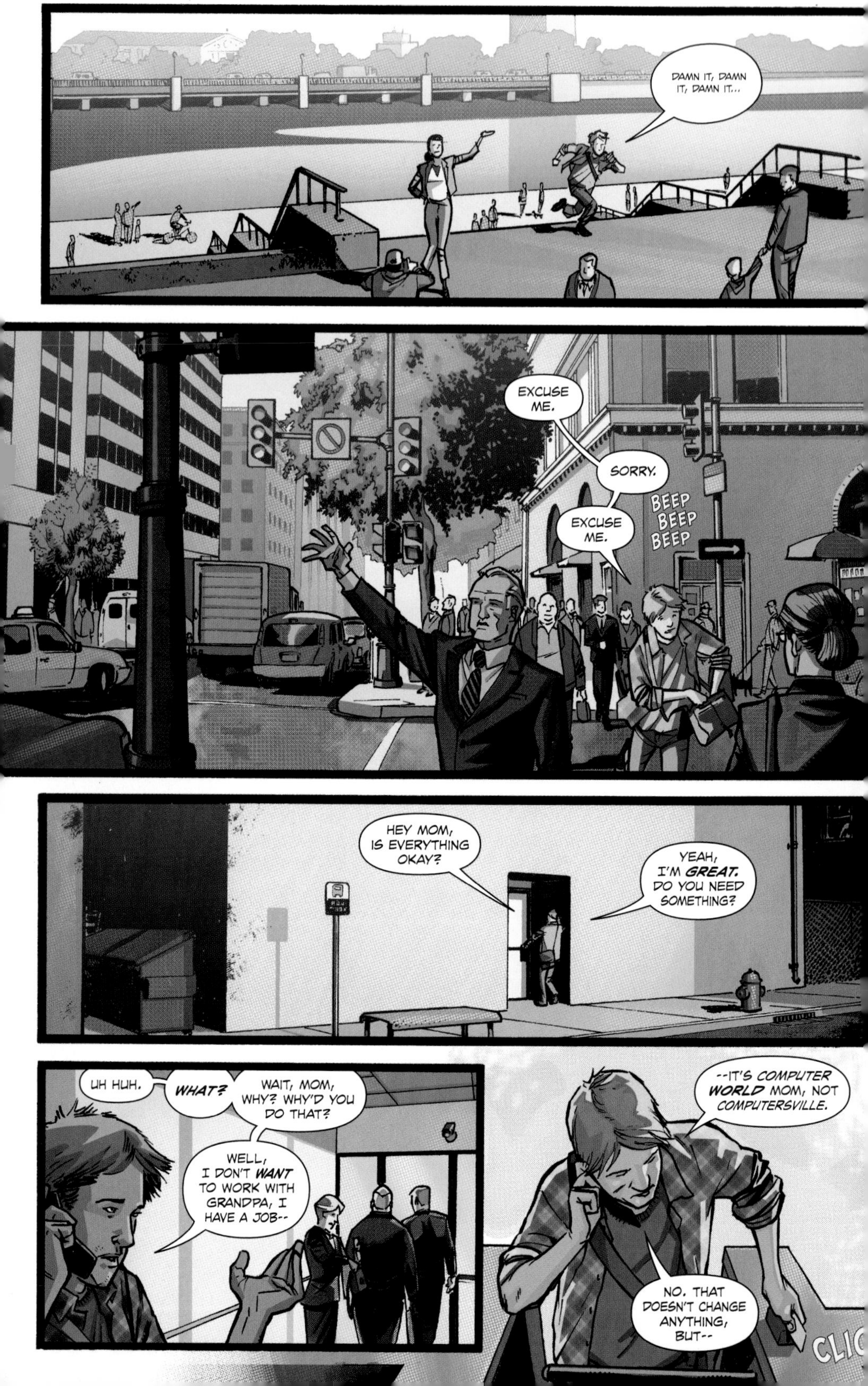
DAMN IT, DAMN IT, DAMN IT...
EXCUSE ME.
SORRY.
EXCUSE ME.
BEEP BEEP BEEP
HEY MOM, IS EVERYTHING OKAY?
YEAH, I'M *GREAT.* DO YOU NEED SOMETHING?
UH HUH.
WHAT?
WAIT, MOM, WHY? WHY'D YOU DO THAT?
WELL, I DON'T *WANT* TO WORK WITH GRANDPA, I HAVE A JOB--
--IT'S *COMPUTER WORLD* MOM, NOT COMPUTERSVILLE.
NO. THAT DOESN'T CHANGE ANYTHING, BUT--
CLIC

--YES, I KNOW IT'S NOT THE *GREATEST* OPPORTUNITY FOR ADVANCEMENT AND YES, I ALSO KNOW IT ISN'T A GOOD USE OF A BRAIN LIKE MINE, BUT I LIKE MY JOB...

I DO TOO!

LISTEN, MOM? I HAVE TO HANG UP NOW, OKAY?

I DO.

I DID SAY IT. JUST A SECOND AGO.

I LOVE YOU TOO, MOM.

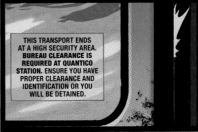

THIS TRANSPORT ENDS AT A HIGH SECURITY AREA. BUREAU CLEARANCE IS REQUIRED AT QUANTICO STATION. ENSURE YOU HAVE PROPER CLEARANCE AND IDENTIFICATION OR YOU WILL BE DETAINED.

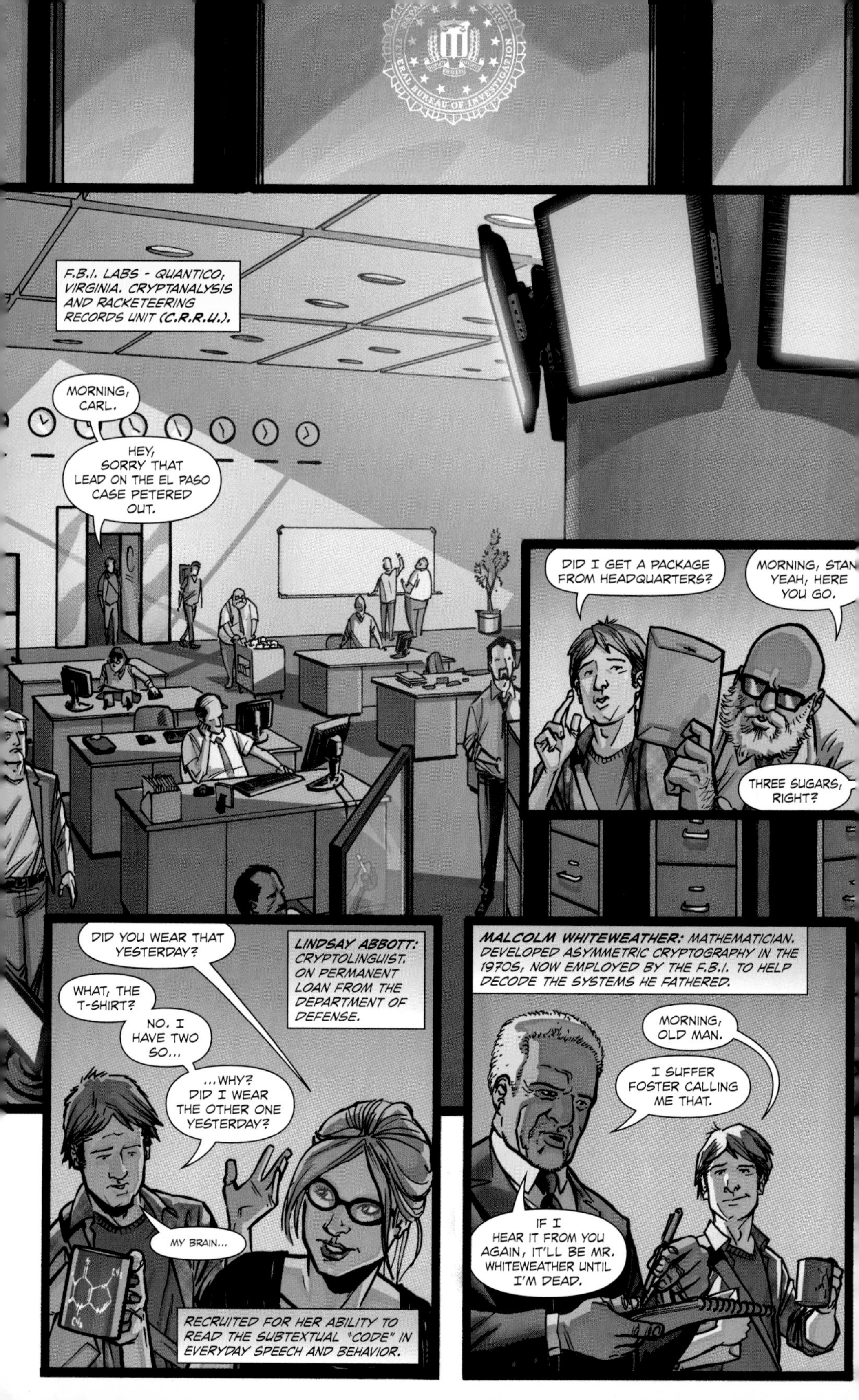
F.B.I. LABS - QUANTICO, VIRGINIA. CRYPTANALYSIS AND RACKETEERING RECORDS UNIT (C.R.R.U.).
MORNING, CARL.
HEY, SORRY THAT LEAD ON THE EL PASO CASE PETERED OUT.
DID I GET A PACKAGE FROM HEADQUARTERS?
MORNING, STAN YEAH, HERE YOU GO.
THREE SUGARS, RIGHT?
DID YOU WEAR THAT YESTERDAY?
LINDSAY ABBOTT: CRYPTOLINGUIST. ON PERMANENT LOAN FROM THE DEPARTMENT OF DEFENSE.
WHAT, THE T-SHIRT?
NO. I HAVE TWO SO...
...WHY? DID I WEAR THE OTHER ONE YESTERDAY?
MY BRAIN...
RECRUITED FOR HER ABILITY TO READ THE SUBTEXTUAL "CODE" IN EVERYDAY SPEECH AND BEHAVIOR.
MALCOLM WHITEWEATHER: MATHEMATICIAN. DEVELOPED ASYMMETRIC CRYPTOGRAPHY IN THE 1970S, NOW EMPLOYED BY THE F.B.I. TO HELP DECODE THE SYSTEMS HE FATHERED.
MORNING, OLD MAN.
I SUFFER FOSTER CALLING ME THAT.
IF I HEAR IT FROM YOU AGAIN, IT'LL BE MR. WHITEWEATHER UNTIL I'M DEAD.

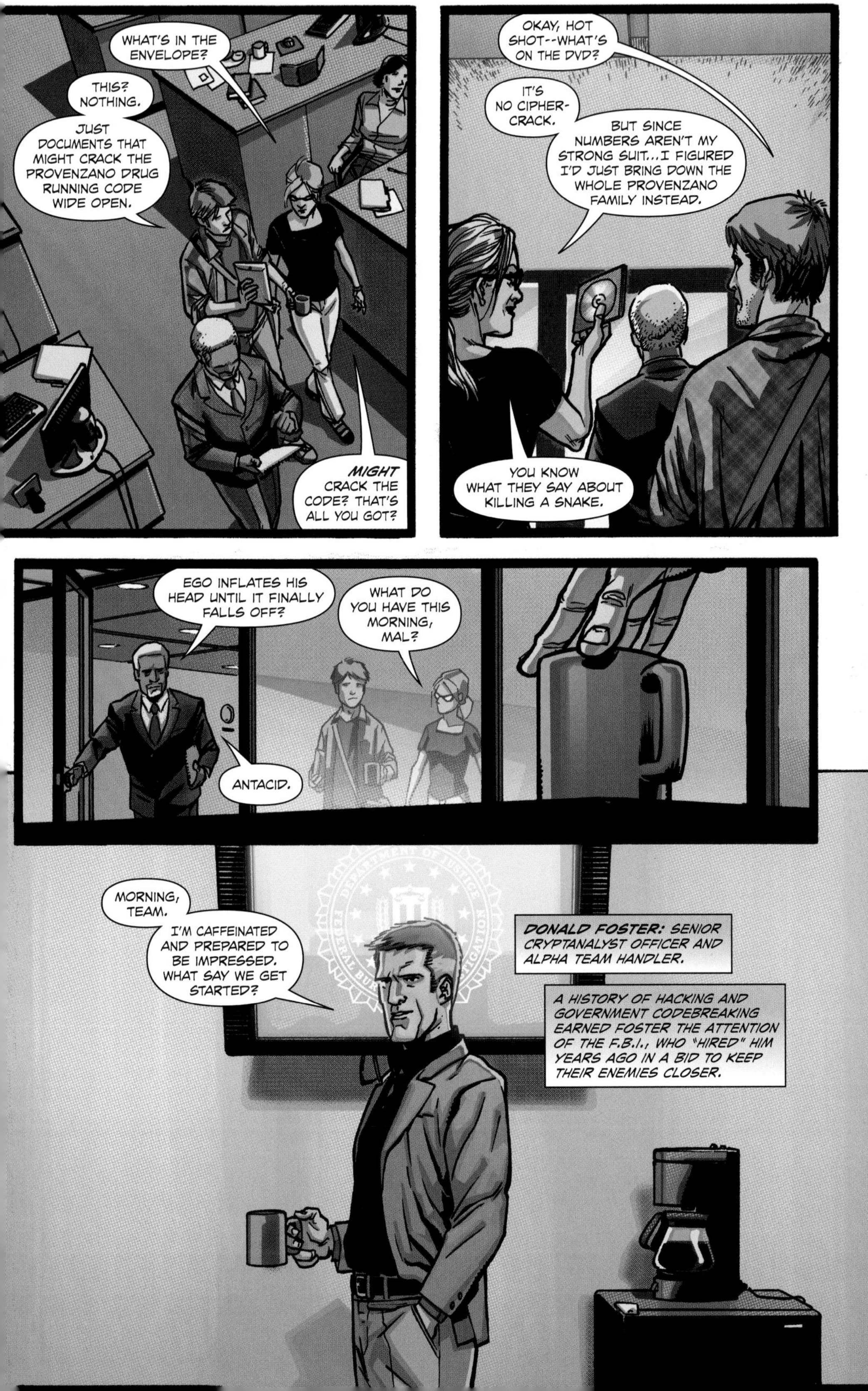
WHAT'S IN THE ENVELOPE?
THIS? NOTHING.
JUST DOCUMENTS THAT MIGHT CRACK THE PROVENZANO DRUG RUNNING CODE WIDE OPEN.
MIGHT CRACK THE CODE? THAT'S ALL YOU GOT?
OKAY, HOT SHOT--WHAT'S ON THE DVD?
IT'S NO CIPHER-CRACK.
BUT SINCE NUMBERS AREN'T MY STRONG SUIT...I FIGURED I'D JUST BRING DOWN THE WHOLE PROVENZANO FAMILY INSTEAD.
YOU KNOW WHAT THEY SAY ABOUT KILLING A SNAKE.
EGO INFLATES HIS HEAD UNTIL IT FINALLY FALLS OFF?
WHAT DO YOU HAVE THIS MORNING, MAL?
ANTACID.
MORNING, TEAM.
I'M CAFFEINATED AND PREPARED TO BE IMPRESSED. WHAT SAY WE GET STARTED?
DONALD FOSTER: SENIOR CRYPTANALYST OFFICER AND ALPHA TEAM HANDLER.
A HISTORY OF HACKING AND GOVERNMENT CODEBREAKING EARNED FOSTER THE ATTENTION OF THE F.B.I., WHO "HIRED" HIM YEARS AGO IN A BID TO KEEP THEIR ENEMIES CLOSER.

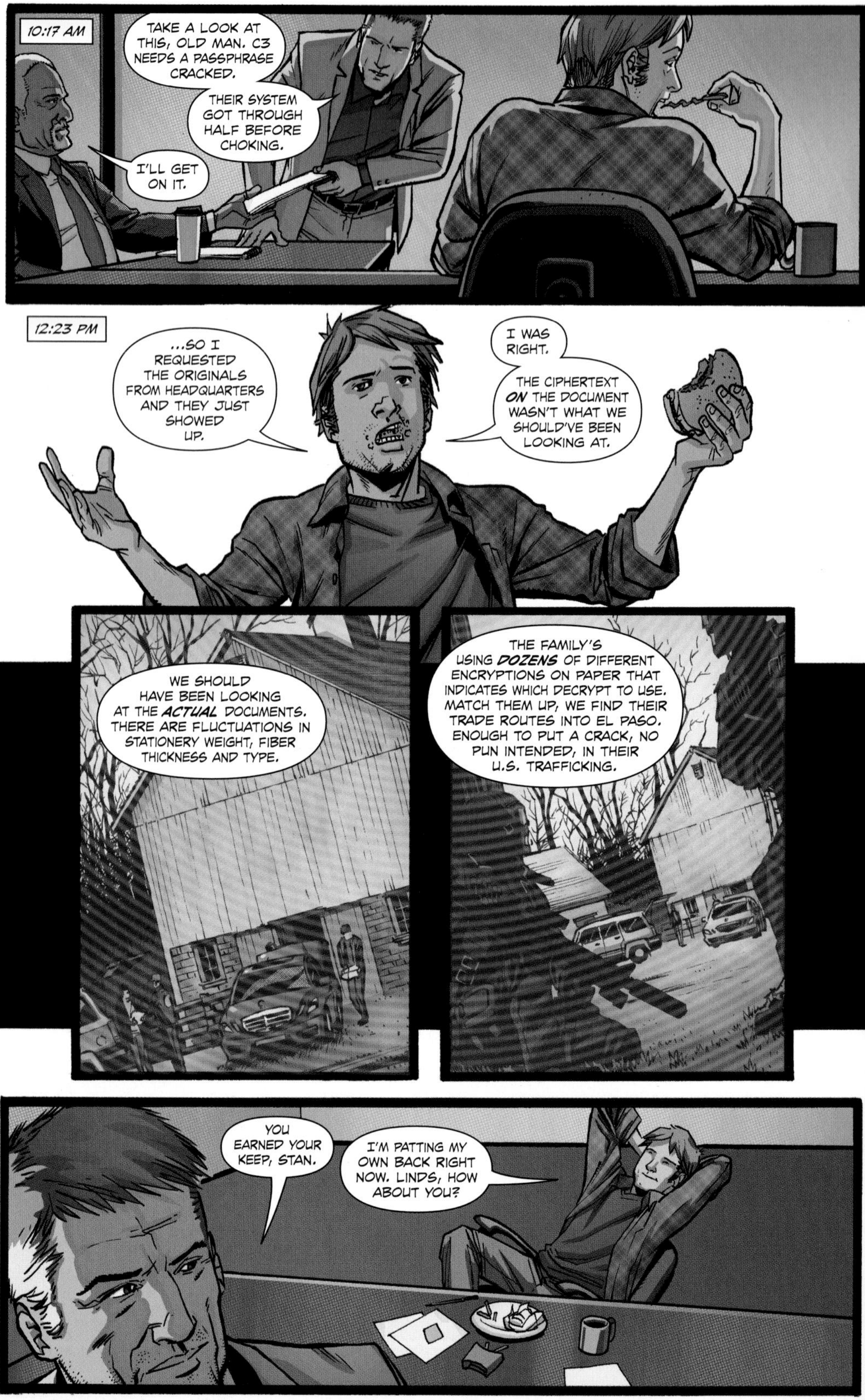
10:17 AM
TAKE A LOOK AT THIS, OLD MAN. C3 NEEDS A PASSPHRASE CRACKED.
THEIR SYSTEM GOT THROUGH HALF BEFORE CHOKING.
I'LL GET ON IT.
12:23 PM
...SO I REQUESTED THE ORIGINALS FROM HEADQUARTERS AND THEY JUST SHOWED UP.
I WAS RIGHT.
THE CIPHERTEXT *ON* THE DOCUMENT WASN'T WHAT WE SHOULD'VE BEEN LOOKING AT.
WE SHOULD HAVE BEEN LOOKING AT THE *ACTUAL* DOCUMENTS. THERE ARE FLUCTUATIONS IN STATIONERY WEIGHT, FIBER THICKNESS AND TYPE.
THE FAMILY'S USING *DOZENS* OF DIFFERENT ENCRYPTIONS ON PAPER THAT INDICATES WHICH DECRYPT TO USE. MATCH THEM UP, WE FIND THEIR TRADE ROUTES INTO EL PASO. ENOUGH TO PUT A CRACK, NO PUN INTENDED, IN THEIR U.S. TRAFFICKING.
YOU EARNED YOUR KEEP, STAN.
I'M PATTING MY OWN BACK RIGHT NOW. LINDS, HOW ABOUT YOU?

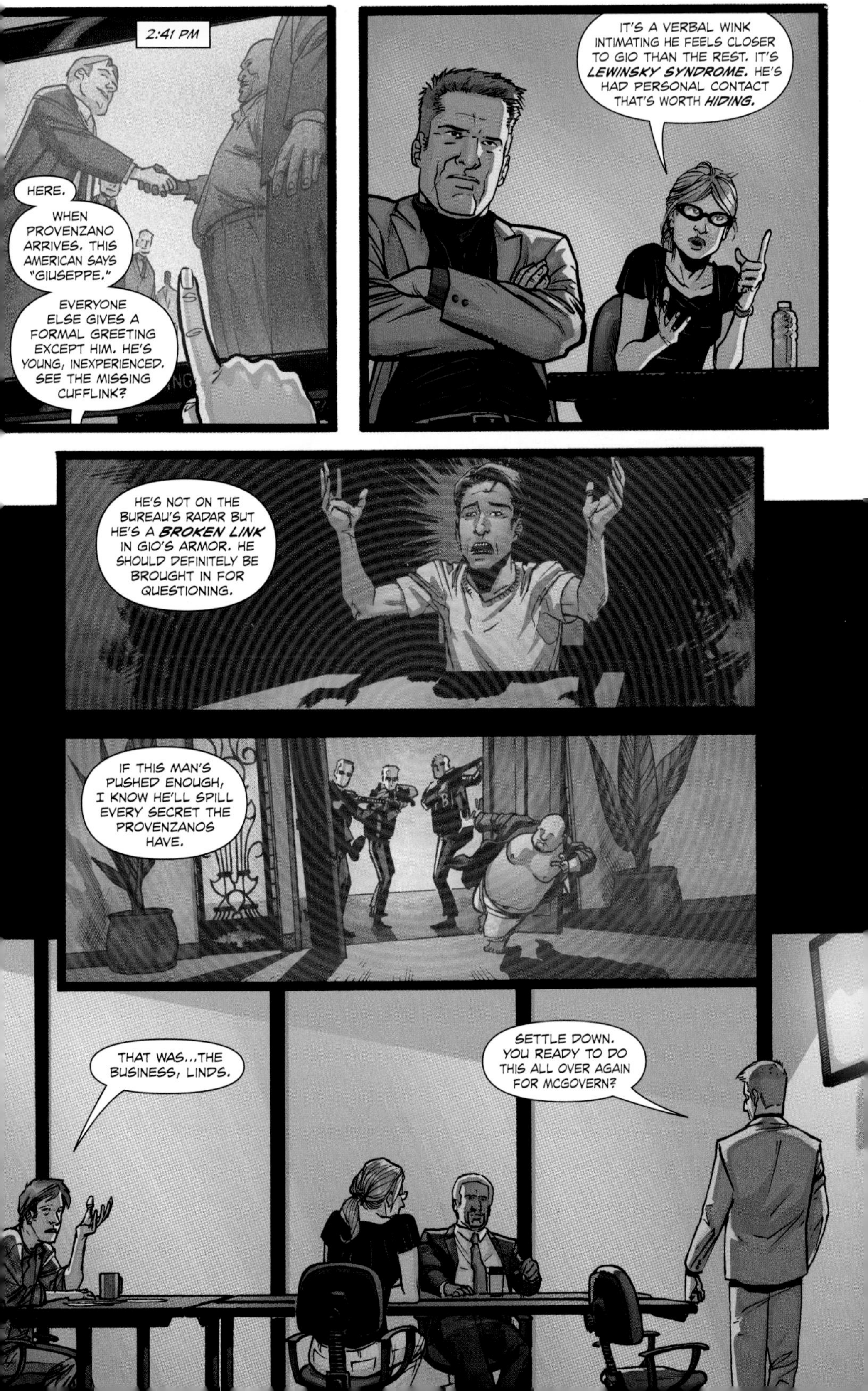
2:41 PM
HERE.
WHEN PROVENZANO ARRIVES, THIS AMERICAN SAYS "GIUSEPPE."
EVERYONE ELSE GIVES A FORMAL GREETING EXCEPT HIM. HE'S YOUNG, INEXPERIENCED. SEE THE MISSING CUFFLINK?
IT'S A VERBAL WINK INTIMATING HE FEELS CLOSER TO GIO THAN THE REST. IT'S LEWINSKY SYNDROME. HE'S HAD PERSONAL CONTACT THAT'S WORTH HIDING.
HE'S NOT ON THE BUREAU'S RADAR BUT HE'S A BROKEN LINK IN GIO'S ARMOR. HE SHOULD DEFINITELY BE BROUGHT IN FOR QUESTIONING.
IF THIS MAN'S PUSHED ENOUGH, I KNOW HE'LL SPILL EVERY SECRET THE PROVENZANOS HAVE.
THAT WAS...THE BUSINESS, LINDS.
SETTLE DOWN. YOU READY TO DO THIS ALL OVER AGAIN FOR MCGOVERN?

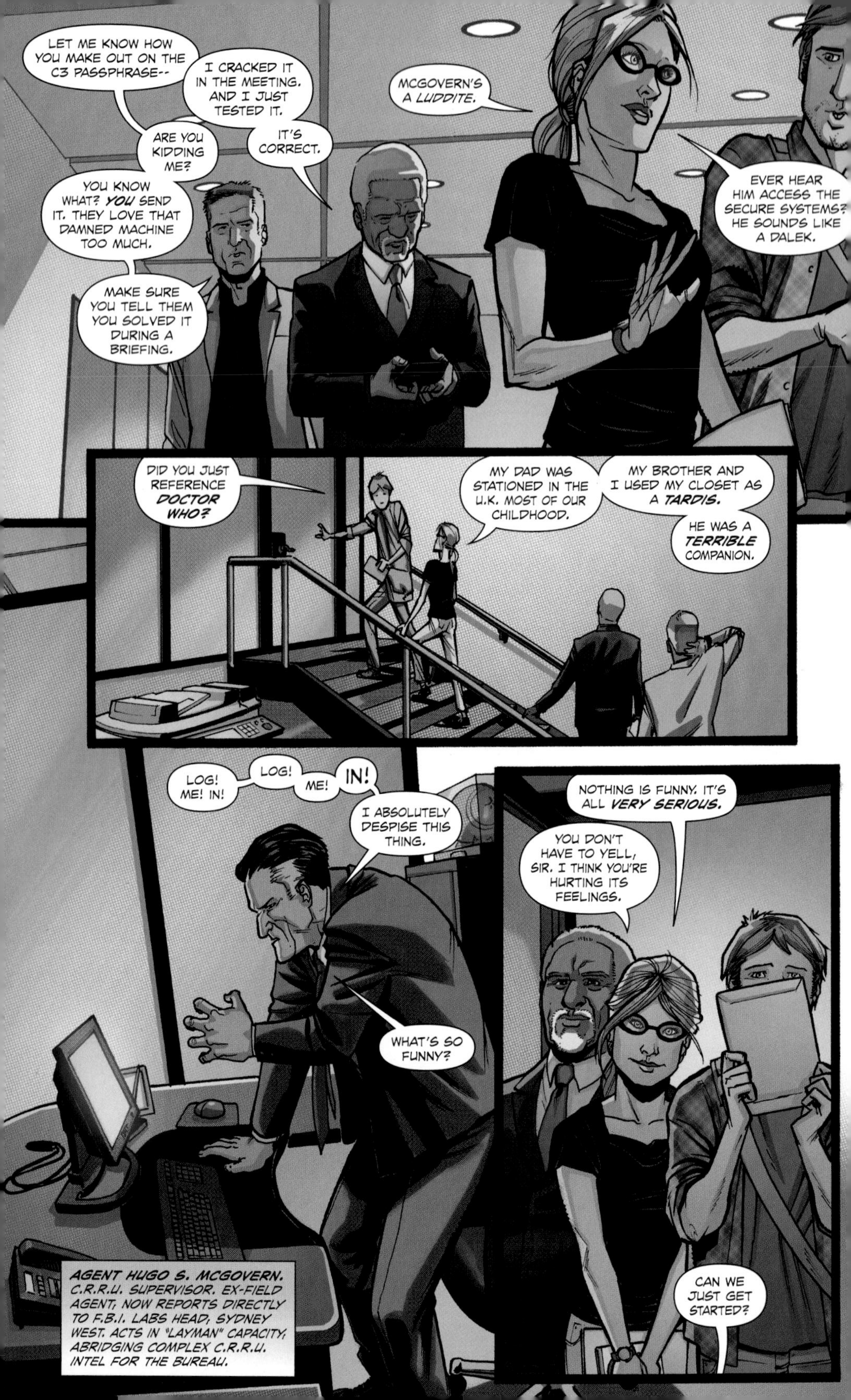
LET ME KNOW HOW YOU MAKE OUT ON THE C3 PASSPHRASE--
I CRACKED IT IN THE MEETING. AND I JUST TESTED IT.
MCGOVERN'S A *LUDDITE.*
ARE YOU KIDDING ME?
IT'S JUST CORRECT.
YOU KNOW WHAT? ***YOU*** SEND IT. THEY LOVE THAT DAMNED MACHINE TOO MUCH.
EVER HEAR HIM ACCESS THE SECURE SYSTEMS? HE SOUNDS LIKE A DALEK.
MAKE SURE YOU TELL THEM YOU SOLVED IT DURING A BRIEFING.
DID YOU JUST REFERENCE ***DOCTOR WHO?***
MY DAD WAS STATIONED IN THE U.K. MOST OF OUR CHILDHOOD.
MY BROTHER AND I USED MY CLOSET AS A ***TARDIS.***
HE WAS A ***TERRIBLE*** COMPANION.
LOG! ME! IN!
LOG!
ME!
IN!
I ABSOLUTELY DESPISE THIS THING.
WHAT'S SO FUNNY?
NOTHING IS FUNNY. IT'S ALL ***VERY SERIOUS.***
YOU DON'T HAVE TO YELL, SIR. I THINK YOU'RE HURTING ITS FEELINGS.
AGENT HUGO S. MCGOVERN. *C.R.R.U. SUPERVISOR. EX-FIELD AGENT, NOW REPORTS DIRECTLY TO F.B.I. LABS HEAD, SYDNEY WEST. ACTS IN "LAYMAN" CAPACITY; ABRIDGING COMPLEX C.R.R.U. INTEL FOR THE BUREAU.*
CAN WE JUST GET STARTED?

7:39 PM

≶sigh≷

"MAY I HOLD THE DOOR FOR YOU, LINDSAY?"

"WHY OF COURSE YOU CAN, *GUY I DON'T KNOW.* I DON'T MEAN TO BE FORWARD, BUT WOULD YOU LIKE TO BE MY COMPANION?"

"I *AM A TIME LORD* AFTER ALL."

✉ **Unknown Sender**
Try and solve this, hotshot.

dwie\eAaa=afjdsldw+w33=3Bm[alWl4
djNmfmaKerikwg[a[Pdsfw[a[dmSdslmf
pgvkdmklepfvpogktlelso\skwklrpvock
w=FOvkfrfsxlcklekpw+Epfkvpr5tk0mn
zsqw2p40yjthLAldleMl4lkpaodKN\wel
bndnekklerrgsbx,dlkmwkojeomdfm+sa
fniero+pDmmdmlskweeort98GjhnasH
wgerm4vamsdsmemlrgsmwlmeelmlgl
smwelrmr21+\e35mbgkdj3hwhpky7m
                        \g1mxi4ufDRiPkN

SERIOUSLY, MALCOLM?

I APPRECIATE THE EFFORT, BUT...

...CHALLENGE ACCEPTED!

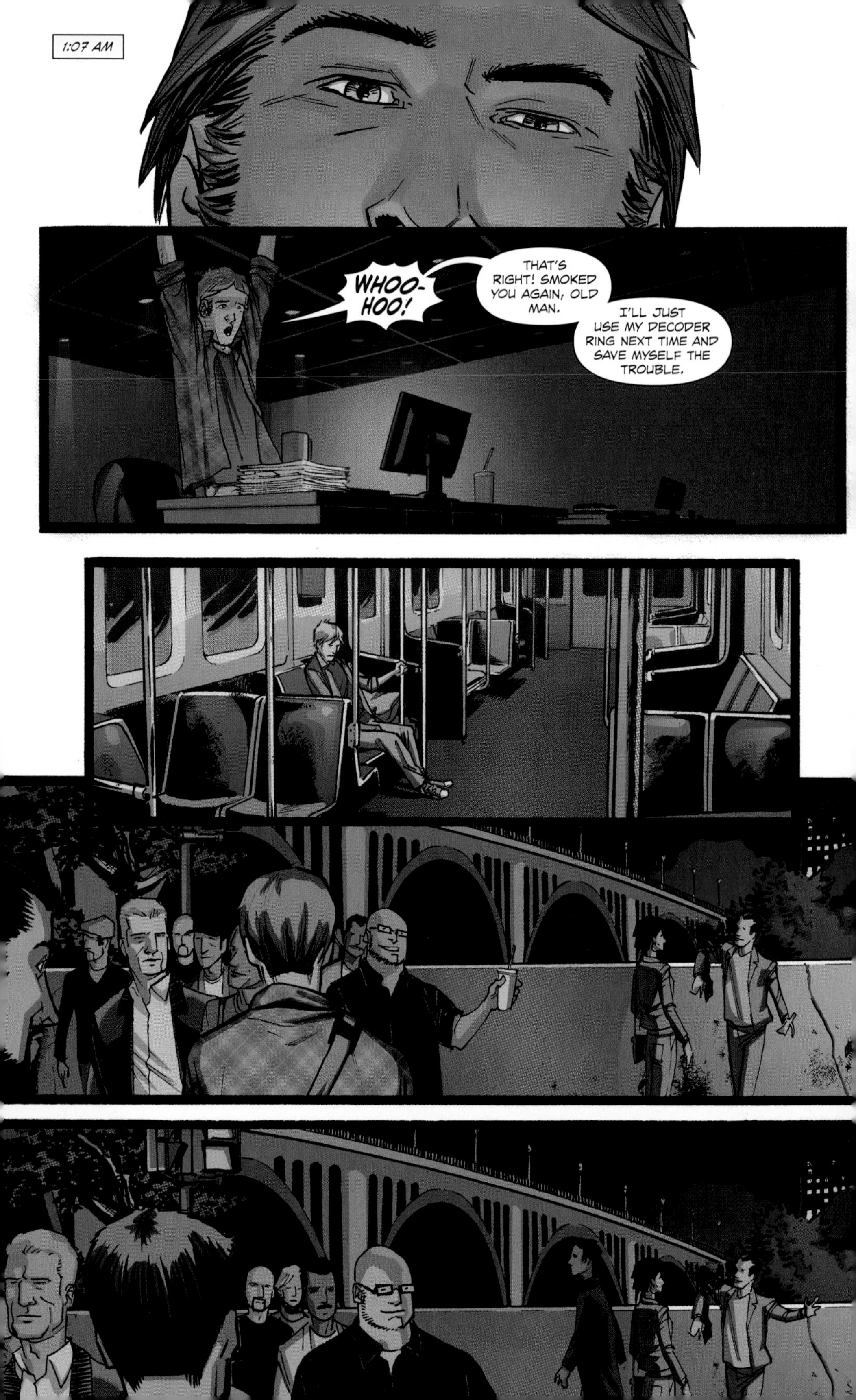
1:07 AM
WHOO-HOO!
THAT'S RIGHT! SMOKED YOU AGAIN, OLD MAN.
I'LL JUST USE MY DECODER RING NEXT TIME AND SAVE MYSELF THE TROUBLE.

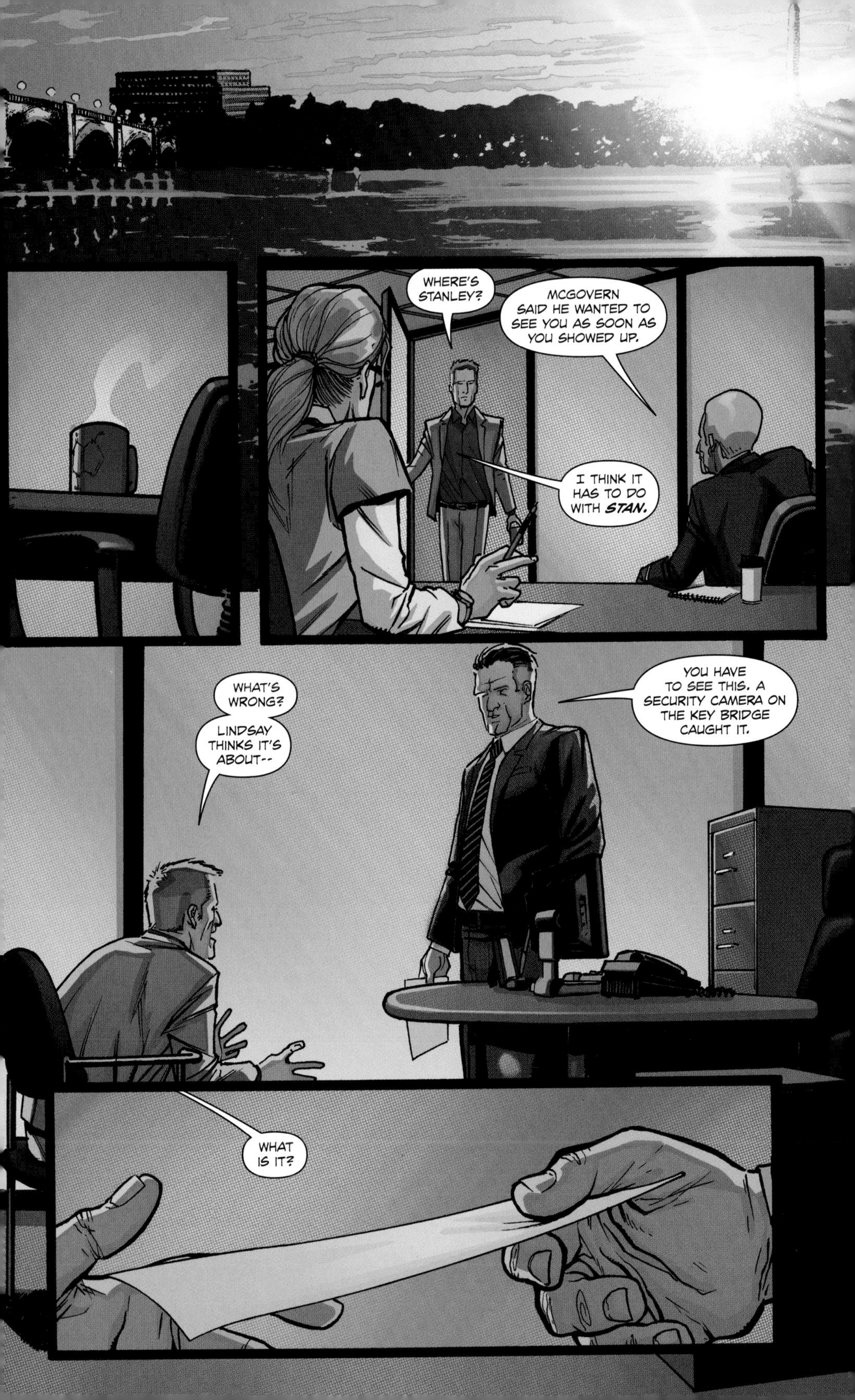
WHERE'S STANLEY?
MCGOVERN SAID HE WANTED TO SEE YOU AS SOON AS YOU SHOWED UP.
I THINK IT HAS TO DO WITH *STAN.*
WHAT'S WRONG?
LINDSAY THINKS IT'S ABOUT--
YOU HAVE TO SEE THIS. A SECURITY CAMERA ON THE KEY BRIDGE CAUGHT IT.
WHAT IS IT?

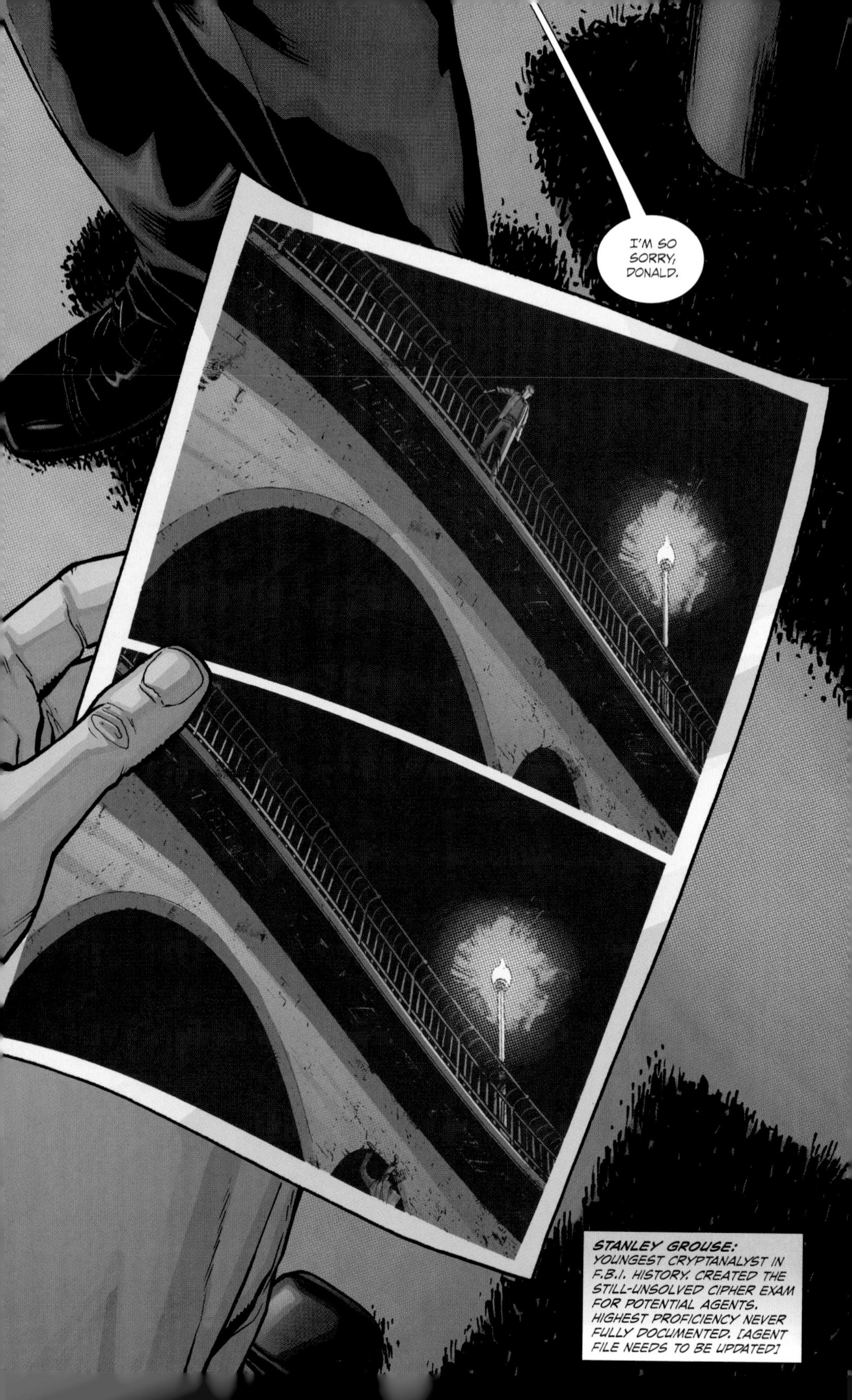
I'M SO SORRY, DONALD.
STANLEY GROUSE: YOUNGEST CRYPTANALYST IN F.B.I. HISTORY. CREATED THE STILL-UNSOLVED CIPHER EXAM FOR POTENTIAL AGENTS. HIGHEST PROFICIENCY NEVER FULLY DOCUMENTED. [AGENT FILE NEEDS TO BE UPDATED]

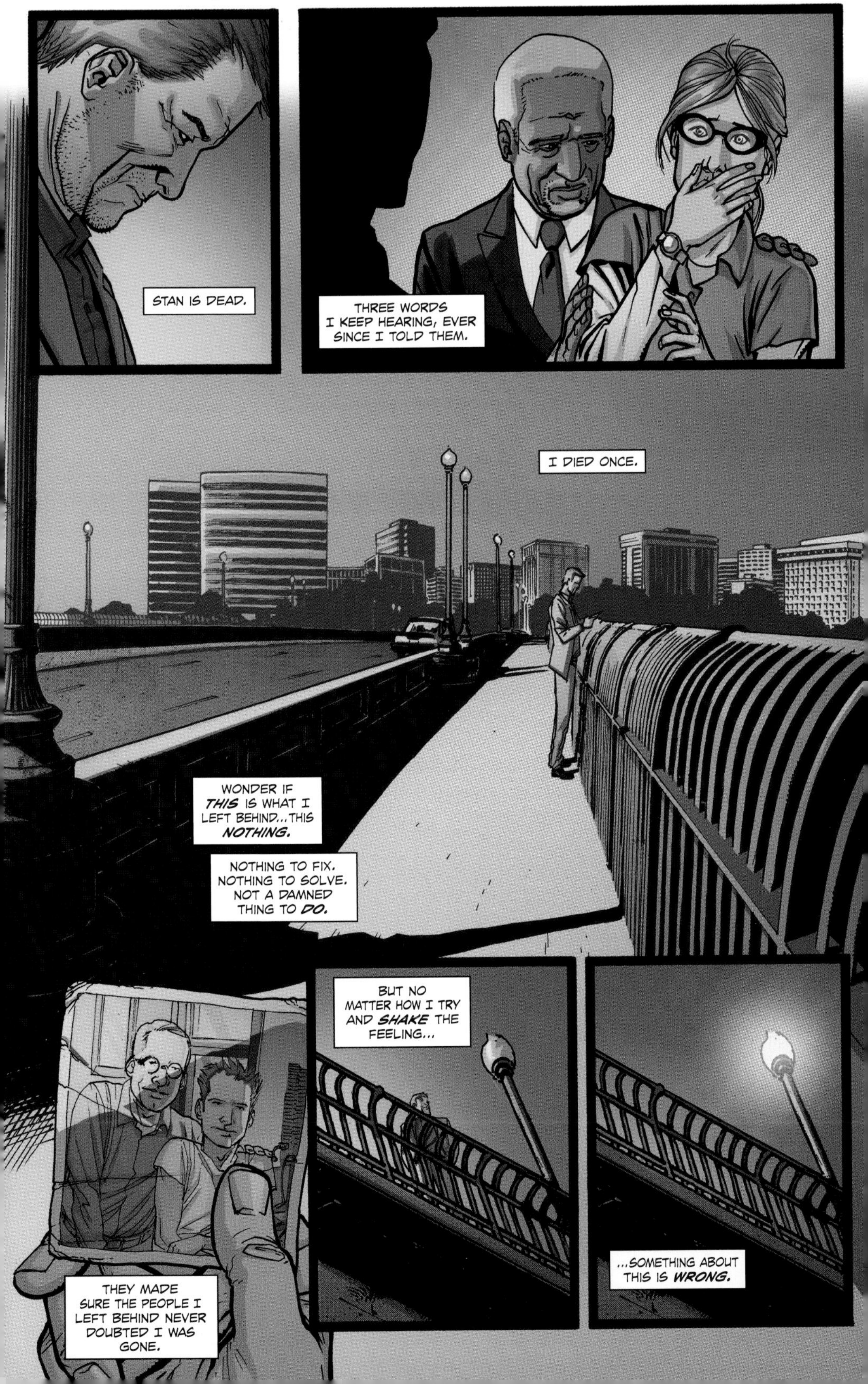
STAN IS DEAD.
THREE WORDS I KEEP HEARING, EVER SINCE I TOLD THEM.
I DIED ONCE.
WONDER IF THIS IS WHAT I LEFT BEHIND...THIS NOTHING.
NOTHING TO FIX. NOTHING TO SOLVE. NOT A DAMNED THING TO DO.
THEY MADE SURE THE PEOPLE I LEFT BEHIND NEVER DOUBTED I WAS GONE.
BUT NO MATTER HOW I TRY AND SHAKE THE FEELING...
...SOMETHING ABOUT THIS IS WRONG.

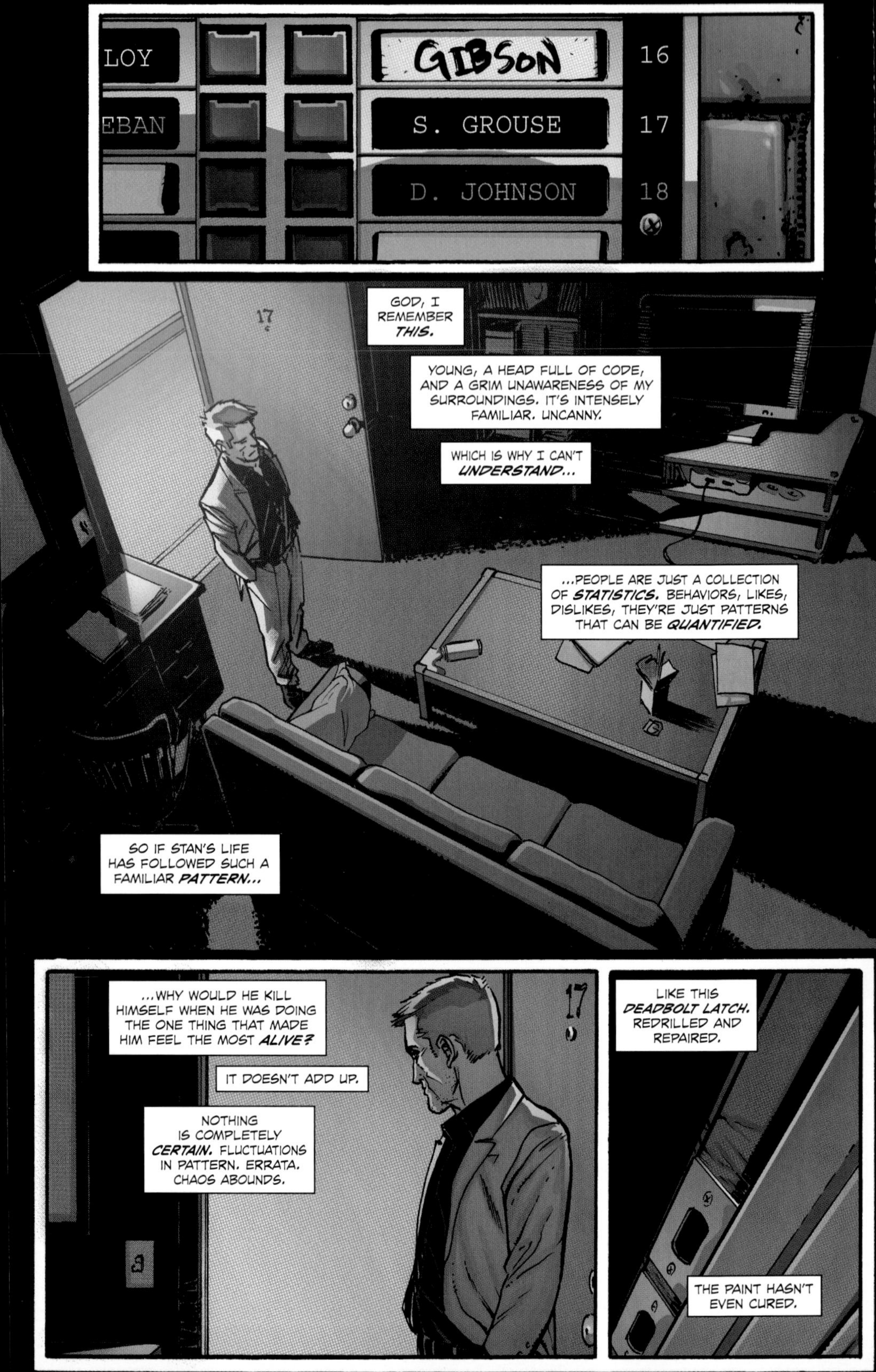
LOY
GIBSON
16
EBAN
S. GROUSE
17
D. JOHNSON
18
17
GOD, I REMEMBER THIS.
YOUNG, A HEAD FULL OF CODE, AND A GRIM UNAWARENESS OF MY SURROUNDINGS. IT'S INTENSELY FAMILIAR. UNCANNY.
WHICH IS WHY I CAN'T UNDERSTAND...
...PEOPLE ARE JUST A COLLECTION OF STATISTICS. BEHAVIORS, LIKES, DISLIKES, THEY'RE JUST PATTERNS THAT CAN BE QUANTIFIED.
SO IF STAN'S LIFE HAS FOLLOWED SUCH A FAMILIAR PATTERN...
...WHY WOULD HE KILL HIMSELF WHEN HE WAS DOING THE ONE THING THAT MADE HIM FEEL THE MOST ALIVE?
IT DOESN'T ADD UP.
NOTHING IS COMPLETELY CERTAIN. FLUCTUATIONS IN PATTERN. ERRATA. CHAOS ABOUNDS.
17
LIKE THIS DEADBOLT LATCH. REDRILLED AND REPAIRED.
THE PAINT HASN'T EVEN CURED.

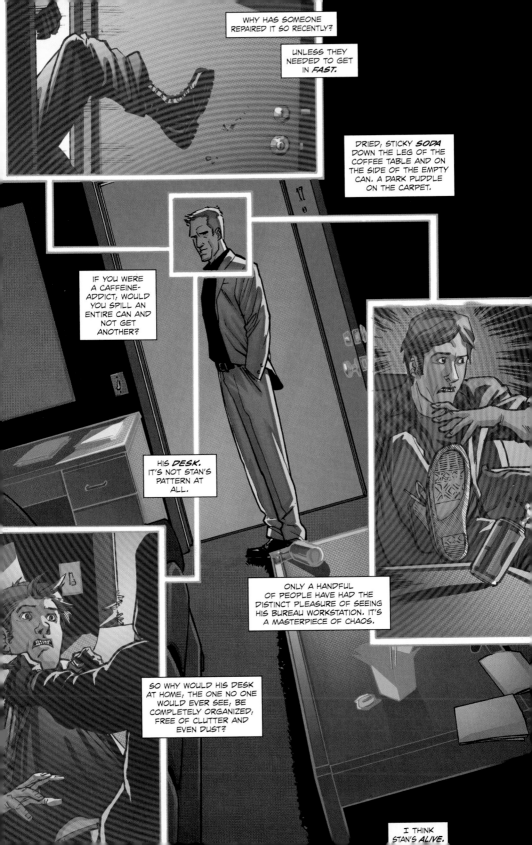

WHY HAS SOMEONE REPAIRED IT SO RECENTLY?

UNLESS THEY NEEDED TO GET IN *FAST.*

DRIED, STICKY *SODA* DOWN THE LEG OF THE COFFEE TABLE AND ON THE SIDE OF THE EMPTY CAN. A DARK PUDDLE ON THE CARPET.

IF YOU WERE A CAFFEINE-ADDICT, WOULD YOU SPILL AN ENTIRE CAN AND NOT GET ANOTHER?

HIS *DESK.* IT'S NOT STAN'S PATTERN AT ALL.

ONLY A HANDFUL OF PEOPLE HAVE HAD THE DISTINCT PLEASURE OF SEEING HIS BUREAU WORKSTATION. IT'S A MASTERPIECE OF CHAOS.

SO WHY WOULD HIS DESK AT HOME, THE ONE NO ONE WOULD EVER SEE, BE COMPLETELY ORGANIZED, FREE OF CLUTTER AND EVEN DUST?

I THINK STAN'S *ALIVE.*

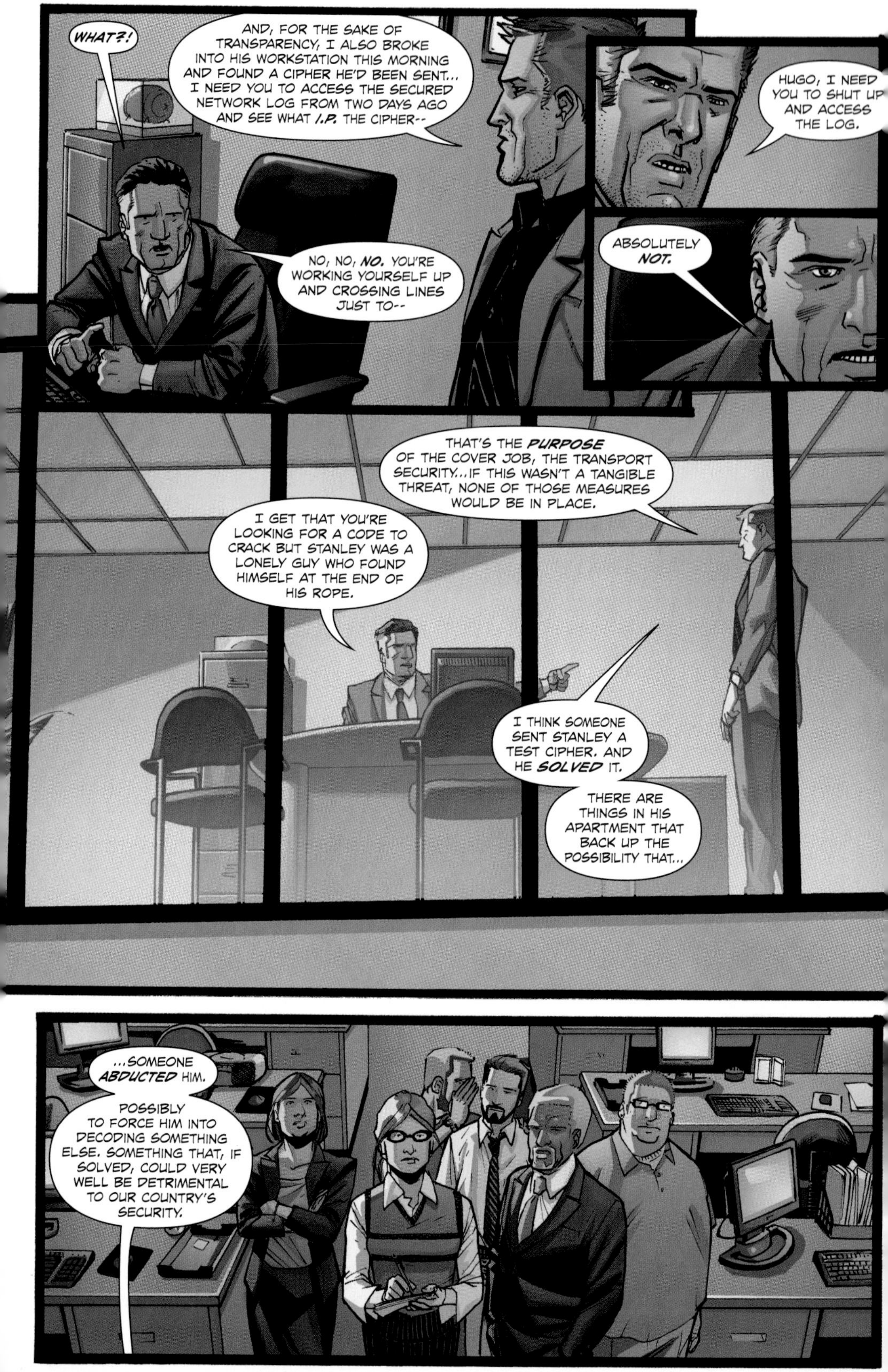
WHAT?!
AND, FOR THE SAKE OF TRANSPARENCY, I ALSO BROKE INTO HIS WORKSTATION THIS MORNING AND FOUND A CIPHER HE'D BEEN SENT... I NEED YOU TO ACCESS THE SECURED NETWORK LOG FROM TWO DAYS AGO AND SEE WHAT I.P. THE CIPHER--
NO, NO, NO. YOU'RE WORKING YOURSELF UP AND CROSSING LINES JUST TO--
HUGO, I NEED YOU TO SHUT UP AND ACCESS THE LOG.
ABSOLUTELY NOT.
THAT'S THE PURPOSE OF THE COVER JOB, THE TRANSPORT SECURITY...IF THIS WASN'T A TANGIBLE THREAT, NONE OF THOSE MEASURES WOULD BE IN PLACE.
I GET THAT YOU'RE LOOKING FOR A CODE TO CRACK BUT STANLEY WAS A LONELY GUY WHO FOUND HIMSELF AT THE END OF HIS ROPE.
I THINK SOMEONE SENT STANLEY A TEST CIPHER. AND HE SOLVED IT.
THERE ARE THINGS IN HIS APARTMENT THAT BACK UP THE POSSIBILITY THAT...
...SOMEONE ABDUCTED HIM.
POSSIBLY TO FORCE HIM INTO DECODING SOMETHING ELSE. SOMETHING THAT, IF SOLVED, COULD VERY WELL BE DETRIMENTAL TO OUR COUNTRY'S SECURITY.

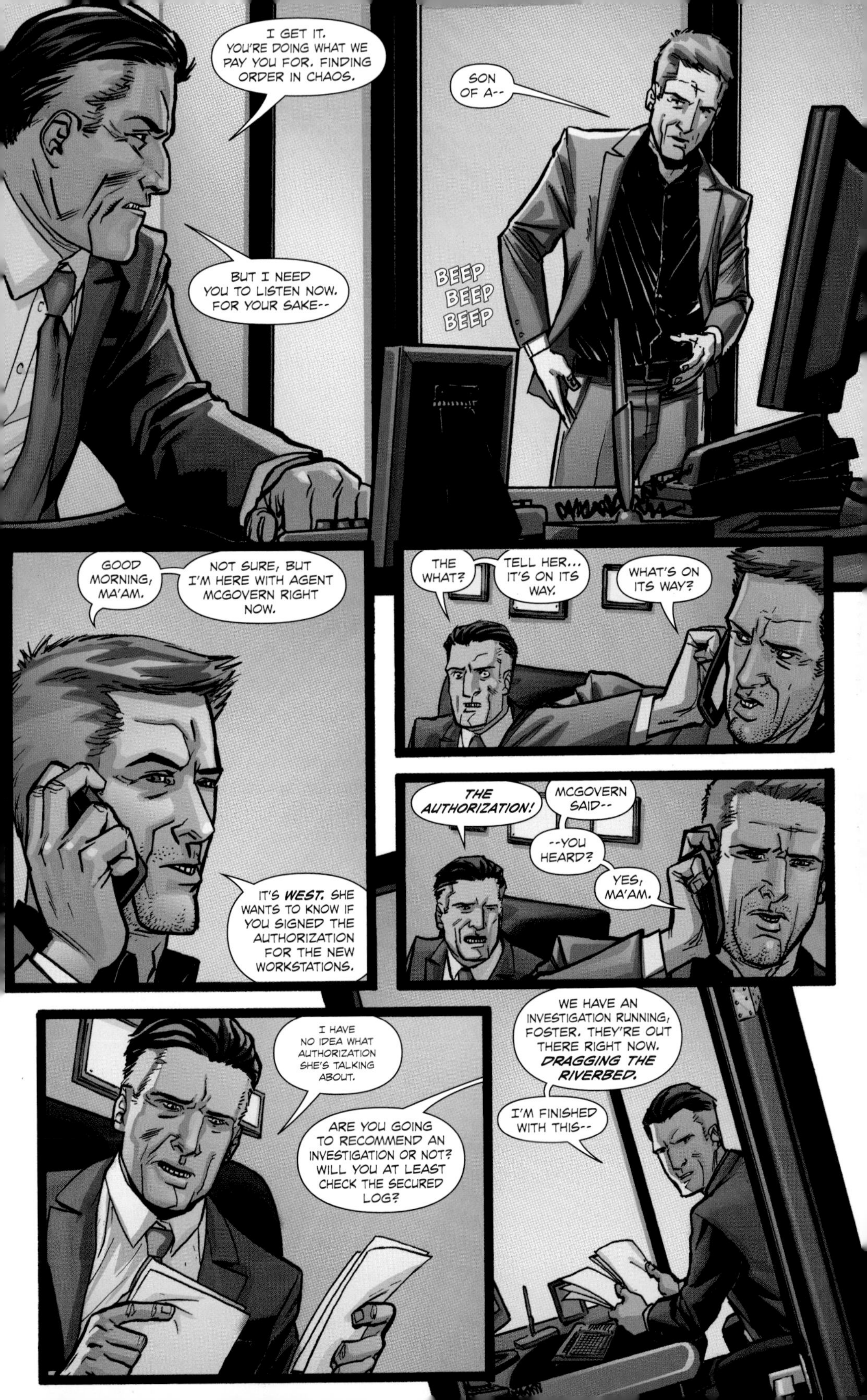
I GET IT. YOU'RE DOING WHAT WE PAY YOU FOR. FINDING ORDER IN CHAOS.
BUT I NEED YOU TO LISTEN NOW. FOR YOUR SAKE--
SON OF A--
BEEP BEEP BEEP
GOOD MORNING, MA'AM.
NOT SURE, BUT I'M HERE WITH AGENT MCGOVERN RIGHT NOW.
IT'S WEST. SHE WANTS TO KNOW IF YOU SIGNED THE AUTHORIZATION FOR THE NEW WORKSTATIONS.
THE WHAT?
TELL HER... IT'S ON ITS WAY.
WHAT'S ON ITS WAY?
THE AUTHORIZATION!
MCGOVERN SAID--
--YOU HEARD?
YES, MA'AM.
I HAVE NO IDEA WHAT AUTHORIZATION SHE'S TALKING ABOUT.
ARE YOU GOING TO RECOMMEND AN INVESTIGATION OR NOT? WILL YOU AT LEAST CHECK THE SECURED LOG?
WE HAVE AN INVESTIGATION RUNNING, FOSTER. THEY'RE OUT THERE RIGHT NOW. DRAGGING THE RIVERBED.
I'M FINISHED WITH THIS--

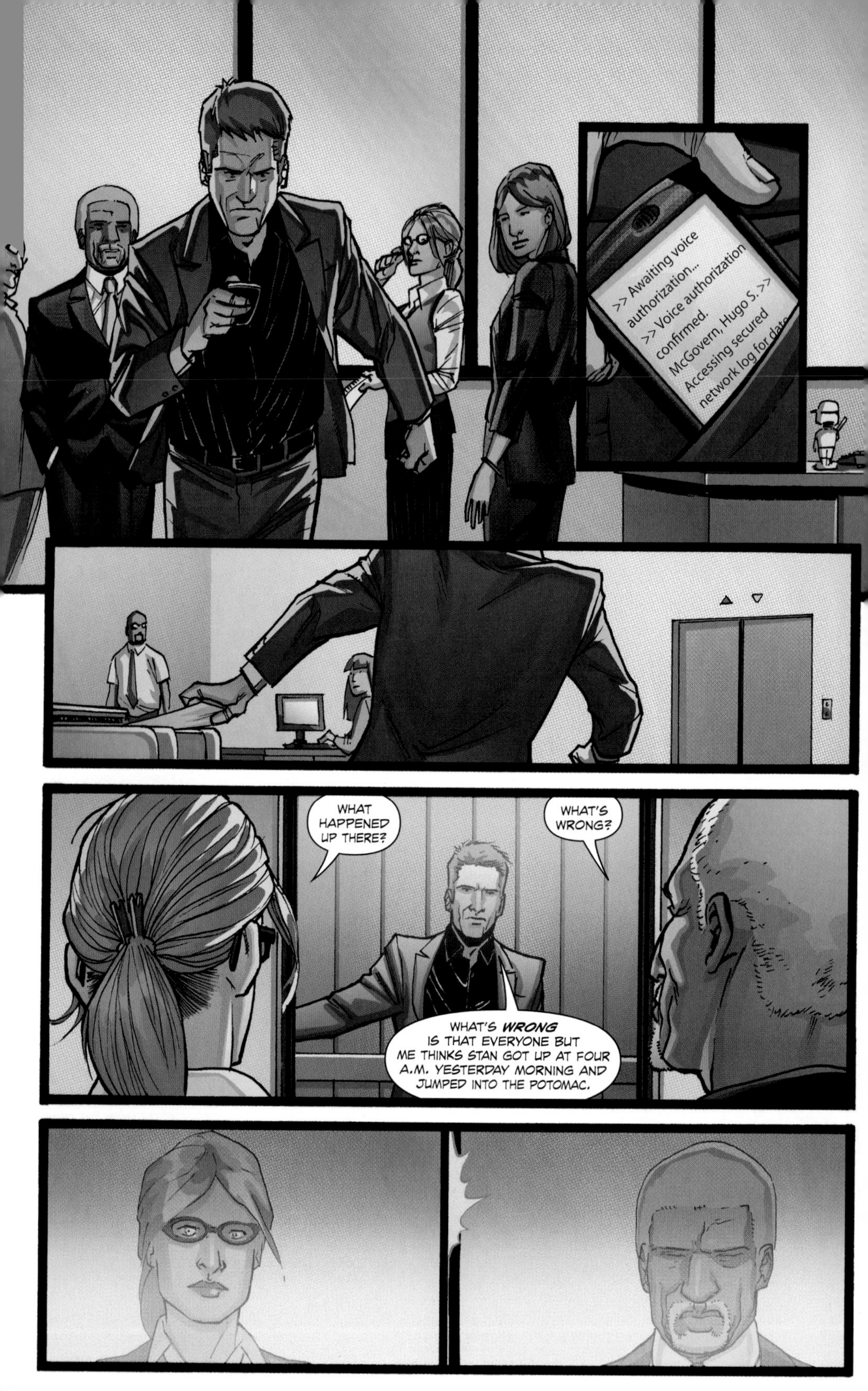
>> Awaiting voice authorization...
>> Voice authorization confirmed.
McGovern, Hugo S. >>
Accessing secured network log for
WHAT HAPPENED UP THERE?
WHAT'S WRONG?
WHAT'S ***WRONG*** IS THAT EVERYONE BUT ME THINKS STAN GOT UP AT FOUR A.M. YESTERDAY MORNING AND JUMPED INTO THE POTOMAC.

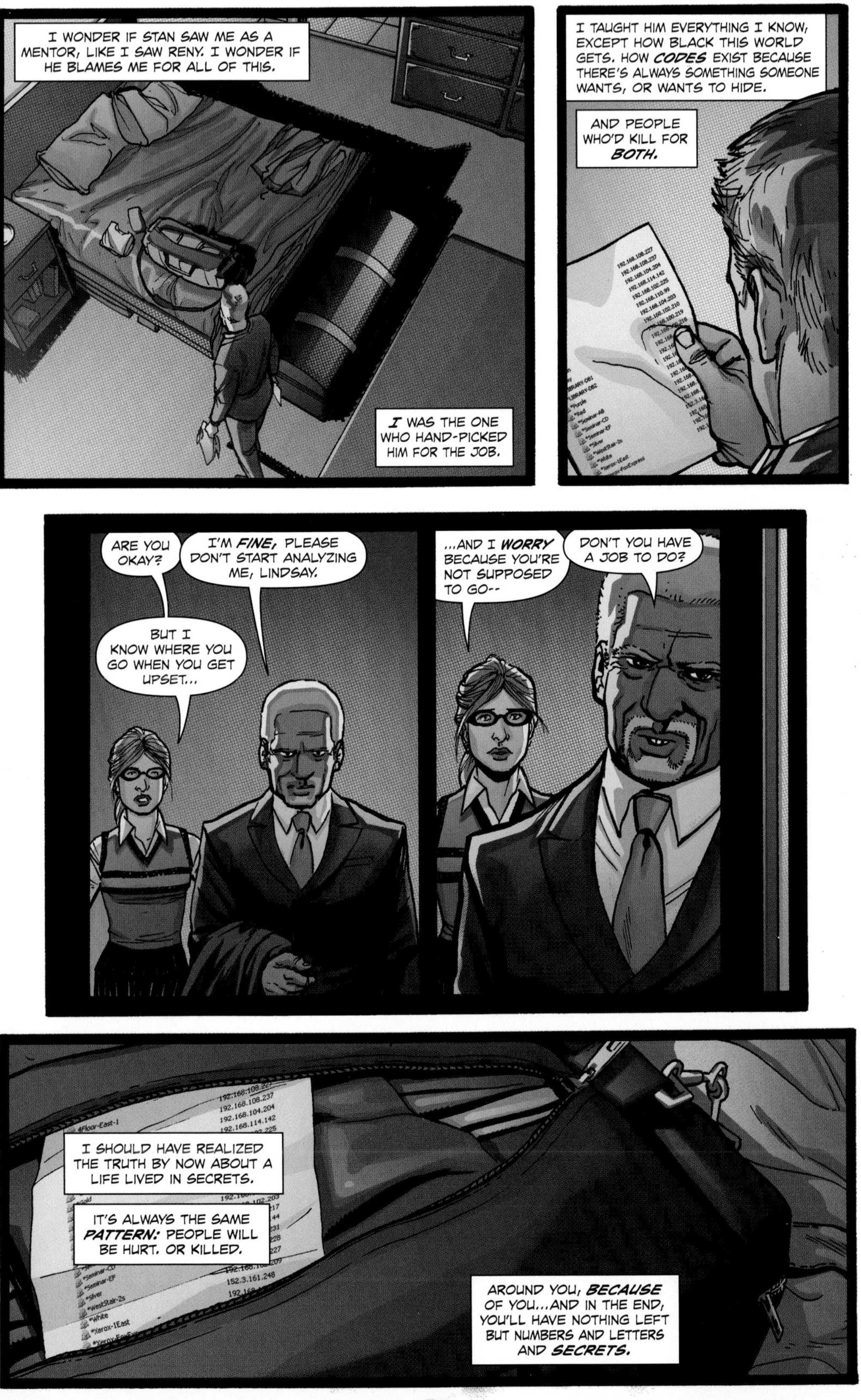
I WONDER IF STAN SAW ME AS A MENTOR, LIKE I SAW RENY. I WONDER IF HE BLAMES ME FOR ALL OF THIS.
I WAS THE ONE WHO HAND-PICKED HIM FOR THE JOB.
I TAUGHT HIM EVERYTHING I KNOW, EXCEPT HOW BLACK THIS WORLD GETS. HOW ***CODES*** EXIST BECAUSE THERE'S ALWAYS SOMETHING SOMEONE WANTS, OR WANTS TO HIDE.
AND PEOPLE WHO'D KILL FOR ***BOTH.***
ARE YOU OKAY?
I'M ***FINE,*** PLEASE DON'T START ANALYZING ME, LINDSAY.
BUT I KNOW WHERE YOU GO WHEN YOU GET UPSET...
...AND I ***WORRY*** BECAUSE YOU'RE NOT SUPPOSED TO GO--
DON'T YOU HAVE A JOB TO DO?
I SHOULD HAVE REALIZED THE TRUTH BY NOW ABOUT A LIFE LIVED IN SECRETS.
IT'S ALWAYS THE SAME ***PATTERN:*** PEOPLE WILL BE HURT. OR KILLED.
AROUND YOU, ***BECAUSE*** OF YOU...AND IN THE END, YOU'LL HAVE NOTHING LEFT BUT NUMBERS AND LETTERS AND ***SECRETS.***

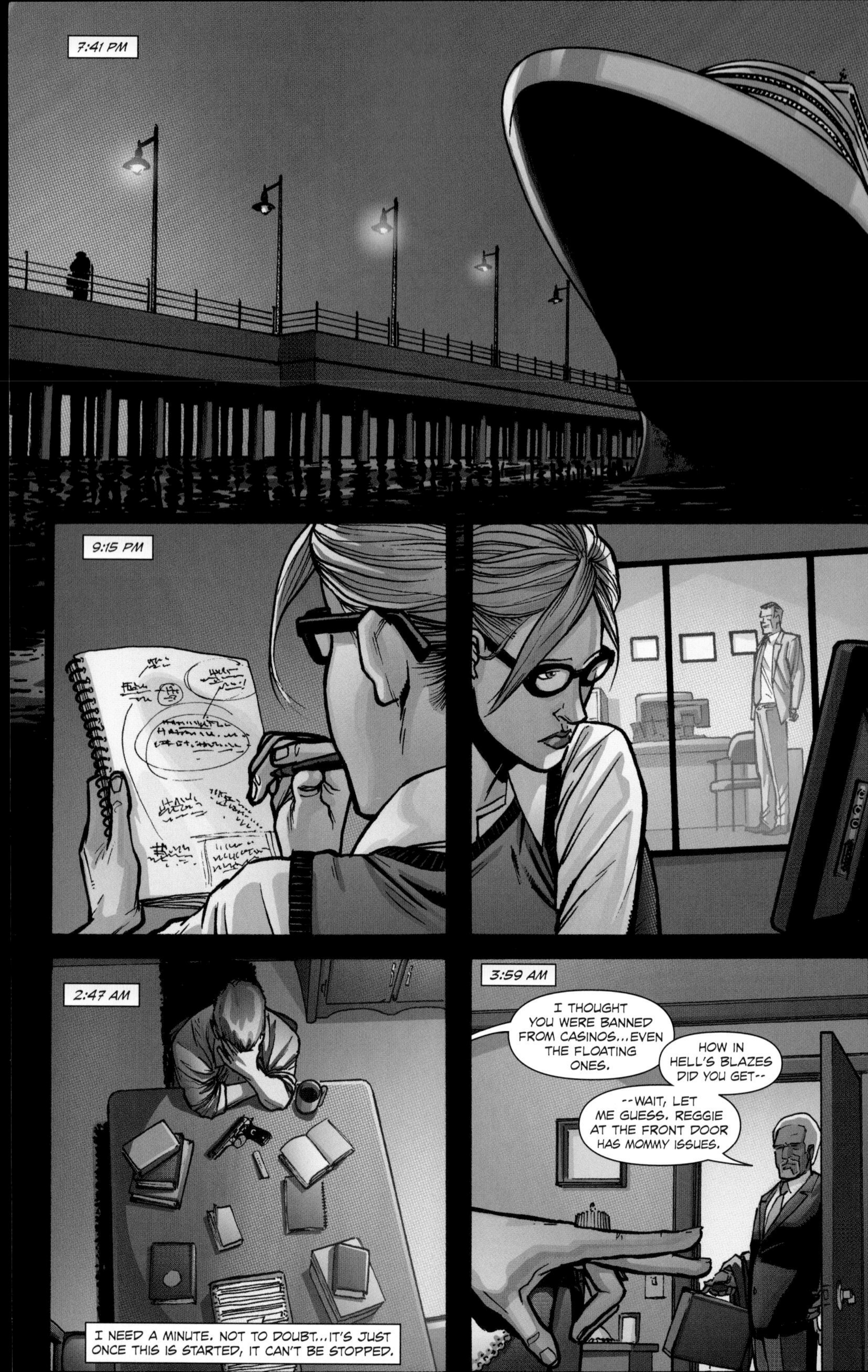
7:41 PM
9:15 PM
2:47 AM
I NEED A MINUTE. NOT TO DOUBT...IT'S JUST ONCE THIS IS STARTED, IT CAN'T BE STOPPED.
3:59 AM
I THOUGHT YOU WERE BANNED FROM CASINOS...EVEN THE FLOATING ONES.
HOW IN HELL'S BLAZES DID YOU GET--
--WAIT, LET ME GUESS. REGGIE AT THE FRONT DOOR HAS MOMMY ISSUES.

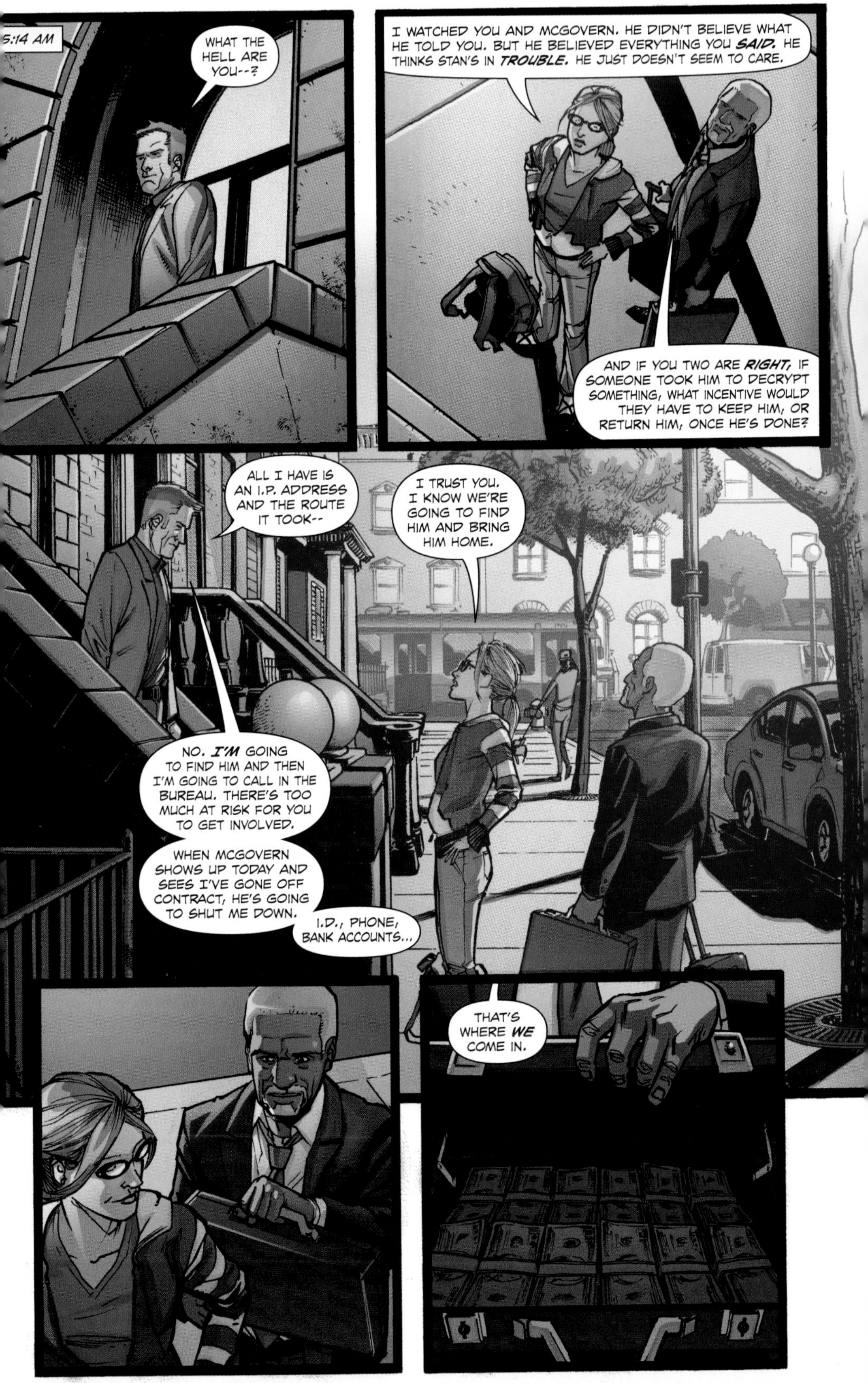
5:14 AM
WHAT THE HELL ARE YOU--?
I WATCHED YOU AND MCGOVERN. HE DIDN'T BELIEVE WHAT HE TOLD YOU. BUT HE BELIEVED EVERYTHING YOU SAID. HE THINKS STAN'S IN TROUBLE. HE JUST DOESN'T SEEM TO CARE.
AND IF YOU TWO ARE RIGHT, IF SOMEONE TOOK HIM TO DECRYPT SOMETHING, WHAT INCENTIVE WOULD THEY HAVE TO KEEP HIM, OR RETURN HIM, ONCE HE'S DONE?
ALL I HAVE IS AN I.P. ADDRESS AND THE ROUTE IT TOOK--
I TRUST YOU. I KNOW WE'RE GOING TO FIND HIM AND BRING HIM HOME.
NO. I'M GOING TO FIND HIM AND THEN I'M GOING TO CALL IN THE BUREAU. THERE'S TOO MUCH AT RISK FOR YOU TO GET INVOLVED.
WHEN MCGOVERN SHOWS UP TODAY AND SEES I'VE GONE OFF CONTRACT, HE'S GOING TO SHUT ME DOWN.
I.D., PHONE, BANK ACCOUNTS...
THAT'S WHERE WE COME IN.

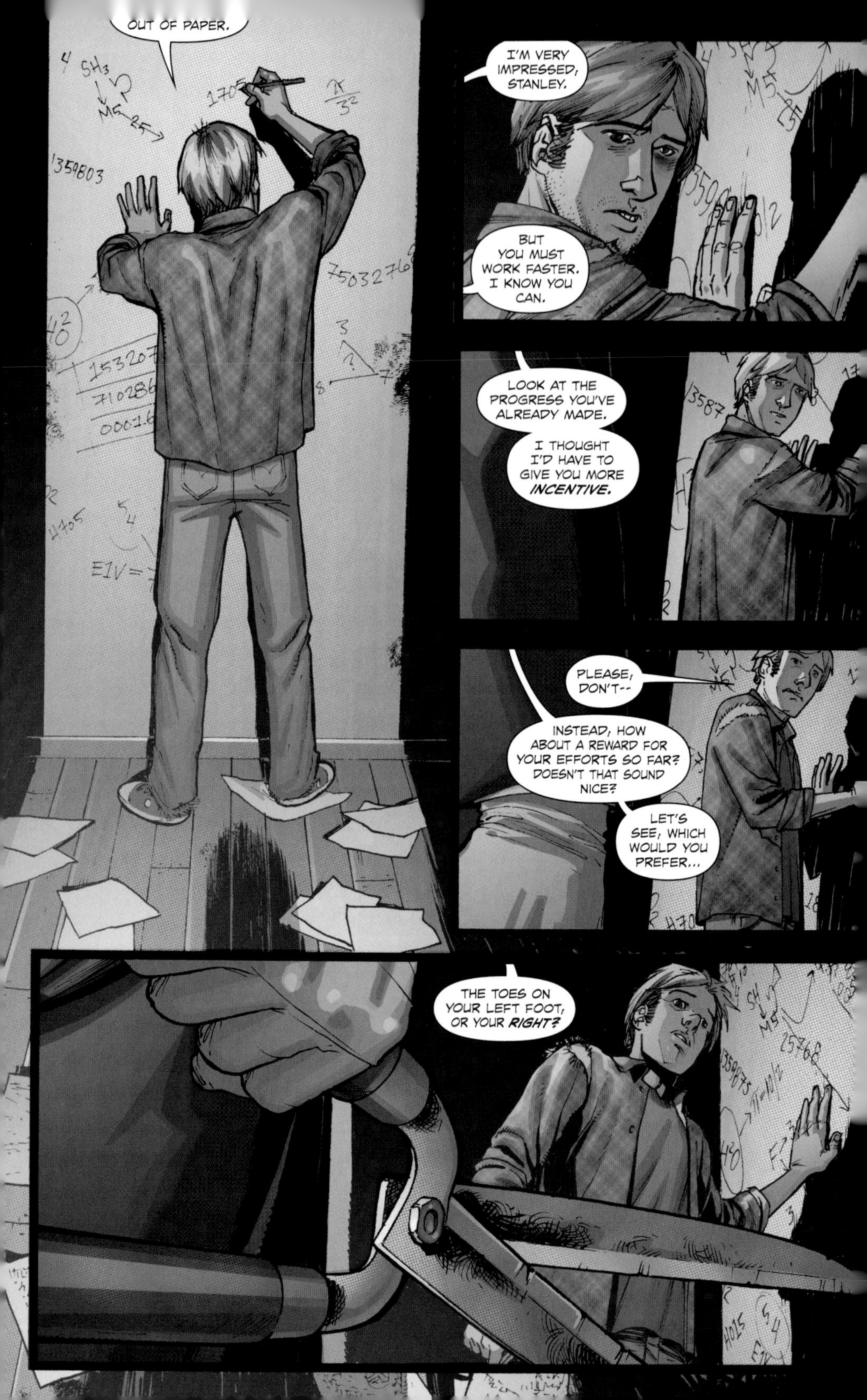
OUT OF PAPER.
I'M VERY IMPRESSED, STANLEY.
BUT YOU MUST WORK FASTER. I KNOW YOU CAN.
LOOK AT THE PROGRESS YOU'VE ALREADY MADE.
I THOUGHT I'D HAVE TO GIVE YOU MORE *INCENTIVE.*
PLEASE, DON'T--
INSTEAD, HOW ABOUT A REWARD FOR YOUR EFFORTS SO FAR? DOESN'T THAT SOUND NICE?
LET'S SEE, WHICH WOULD YOU PREFER...
THE TOES ON YOUR LEFT FOOT, OR YOUR *RIGHT?*

CODEBREAKERS

CHAPTER: TWO

CODE BREAKERS

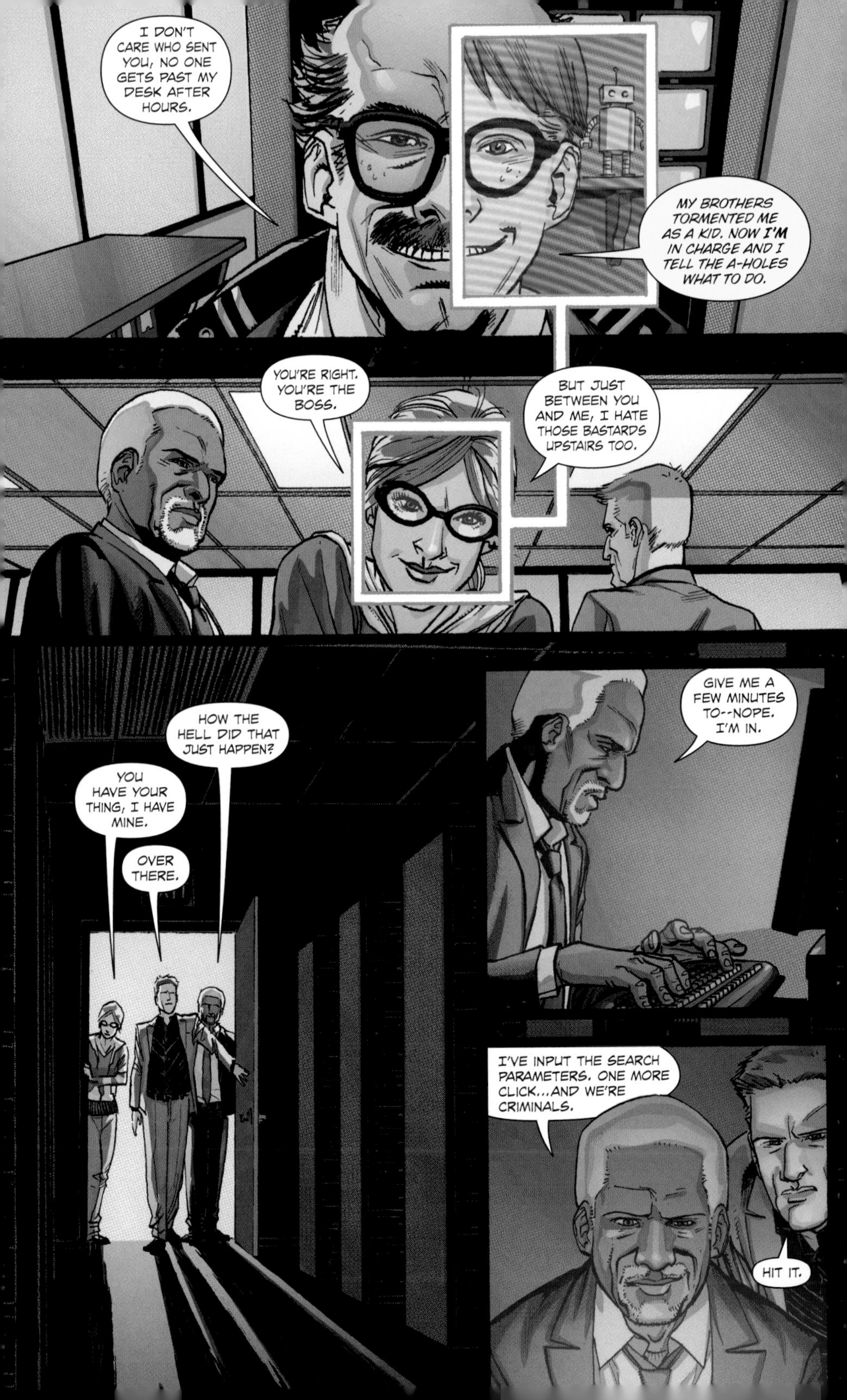

I DON'T CARE WHO SENT YOU, NO ONE GETS PAST MY DESK AFTER HOURS.
MY BROTHERS TORMENTED ME AS A KID. NOW I'M IN CHARGE AND I TELL THE A-HOLES WHAT TO DO.
YOU'RE RIGHT. YOU'RE THE BOSS.
BUT JUST BETWEEN YOU AND ME, I HATE THOSE BASTARDS UPSTAIRS TOO.
HOW THE HELL DID THAT JUST HAPPEN?
YOU HAVE YOUR THING, I HAVE MINE.
OVER THERE.
GIVE ME A FEW MINUTES TO--NOPE. I'M IN.
I'VE INPUT THE SEARCH PARAMETERS. ONE MORE CLICK...AND WE'RE CRIMINALS.
HIT IT.

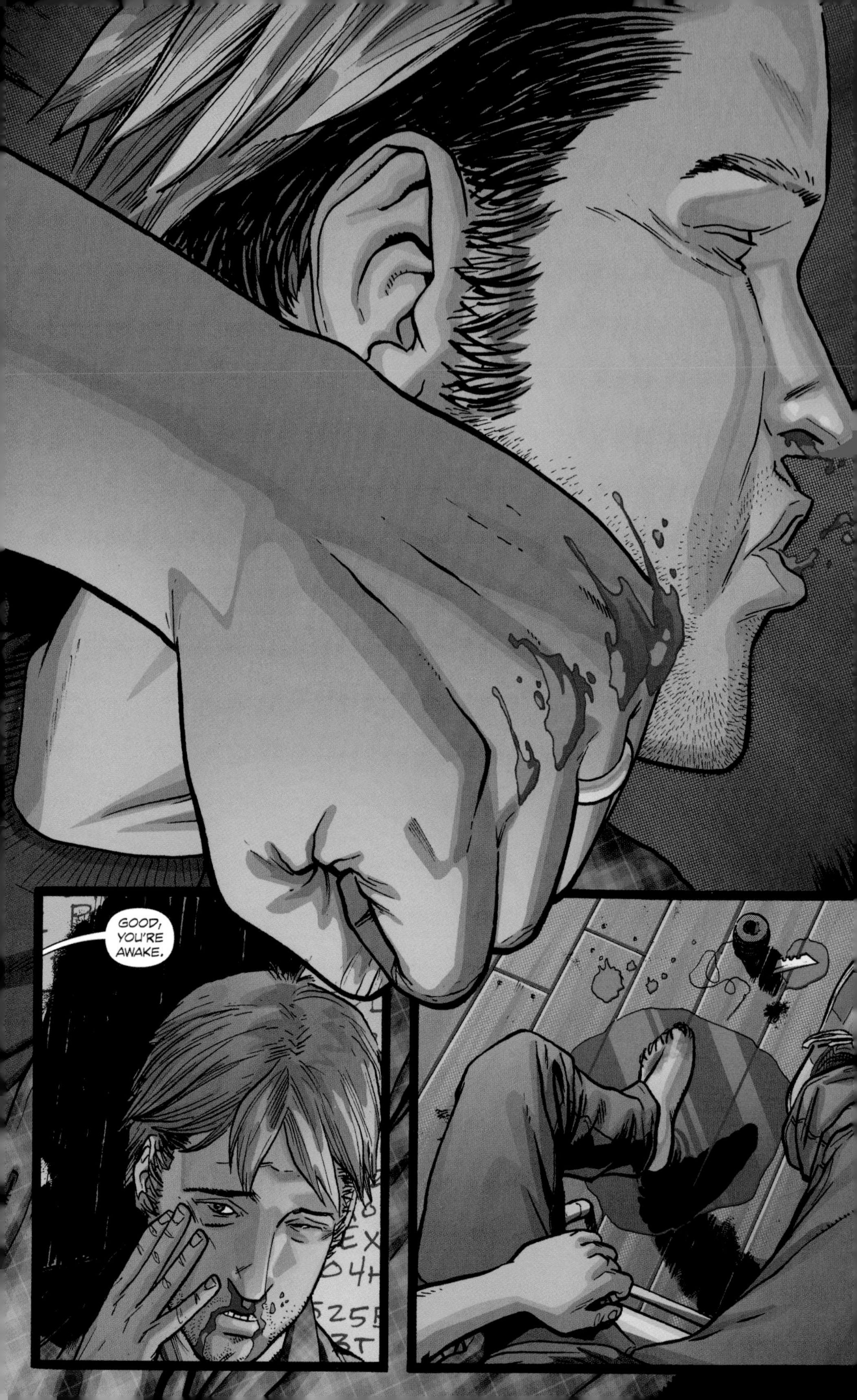
GOOD, YOU'RE AWAKE.

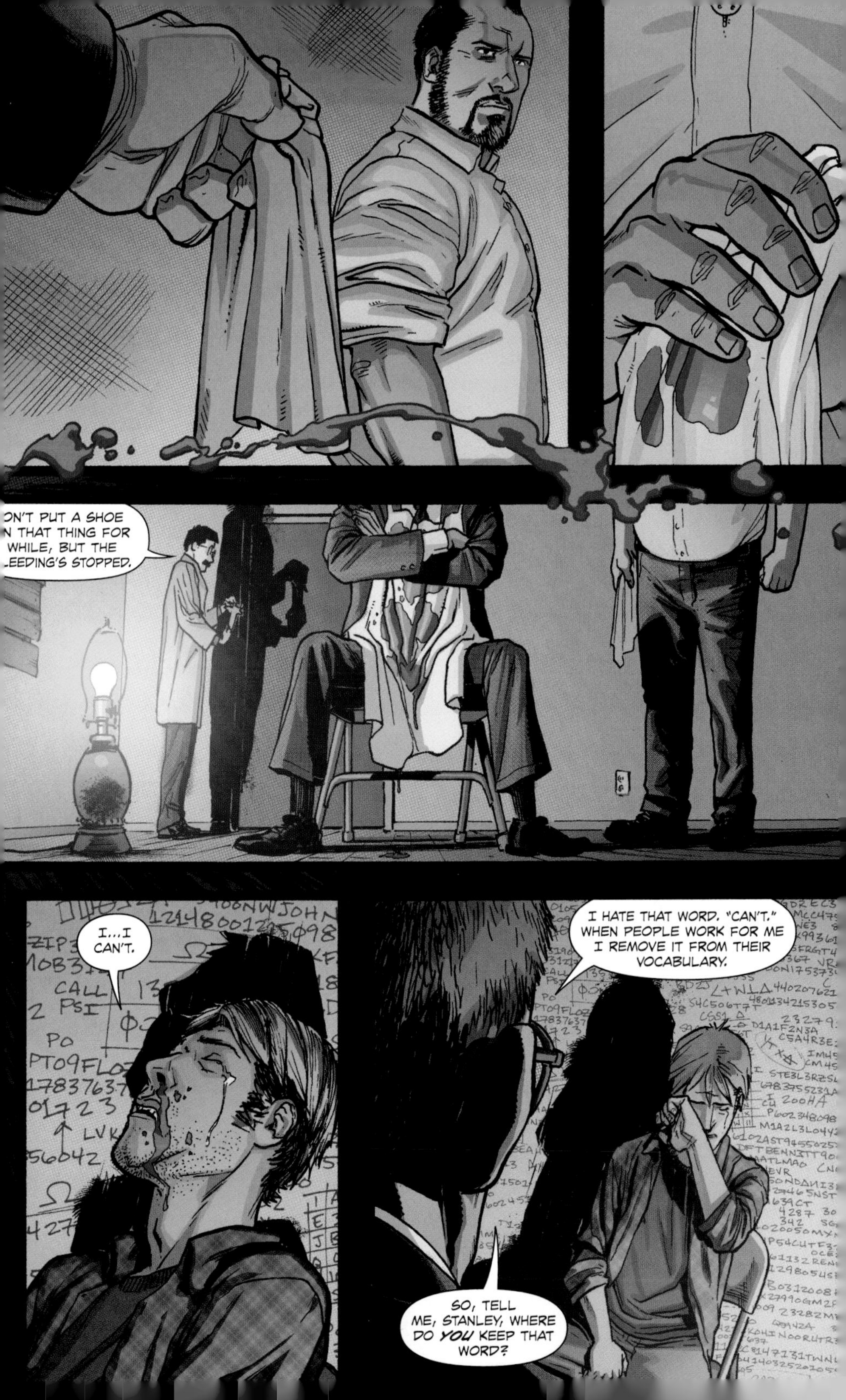
ON'T PUT A SHOE
N THAT THING FOR
WHILE, BUT THE
LEEDING'S STOPPED.
I...I CAN'T.
I HATE THAT WORD. "CAN'T." WHEN PEOPLE WORK FOR ME I REMOVE IT FROM THEIR VOCABULARY.
SO, TELL ME, STANLEY, WHERE DO YOU KEEP THAT WORD?

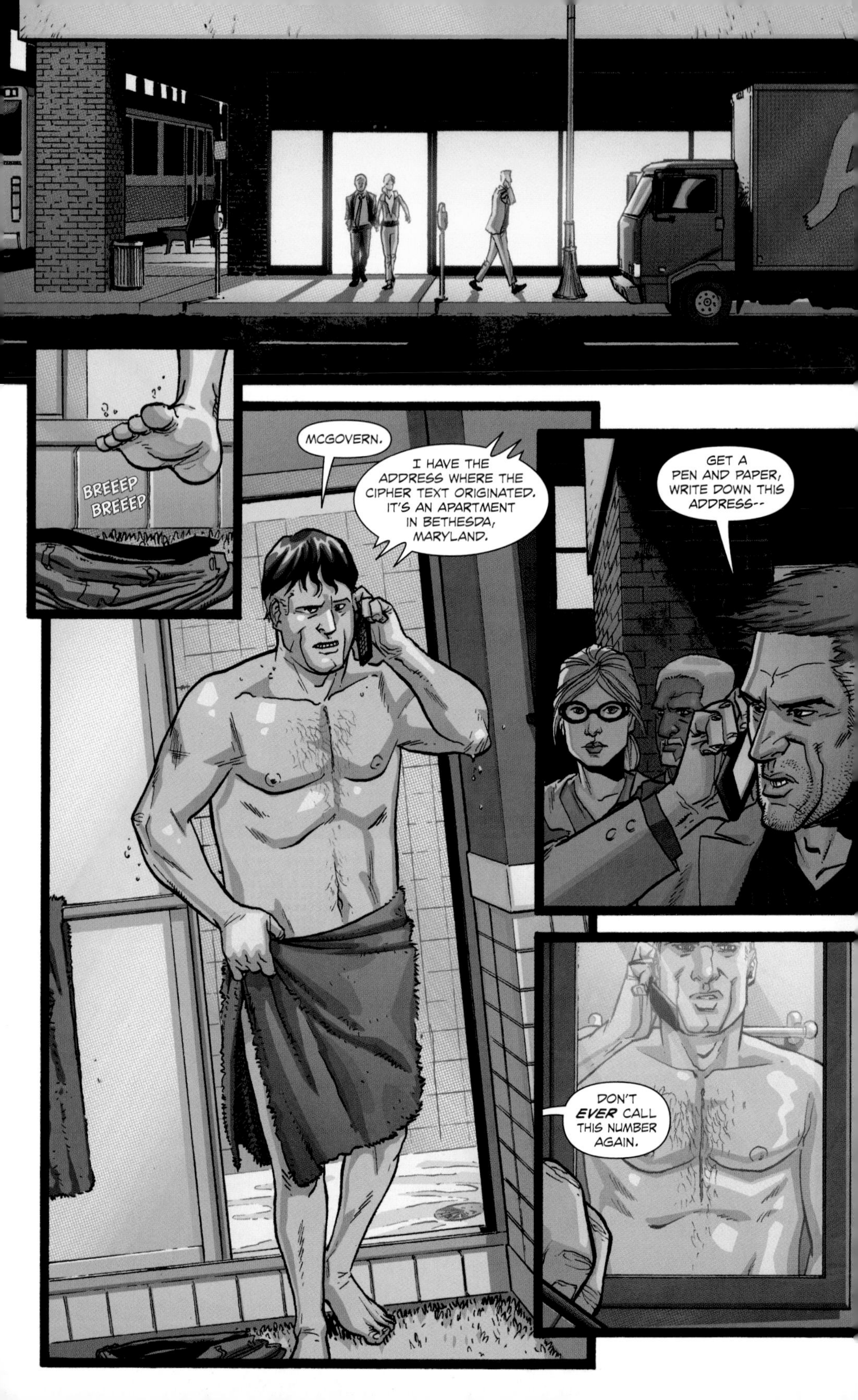
BREEEP
BREEEP
MCGOVERN.
I HAVE THE ADDRESS WHERE THE CIPHER TEXT ORIGINATED. IT'S AN APARTMENT IN BETHESDA, MARYLAND.
GET A PEN AND PAPER, WRITE DOWN THIS ADDRESS--
DON'T EVER CALL THIS NUMBER AGAIN.

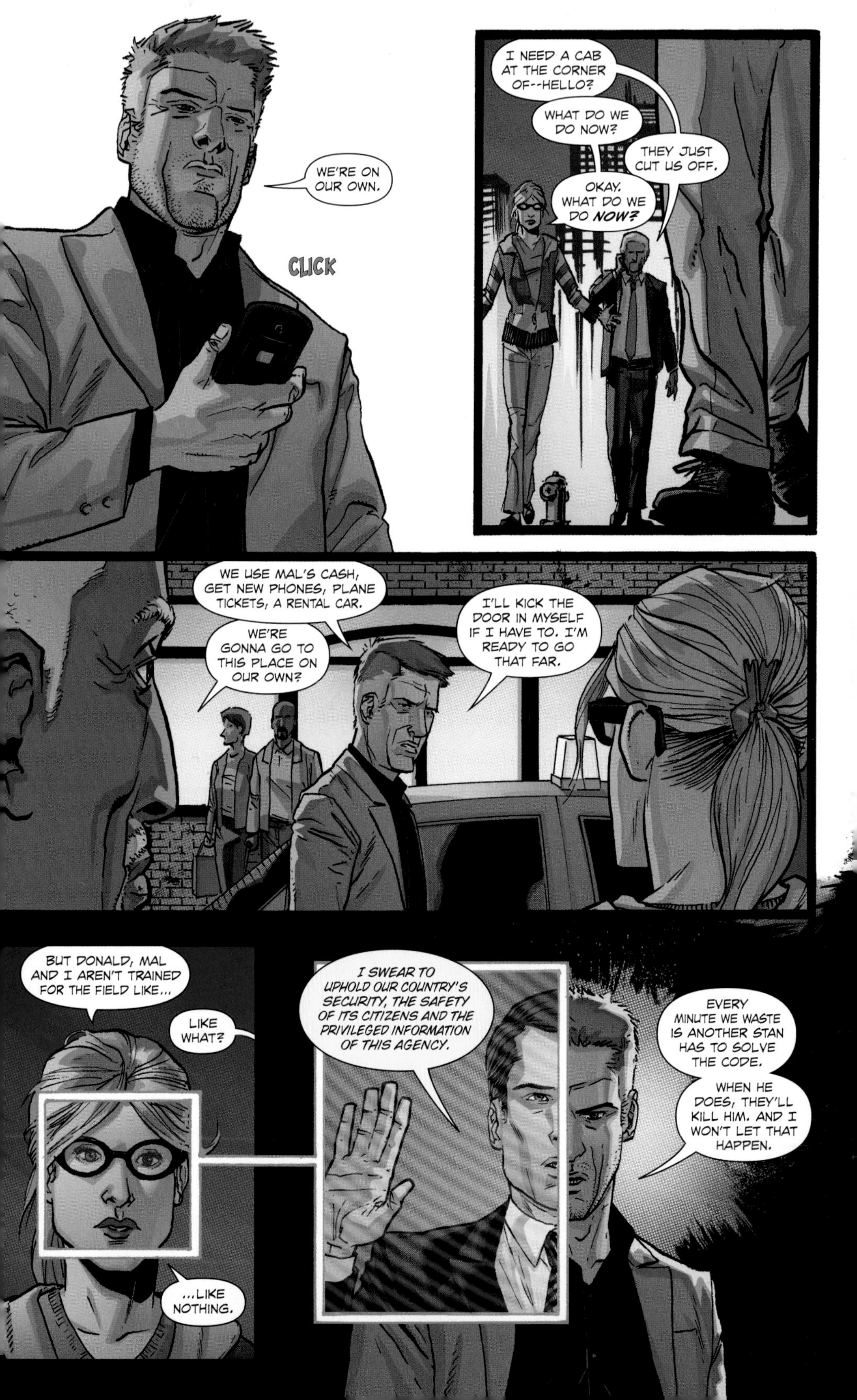
WE'RE ON OUR OWN.
CLICK
I NEED A CAB AT THE CORNER OF--HELLO?
WHAT DO WE DO NOW?
THEY JUST CUT US OFF.
OKAY. WHAT DO WE DO *NOW?*
WE USE MAL'S CASH, GET NEW PHONES, PLANE TICKETS, A RENTAL CAR.
WE'RE GONNA GO TO THIS PLACE ON OUR OWN?
I'LL KICK THE DOOR IN MYSELF IF I HAVE TO. I'M READY TO GO THAT FAR.
BUT DONALD, MAL AND I AREN'T TRAINED FOR THE FIELD LIKE...
LIKE WHAT?
...LIKE NOTHING.
I SWEAR TO UPHOLD OUR COUNTRY'S SECURITY, THE SAFETY OF ITS CITIZENS AND THE PRIVILEGED INFORMATION OF THIS AGENCY.
EVERY MINUTE WE WASTE IS ANOTHER STAN HAS TO SOLVE THE CODE.
WHEN HE DOES, THEY'LL KILL HIM. AND I WON'T LET THAT HAPPEN.

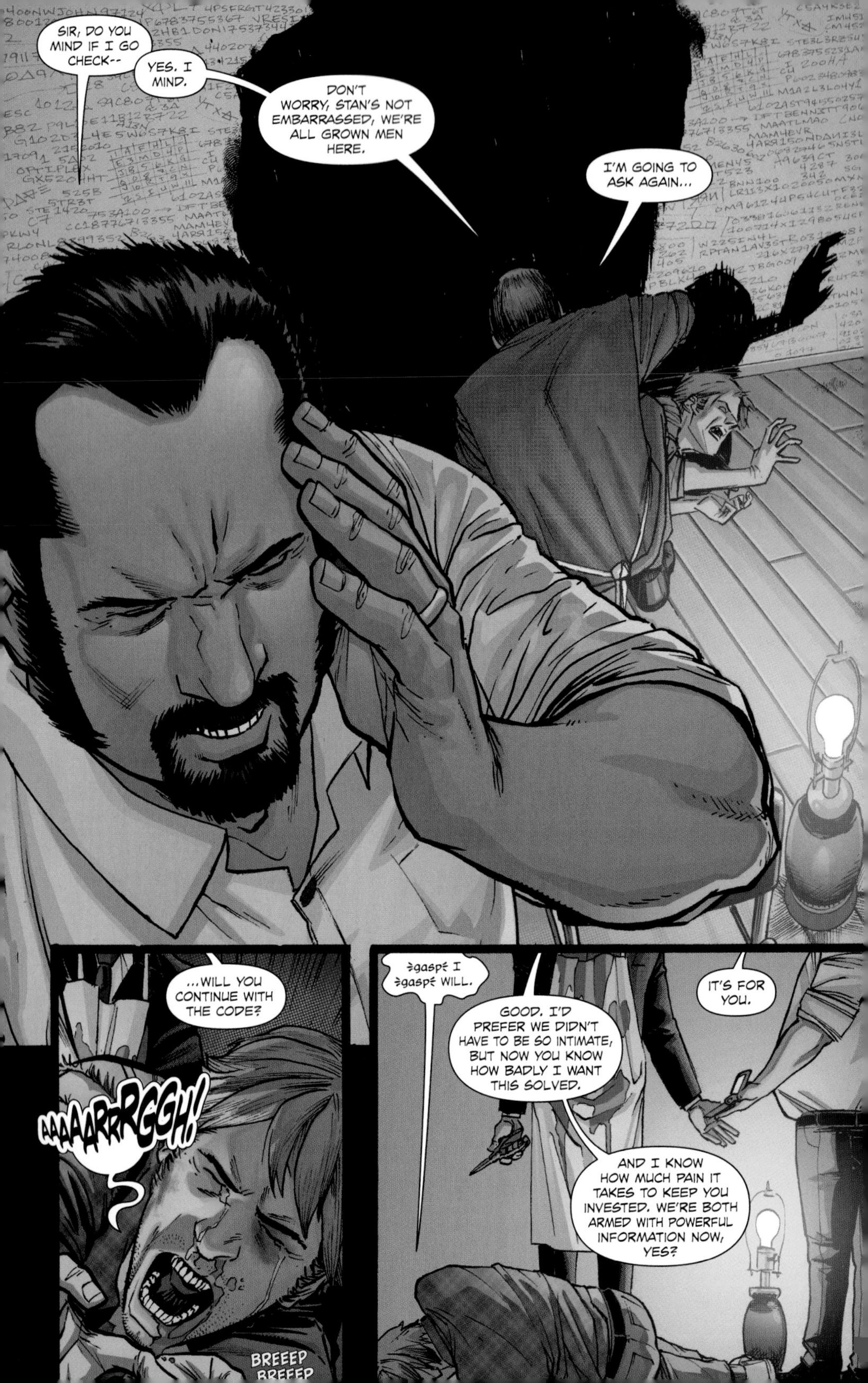
SIR, DO YOU MIND IF I GO CHECK--
YES. I MIND.
DON'T WORRY, STAN'S NOT EMBARRASSED, WE'RE ALL GROWN MEN HERE.
I'M GOING TO ASK AGAIN...
...WILL YOU CONTINUE WITH THE CODE?
AAAAARRRGGH!
BREEEP
gasp I *gasp* WILL.
GOOD. I'D PREFER WE DIDN'T HAVE TO BE SO INTIMATE, BUT NOW YOU KNOW HOW BADLY I WANT THIS SOLVED.
AND I KNOW HOW MUCH PAIN IT TAKES TO KEEP YOU INVESTED. WE'RE BOTH ARMED WITH POWERFUL INFORMATION NOW, YES?
IT'S FOR YOU.

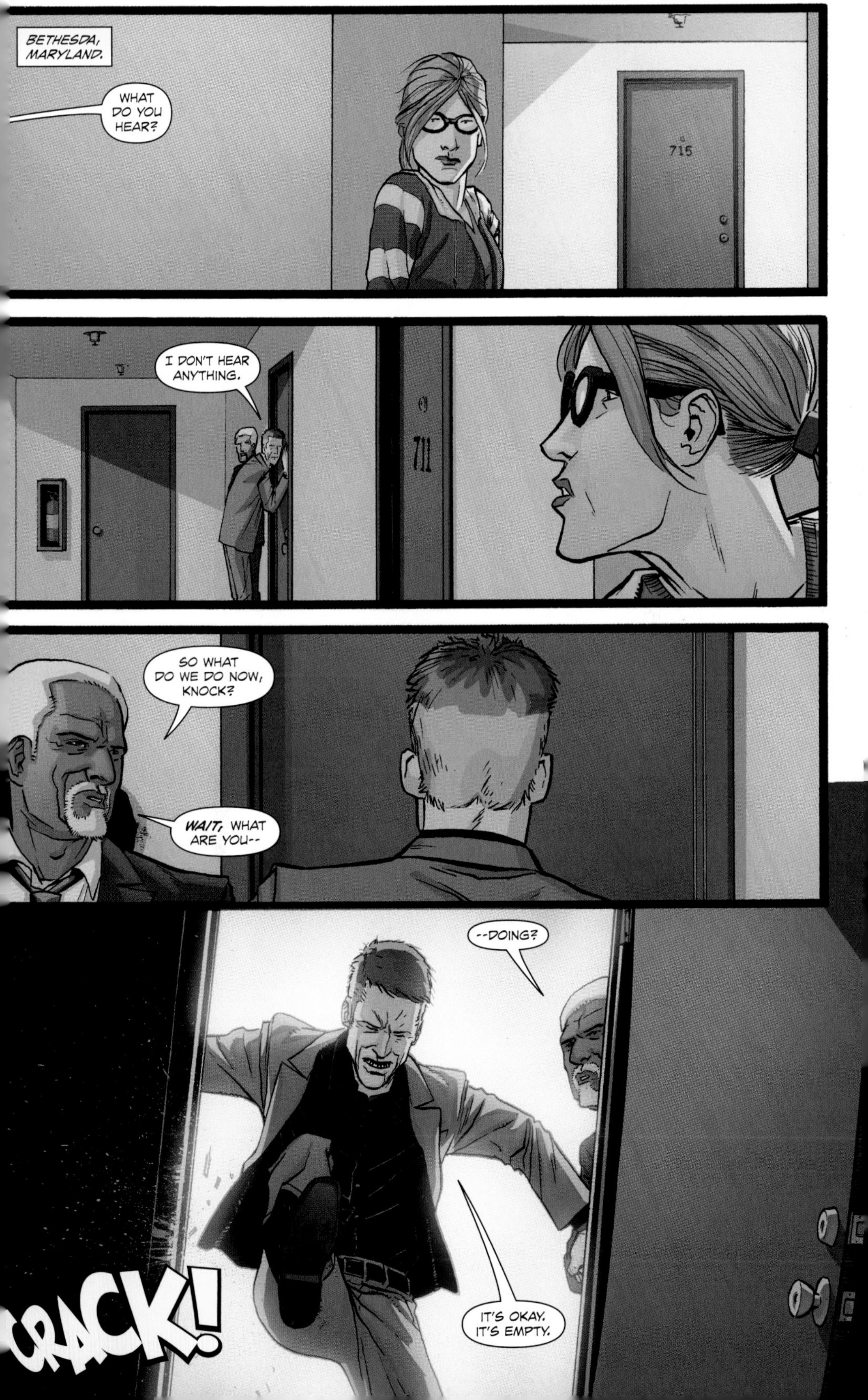
BETHESDA, MARYLAND.
WHAT DO YOU HEAR?
715
I DON'T HEAR ANYTHING.
711
SO WHAT DO WE DO NOW, KNOCK?
WAIT, WHAT ARE YOU--
--DOING?
CRACK!
IT'S OKAY. IT'S EMPTY.

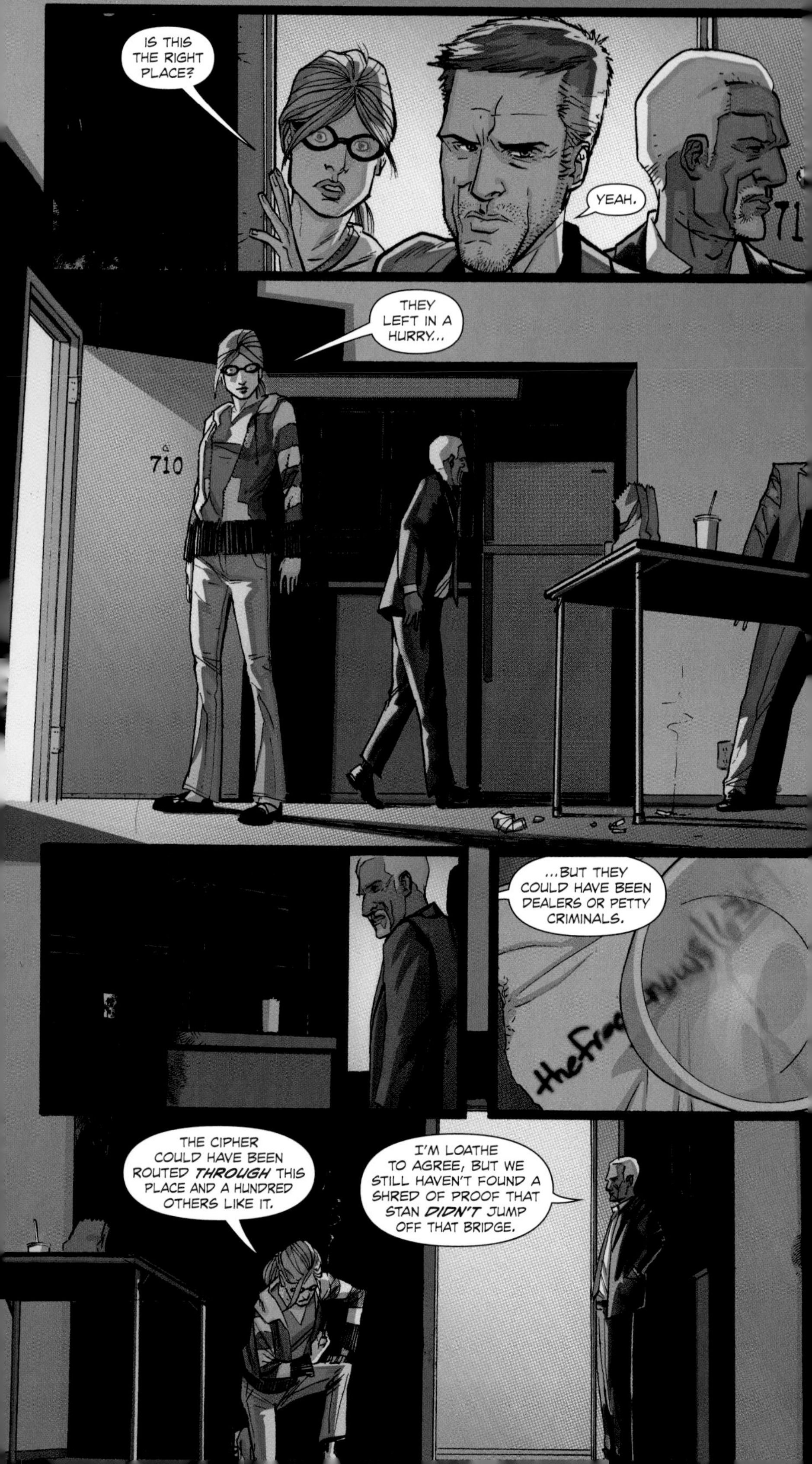
IS THIS THE RIGHT PLACE?
YEAH.
THEY LEFT IN A HURRY...
...BUT THEY COULD HAVE BEEN DEALERS OR PETTY CRIMINALS.
THE CIPHER COULD HAVE BEEN ROUTED *THROUGH* THIS PLACE AND A HUNDRED OTHERS LIKE IT.
I'M LOATHE TO AGREE, BUT WE STILL HAVEN'T FOUND A SHRED OF PROOF THAT STAN *DIDN'T* JUMP OFF THAT BRIDGE.

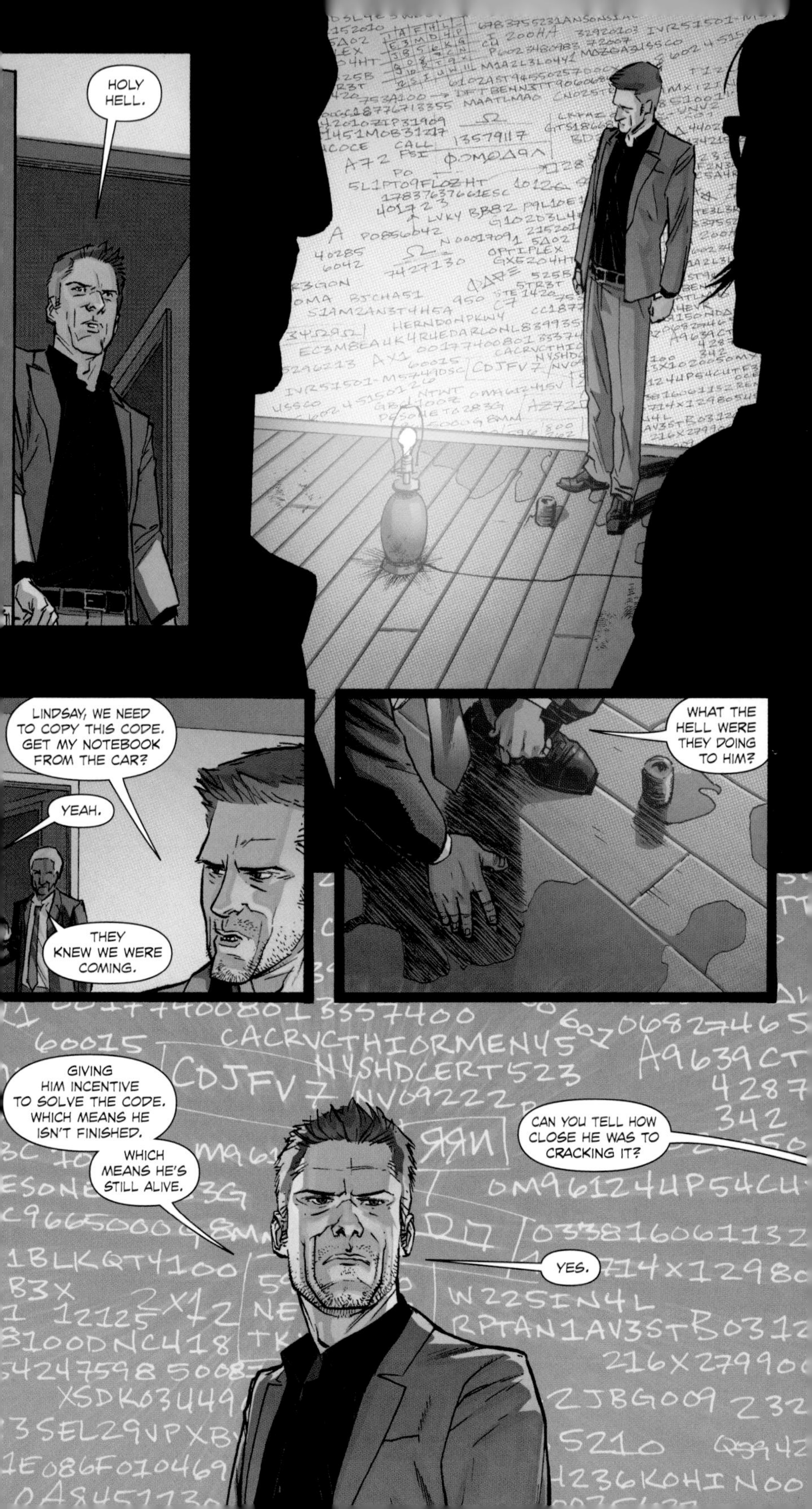
HOLY HELL.
LINDSAY, WE NEED TO COPY THIS CODE. GET MY NOTEBOOK FROM THE CAR?
YEAH.
THEY KNEW WE WERE COMING.
WHAT THE HELL WERE THEY DOING TO HIM?
GIVING HIM INCENTIVE TO SOLVE THE CODE. WHICH MEANS HE ISN'T FINISHED.
WHICH MEANS HE'S STILL ALIVE.
CAN YOU TELL HOW CLOSE HE WAS TO CRACKING IT?
YES.

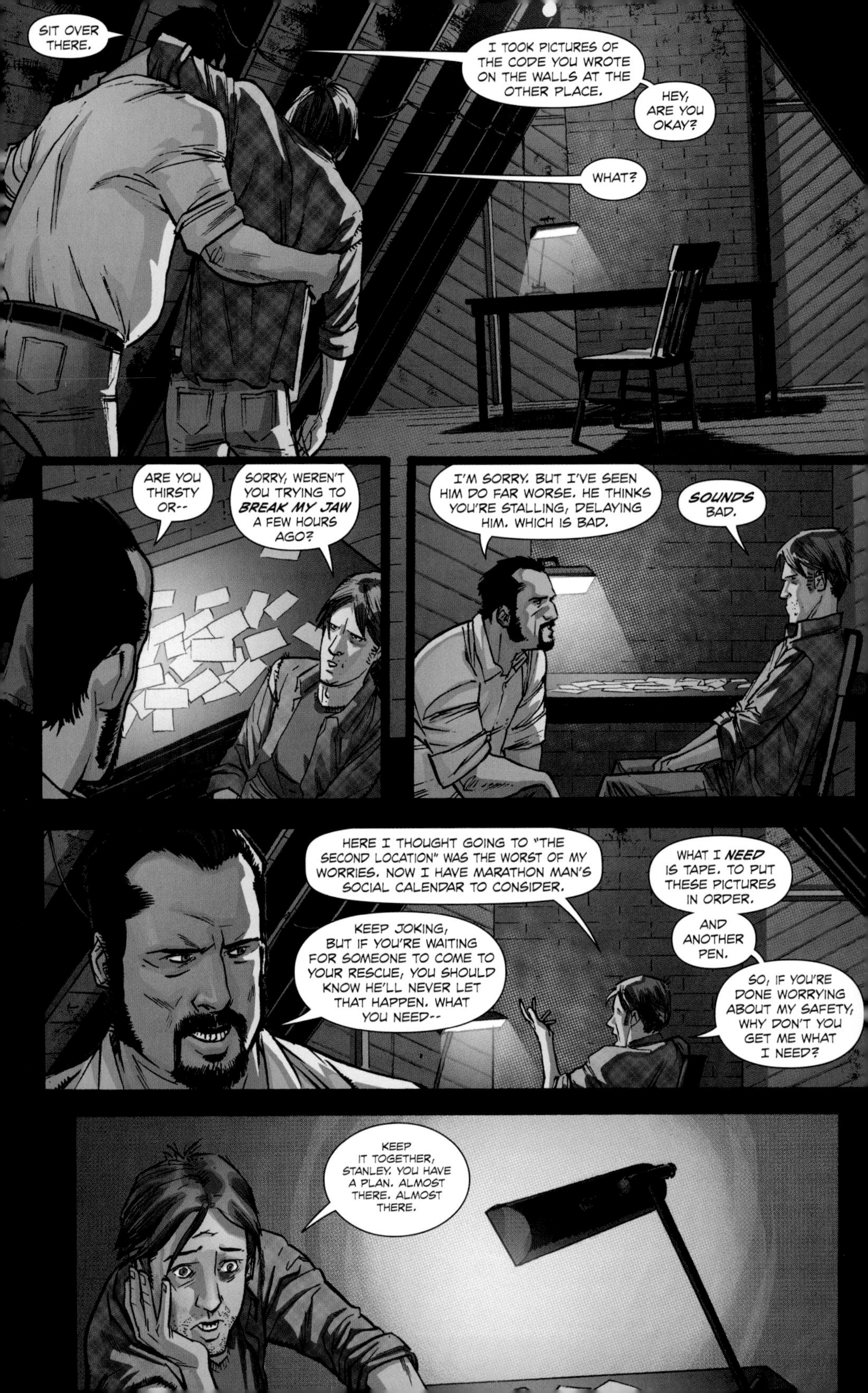
SIT OVER THERE.
I TOOK PICTURES OF THE CODE YOU WROTE ON THE WALLS AT THE OTHER PLACE.
HEY, ARE YOU OKAY?
WHAT?
ARE YOU THIRSTY OR--
SORRY, WEREN'T YOU TRYING TO BREAK MY JAW A FEW HOURS AGO?
I'M SORRY. BUT I'VE SEEN HIM DO FAR WORSE. HE THINKS YOU'RE STALLING, DELAYING HIM. WHICH IS BAD.
SOUNDS BAD.
HERE I THOUGHT GOING TO "THE SECOND LOCATION" WAS THE WORST OF MY WORRIES. NOW I HAVE MARATHON MAN'S SOCIAL CALENDAR TO CONSIDER.
KEEP JOKING, BUT IF YOU'RE WAITING FOR SOMEONE TO COME TO YOUR RESCUE, YOU SHOULD KNOW HE'LL NEVER LET THAT HAPPEN. WHAT YOU NEED--
WHAT I NEED IS TAPE. TO PUT THESE PICTURES IN ORDER.
AND ANOTHER PEN.
SO, IF YOU'RE DONE WORRYING ABOUT MY SAFETY, WHY DON'T YOU GET ME WHAT I NEED?
KEEP IT TOGETHER, STANLEY. YOU HAVE A PLAN. ALMOST THERE. ALMOST THERE.

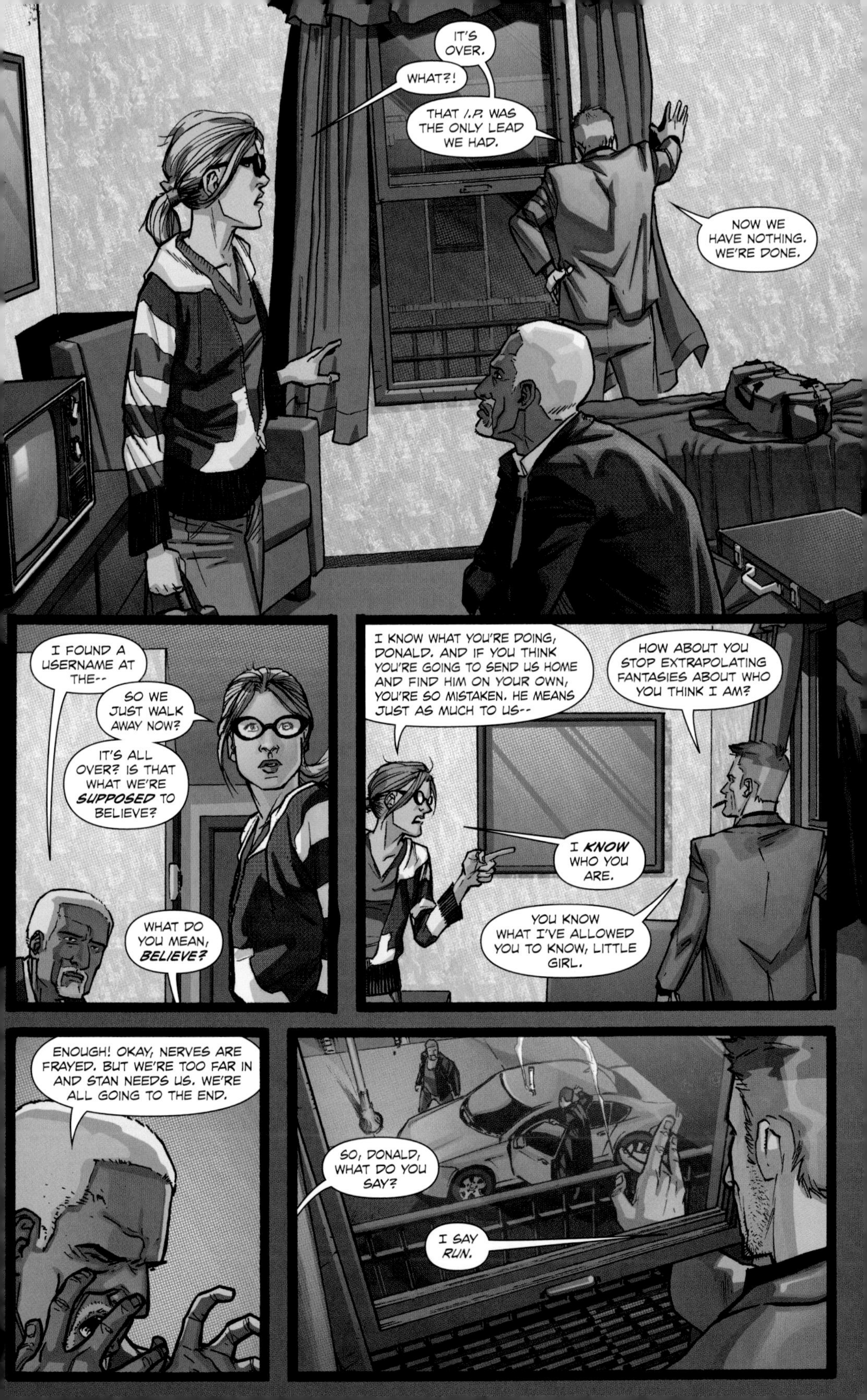
IT'S OVER.
WHAT?!
THAT I.P. WAS THE ONLY LEAD WE HAD.
NOW WE HAVE NOTHING. WE'RE DONE.
I FOUND A USERNAME AT THE--
SO WE JUST WALK AWAY NOW?
IT'S ALL OVER? IS THAT WHAT WE'RE SUPPOSED TO BELIEVE?
WHAT DO YOU MEAN, BELIEVE?
I KNOW WHAT YOU'RE DOING, DONALD. AND IF YOU THINK YOU'RE GOING TO SEND US HOME AND FIND HIM ON YOUR OWN, YOU'RE SO MISTAKEN. HE MEANS JUST AS MUCH TO US--
HOW ABOUT YOU STOP EXTRAPOLATING FANTASIES ABOUT WHO YOU THINK I AM?
I KNOW WHO YOU ARE.
YOU KNOW WHAT I'VE ALLOWED YOU TO KNOW, LITTLE GIRL.
ENOUGH! OKAY, NERVES ARE FRAYED. BUT WE'RE TOO FAR IN AND STAN NEEDS US. WE'RE ALL GOING TO THE END.
SO, DONALD, WHAT DO YOU SAY?
I SAY RUN.

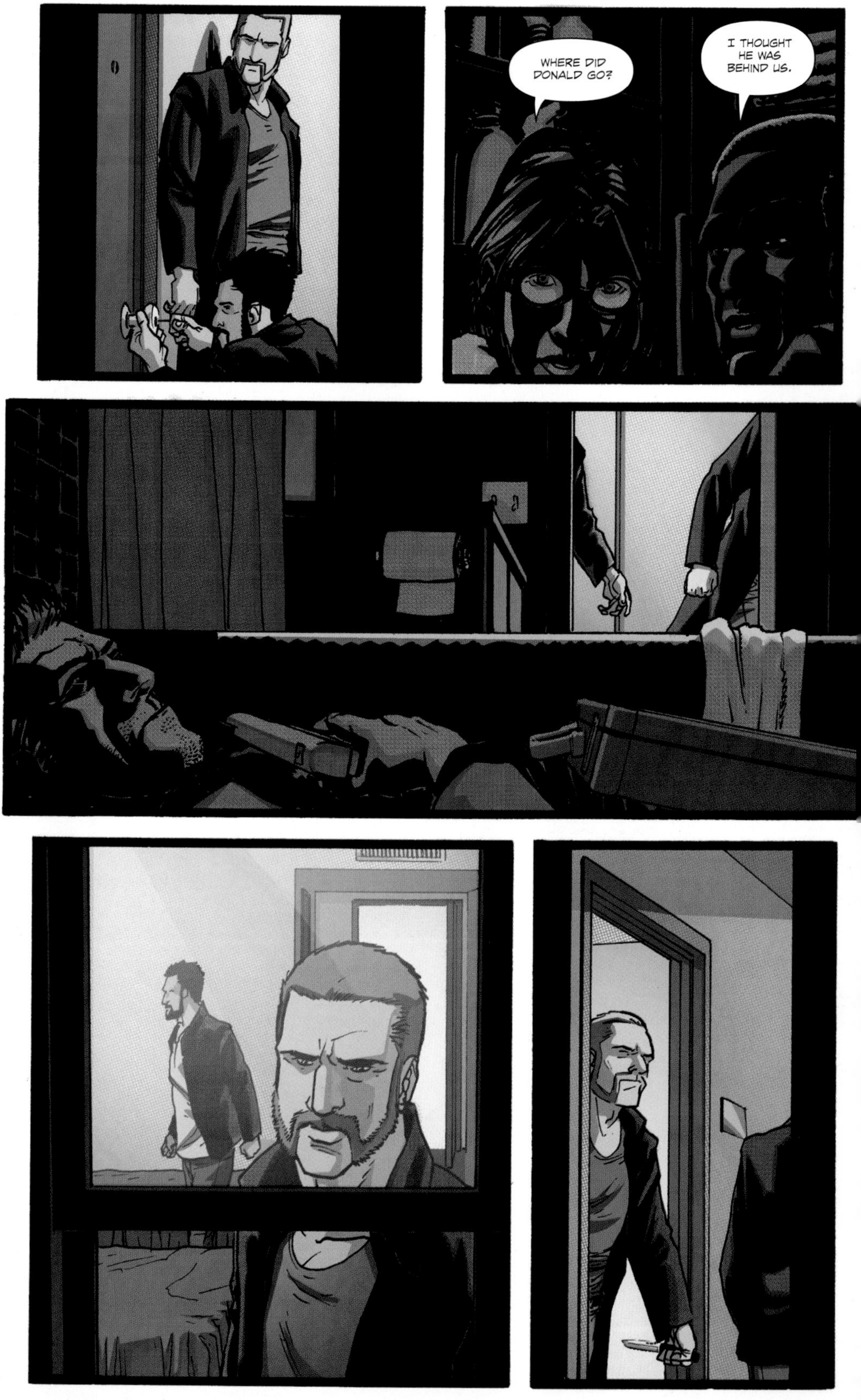
WHERE DID DONALD GO?
I THOUGHT HE WAS BEHIND US.

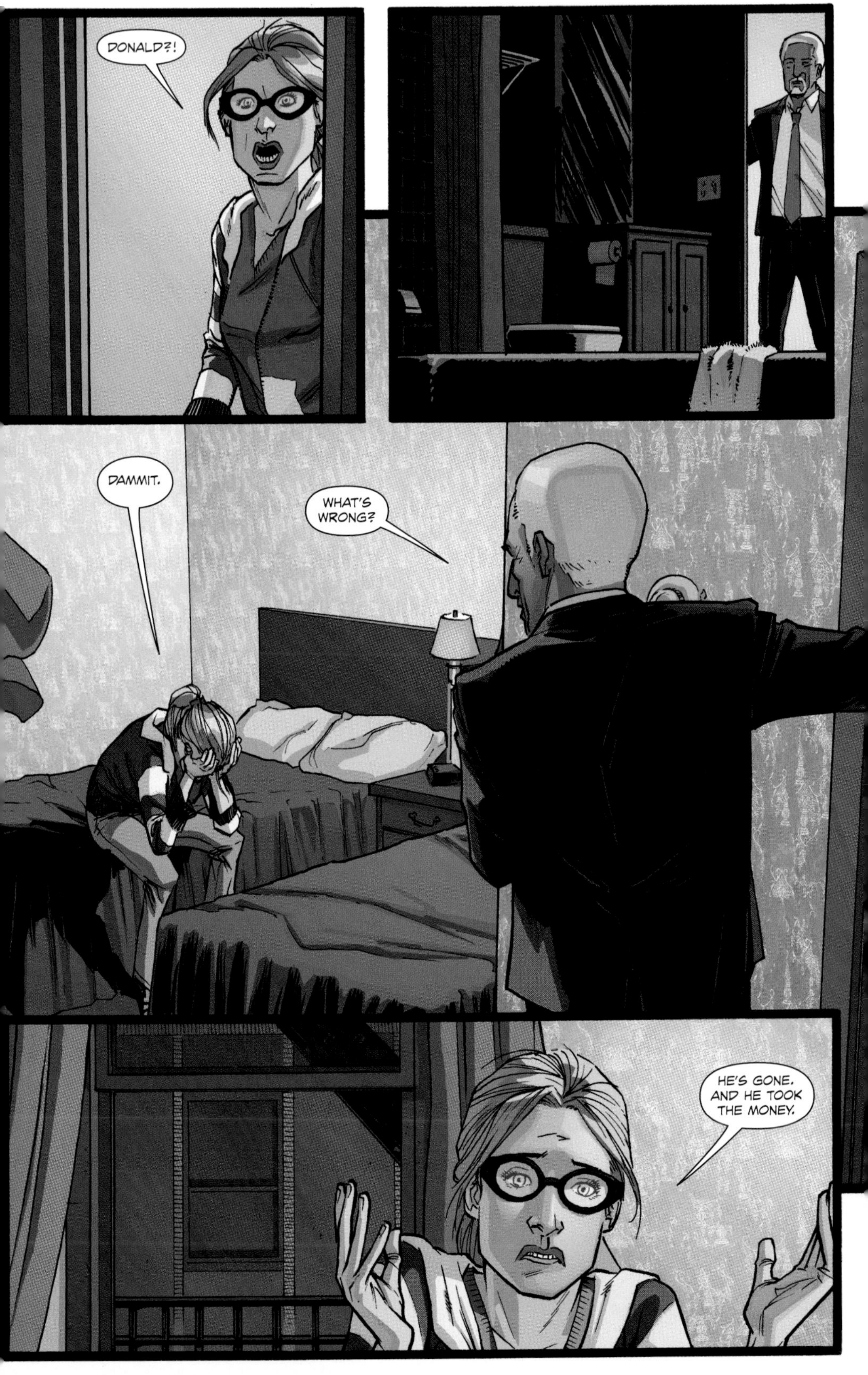
DONALD?!
DAMMIT.
WHAT'S WRONG?
HE'S GONE. AND HE TOOK THE MONEY.

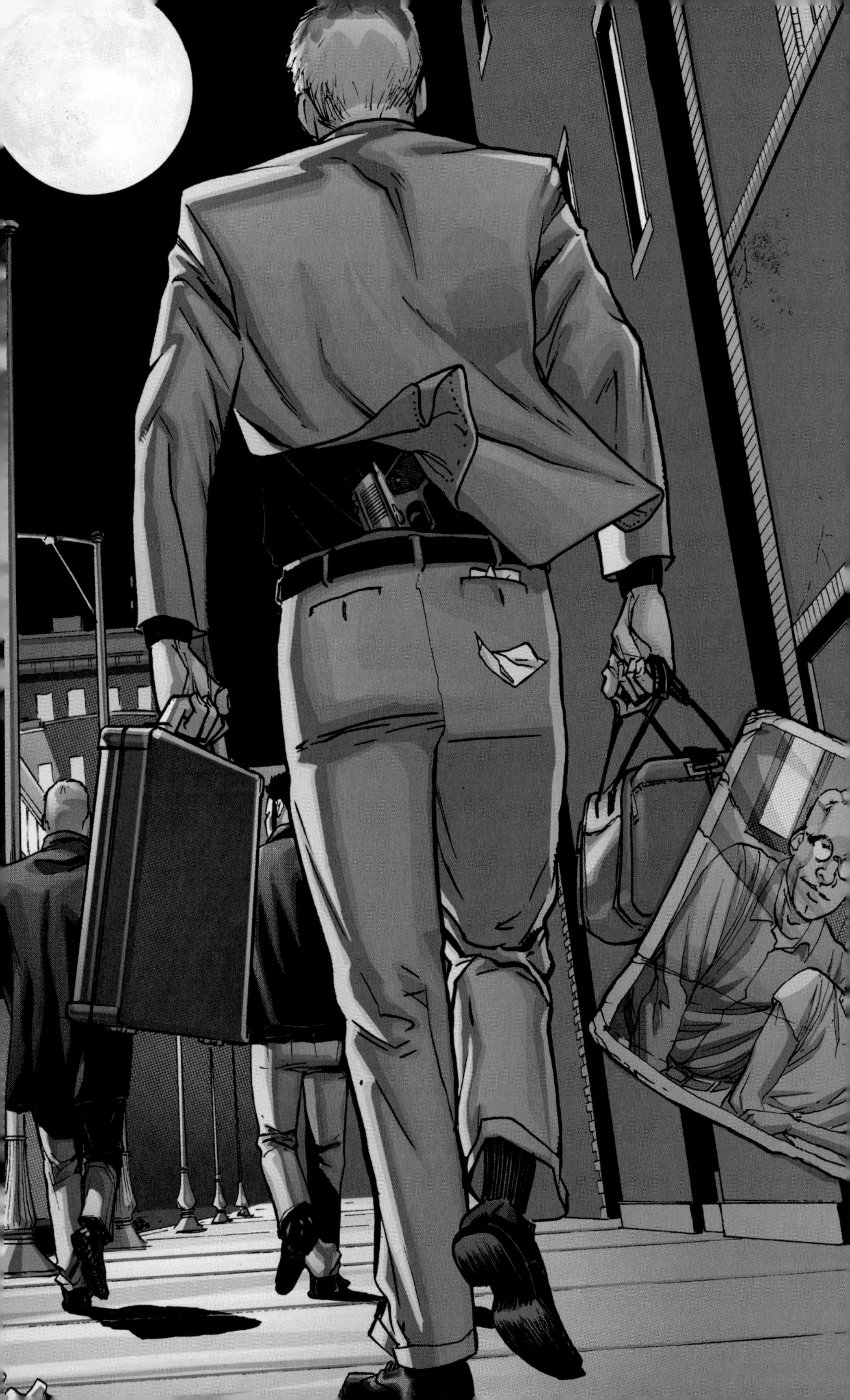

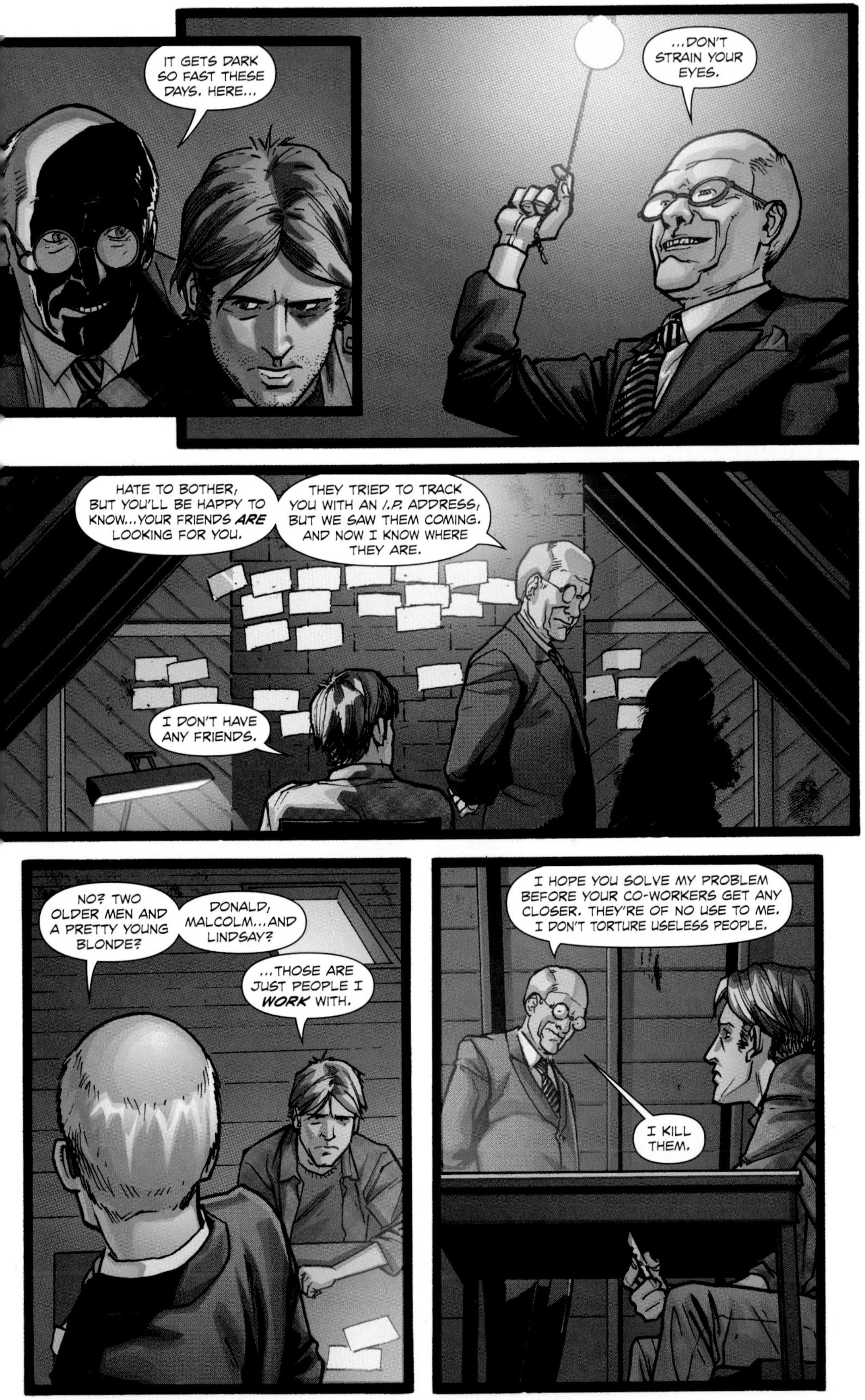
IT GETS DARK SO FAST THESE DAYS. HERE...
...DON'T STRAIN YOUR EYES.
HATE TO BOTHER, BUT YOU'LL BE HAPPY TO KNOW...YOUR FRIENDS **ARE** LOOKING FOR YOU.
THEY TRIED TO TRACK YOU WITH AN *I.P.* ADDRESS, BUT WE SAW THEM COMING. AND NOW I KNOW WHERE THEY ARE.
I DON'T HAVE ANY FRIENDS.
NO? TWO OLDER MEN AND A PRETTY YOUNG BLONDE?
DONALD, MALCOLM...AND LINDSAY?
...THOSE ARE JUST PEOPLE I **WORK** WITH.
I HOPE YOU SOLVE MY PROBLEM BEFORE YOUR CO-WORKERS GET ANY CLOSER. THEY'RE OF NO USE TO ME. I DON'T TORTURE USELESS PEOPLE.
I KILL THEM.

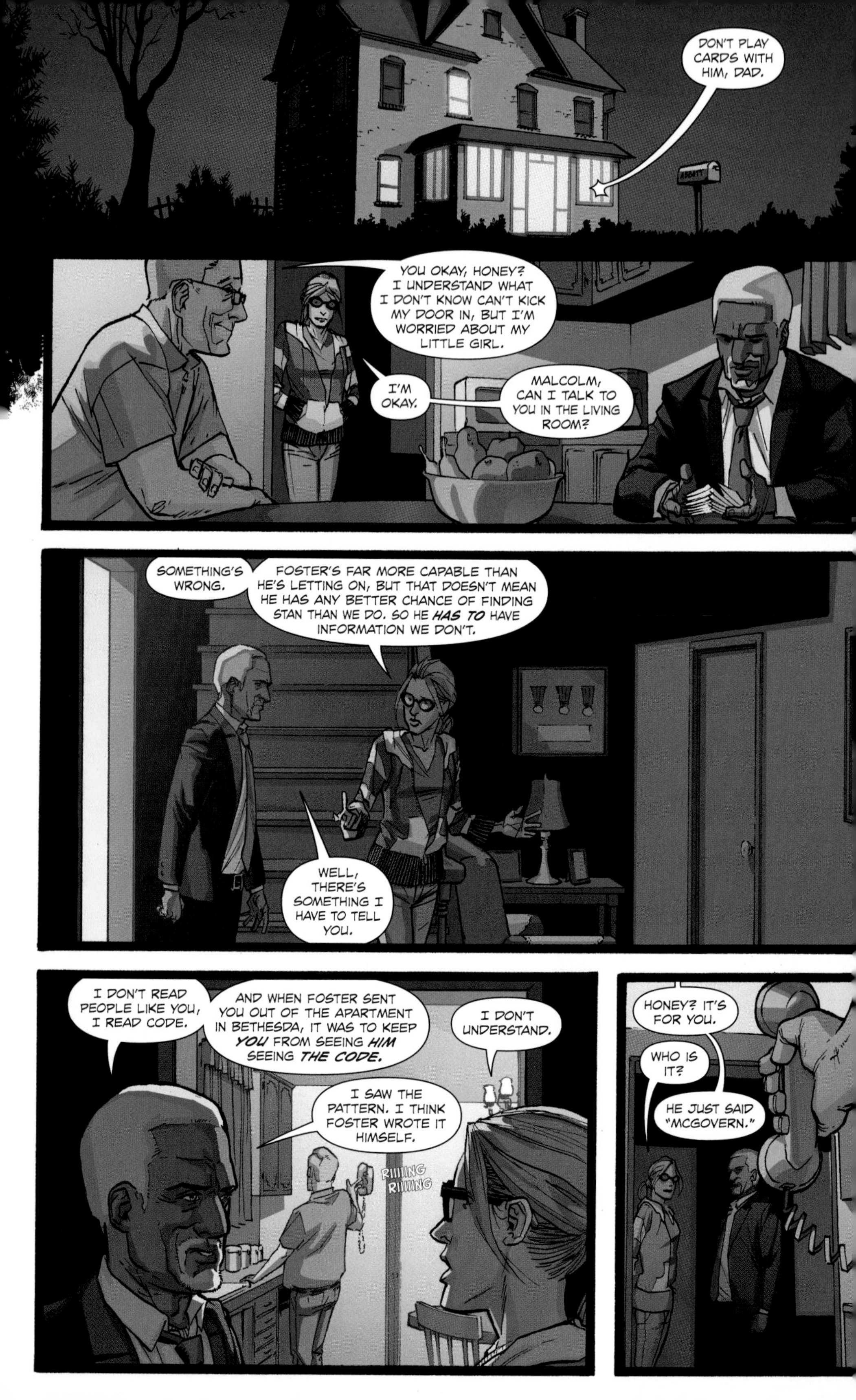

DON'T PLAY CARDS WITH HIM, DAD.
YOU OKAY, HONEY? I UNDERSTAND WHAT I DON'T KNOW CAN'T KICK MY DOOR IN, BUT I'M WORRIED ABOUT MY LITTLE GIRL.
I'M OKAY.
MALCOLM, CAN I TALK TO YOU IN THE LIVING ROOM?
SOMETHING'S WRONG.
FOSTER'S FAR MORE CAPABLE THAN HE'S LETTING ON, BUT THAT DOESN'T MEAN HE HAS ANY BETTER CHANCE OF FINDING STAN THAN WE DO. SO HE *HAS TO* HAVE INFORMATION WE DON'T.
WELL, THERE'S SOMETHING I HAVE TO TELL YOU.
I DON'T READ PEOPLE LIKE YOU, I READ CODE.
AND WHEN FOSTER SENT YOU OUT OF THE APARTMENT IN BETHESDA, IT WAS TO KEEP *YOU* FROM SEEING *HIM* SEEING *THE CODE.*
I DON'T UNDERSTAND.
I SAW THE PATTERN. I THINK FOSTER WROTE IT HIMSELF.
RIIIING
RIIIING
HONEY? IT'S FOR YOU.
WHO IS IT?
HE JUST SAID "MCGOVERN."

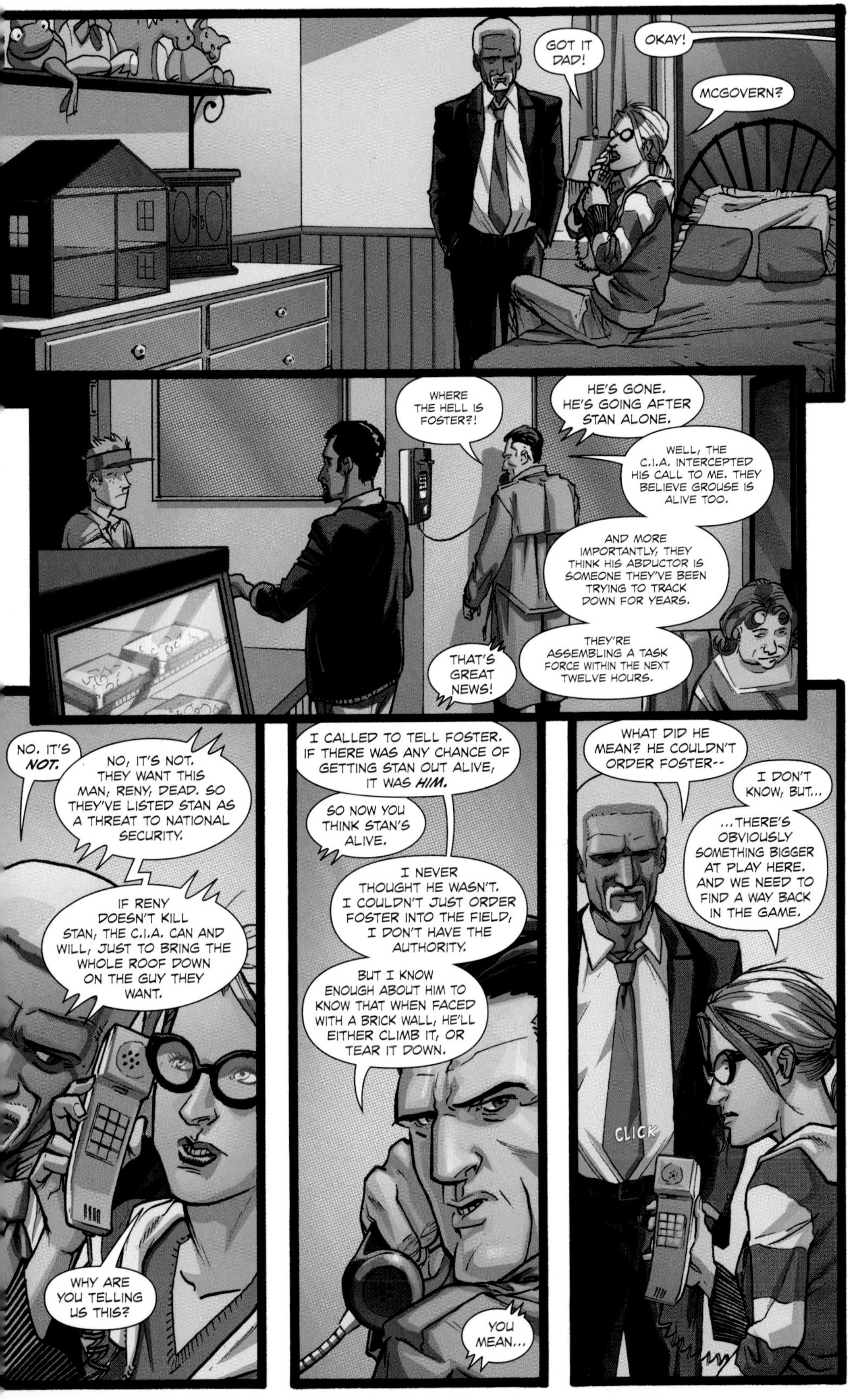
GOT IT DAD!
OKAY!
MCGOVERN?
WHERE THE HELL IS FOSTER?!
HE'S GONE. HE'S GOING AFTER STAN ALONE.
WELL, THE C.I.A. INTERCEPTED HIS CALL TO ME. THEY BELIEVE GROUSE IS ALIVE TOO.
AND MORE IMPORTANTLY, THEY THINK HIS ABDUCTOR IS SOMEONE THEY'VE BEEN TRYING TO TRACK DOWN FOR YEARS.
THEY'RE ASSEMBLING A TASK FORCE WITHIN THE NEXT TWELVE HOURS.
THAT'S GREAT NEWS!
NO. IT'S *NOT.*
NO, IT'S NOT. THEY WANT THIS MAN, RENY, DEAD. SO THEY'VE LISTED STAN AS A THREAT TO NATIONAL SECURITY.
IF RENY DOESN'T KILL STAN, THE C.I.A. CAN AND WILL, JUST TO BRING THE WHOLE ROOF DOWN ON THE GUY THEY WANT.
WHY ARE YOU TELLING US THIS?
I CALLED TO TELL FOSTER. IF THERE WAS ANY CHANCE OF GETTING STAN OUT ALIVE, IT WAS *HIM.*
SO NOW YOU THINK STAN'S ALIVE.
I NEVER THOUGHT HE WASN'T. I COULDN'T JUST ORDER FOSTER INTO THE FIELD, I DON'T HAVE THE AUTHORITY.
BUT I KNOW ENOUGH ABOUT HIM TO KNOW THAT WHEN FACED WITH A BRICK WALL, HE'LL EITHER CLIMB IT, OR TEAR IT DOWN.
YOU MEAN...
CLICK
WHAT DID HE MEAN? HE COULDN'T ORDER FOSTER--
I DON'T KNOW, BUT...
...THERE'S OBVIOUSLY SOMETHING BIGGER AT PLAY HERE. AND WE NEED TO FIND A WAY BACK IN THE GAME.

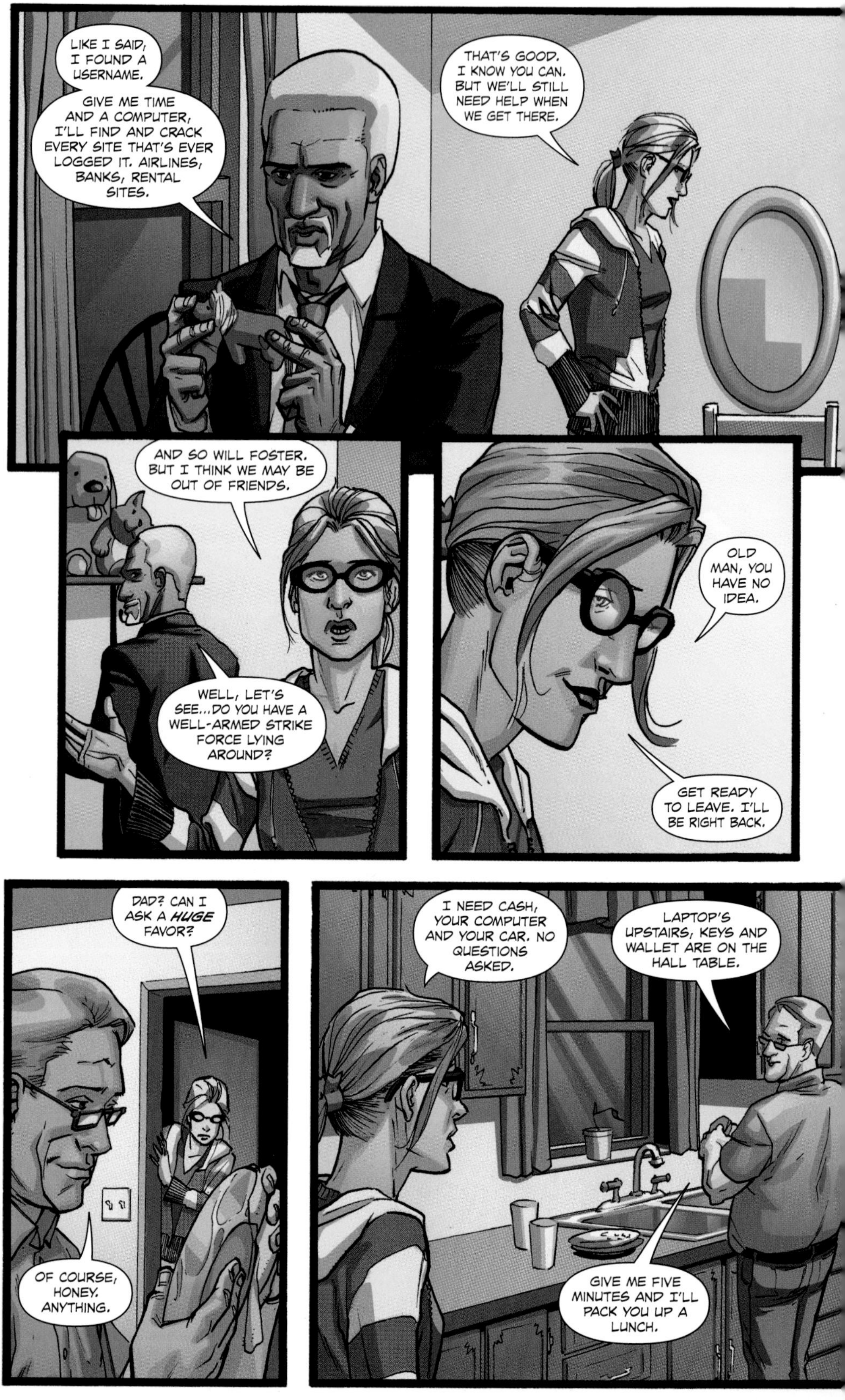
LIKE I SAID, I FOUND A USERNAME.
GIVE ME TIME AND A COMPUTER, I'LL FIND AND CRACK EVERY SITE THAT'S EVER LOGGED IT. AIRLINES, BANKS, RENTAL SITES.
THAT'S GOOD. I KNOW YOU CAN. BUT WE'LL STILL NEED HELP WHEN WE GET THERE.
AND SO WILL FOSTER. BUT I THINK WE MAY BE OUT OF FRIENDS.
WELL, LET'S SEE...DO YOU HAVE A WELL-ARMED STRIKE FORCE LYING AROUND?
OLD MAN, YOU HAVE NO IDEA.
GET READY TO LEAVE. I'LL BE RIGHT BACK.
DAD? CAN I ASK A *HUGE* FAVOR?
OF COURSE, HONEY. ANYTHING.
I NEED CASH, YOUR COMPUTER AND YOUR CAR. NO QUESTIONS ASKED.
LAPTOP'S UPSTAIRS, KEYS AND WALLET ARE ON THE HALL TABLE.
GIVE ME FIVE MINUTES AND I'LL PACK YOU UP A LUNCH.

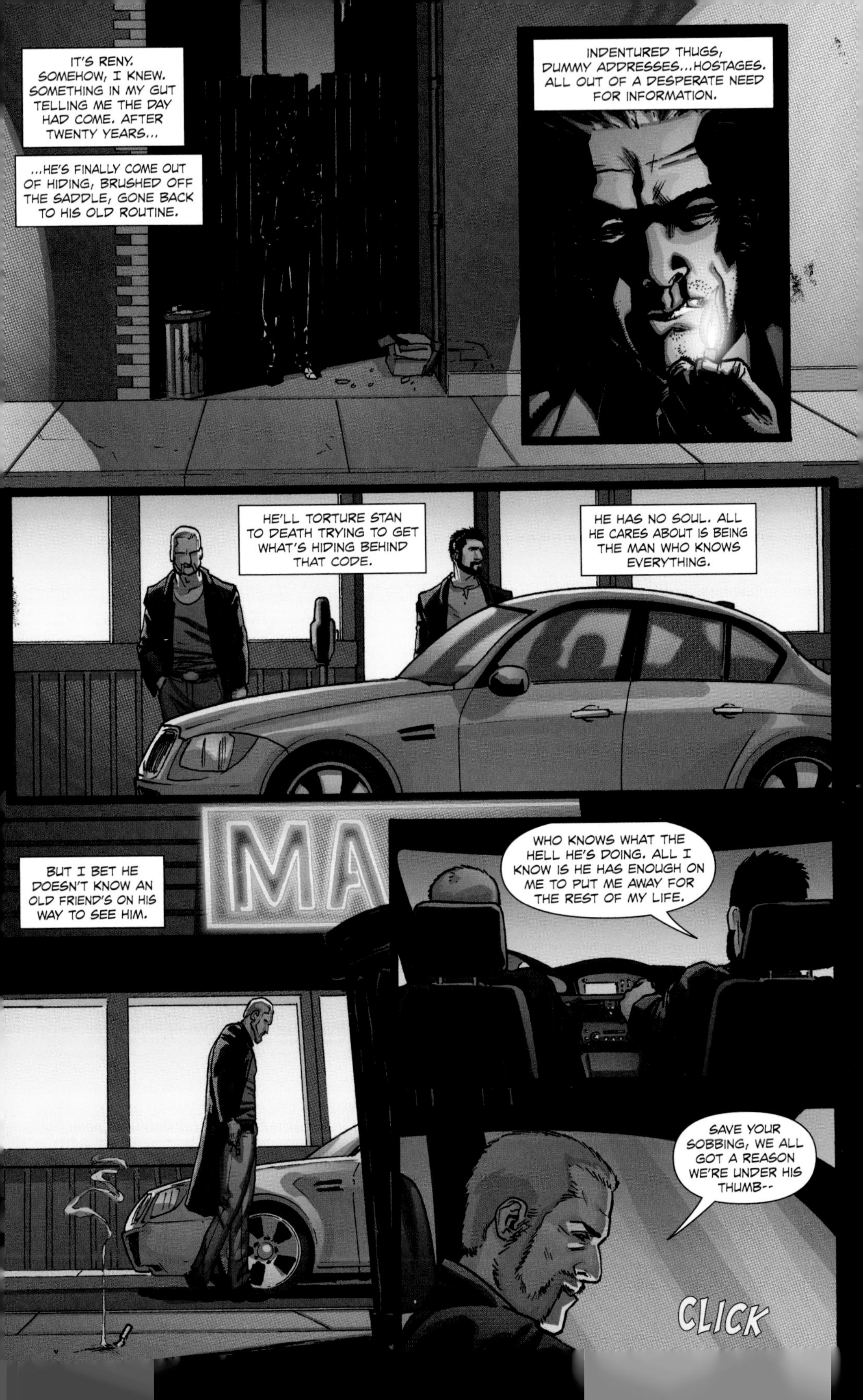
IT'S RENY. SOMEHOW, I KNEW. SOMETHING IN MY GUT TELLING ME THE DAY HAD COME. AFTER TWENTY YEARS...
...HE'S FINALLY COME OUT OF HIDING, BRUSHED OFF THE SADDLE, GONE BACK TO HIS OLD ROUTINE.
INDENTURED THUGS, DUMMY ADDRESSES...HOSTAGES. ALL OUT OF A DESPERATE NEED FOR INFORMATION.
HE'LL TORTURE STAN TO DEATH TRYING TO GET WHAT'S HIDING BEHIND THAT CODE.
HE HAS NO SOUL. ALL HE CARES ABOUT IS BEING THE MAN WHO KNOWS EVERYTHING.
MA
BUT I BET HE DOESN'T KNOW AN OLD FRIEND'S ON HIS WAY TO SEE HIM.
WHO KNOWS WHAT THE HELL HE'S DOING. ALL I KNOW IS HE HAS ENOUGH ON ME TO PUT ME AWAY FOR THE REST OF MY LIFE.
SAVE YOUR SOBBING, WE ALL GOT A REASON WE'RE UNDER HIS THUMB--
CLICK

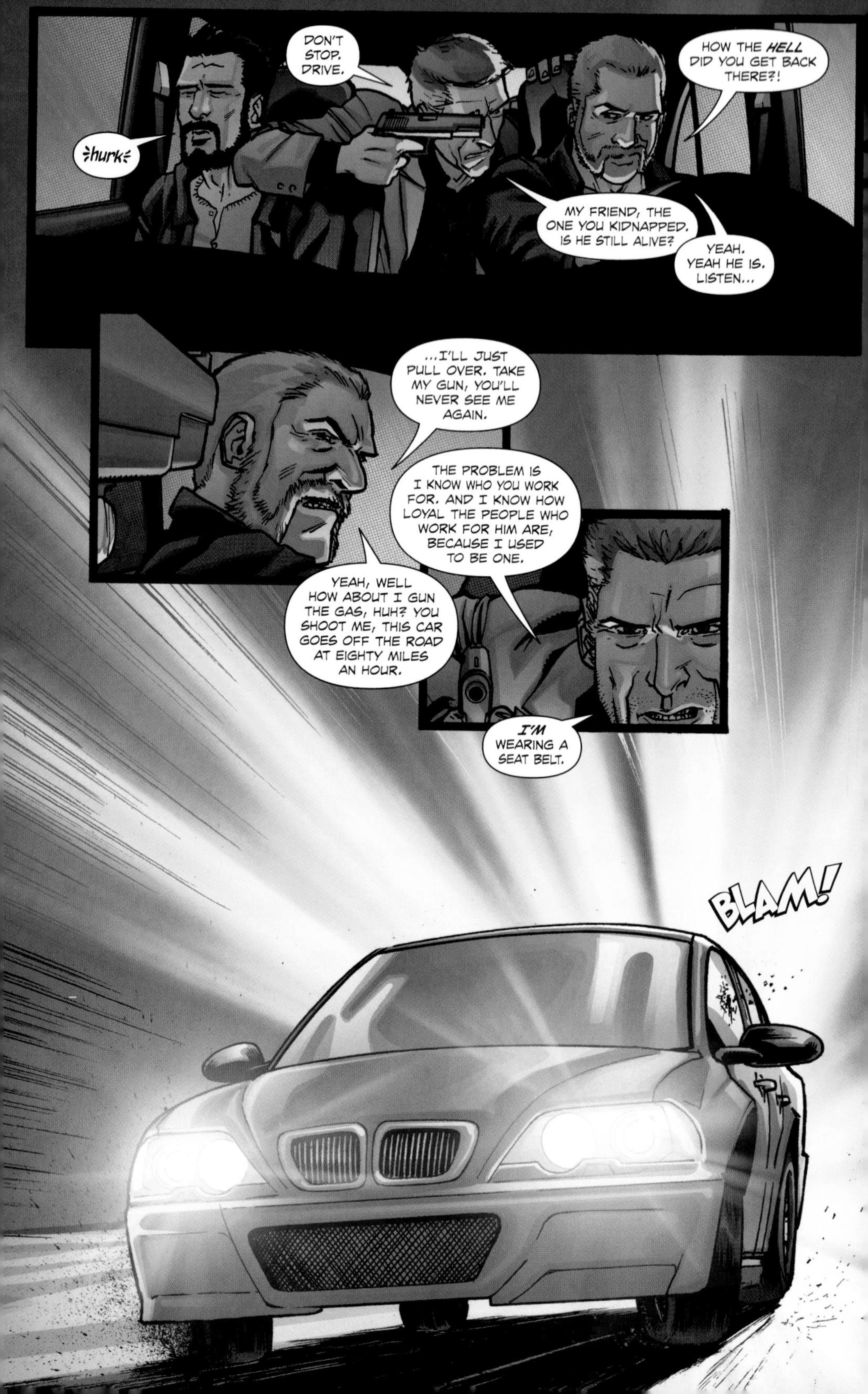
DON'T STOP. DRIVE.
HOW THE *HELL* DID YOU GET BACK THERE?!
hurk
MY FRIEND, THE ONE YOU KIDNAPPED. IS HE STILL ALIVE?
YEAH. YEAH HE IS. LISTEN...
...I'LL JUST PULL OVER. TAKE MY GUN, YOU'LL NEVER SEE ME AGAIN.
THE PROBLEM IS I KNOW WHO YOU WORK FOR. AND I KNOW HOW LOYAL THE PEOPLE WHO WORK FOR HIM ARE, BECAUSE I USED TO BE ONE.
YEAH, WELL HOW ABOUT I GUN THE GAS, HUH? YOU SHOOT ME, THIS CAR GOES OFF THE ROAD AT EIGHTY MILES AN HOUR.
I'M WEARING A SEAT BELT.
BLAM!

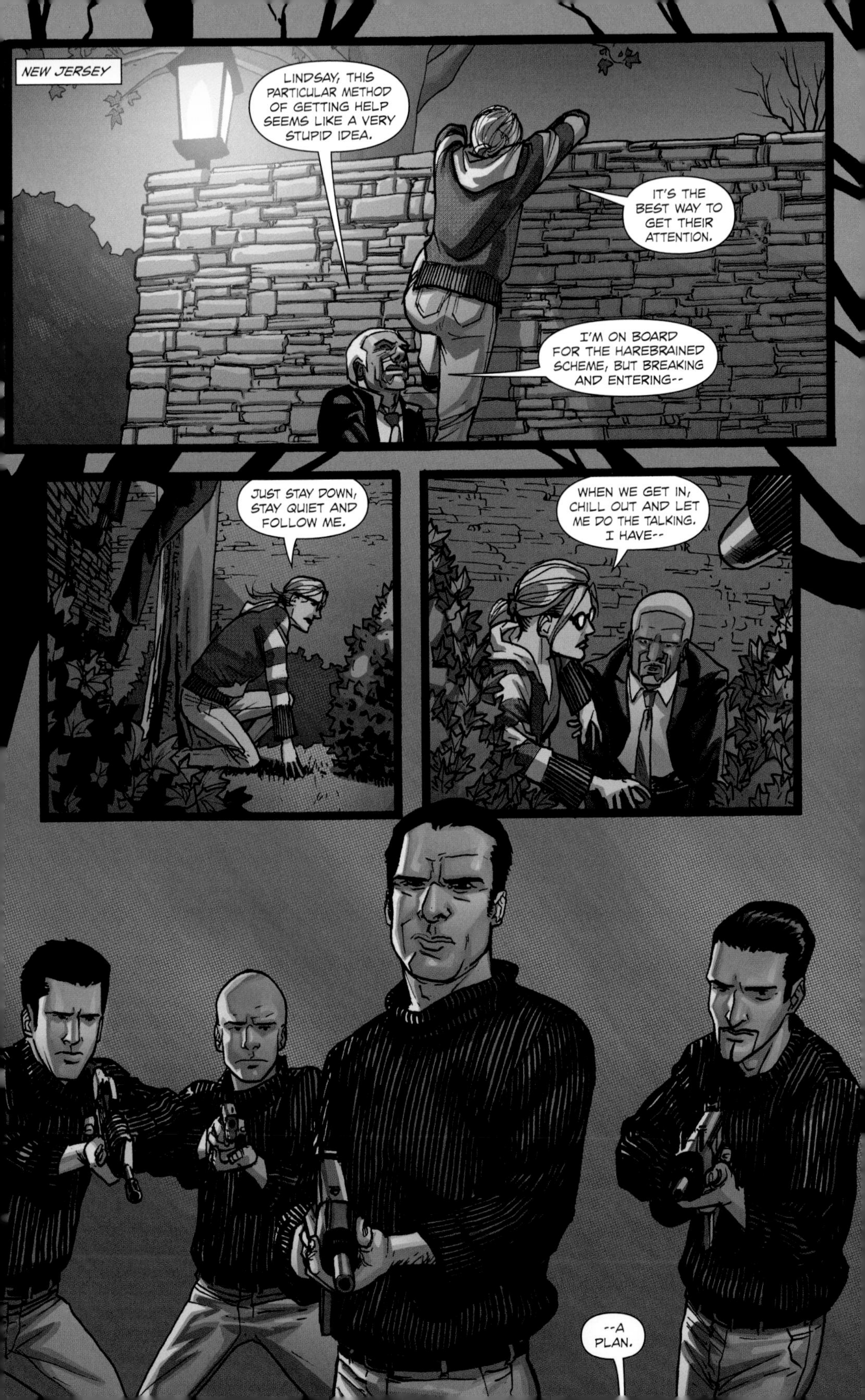
NEW JERSEY
LINDSAY, THIS PARTICULAR METHOD OF GETTING HELP SEEMS LIKE A VERY STUPID IDEA.
IT'S THE BEST WAY TO GET THEIR ATTENTION.
I'M ON BOARD FOR THE HAREBRAINED SCHEME, BUT BREAKING AND ENTERING--
JUST STAY DOWN, STAY QUIET AND FOLLOW ME.
WHEN WE GET IN, CHILL OUT AND LET ME DO THE TALKING. I HAVE--
--A PLAN.

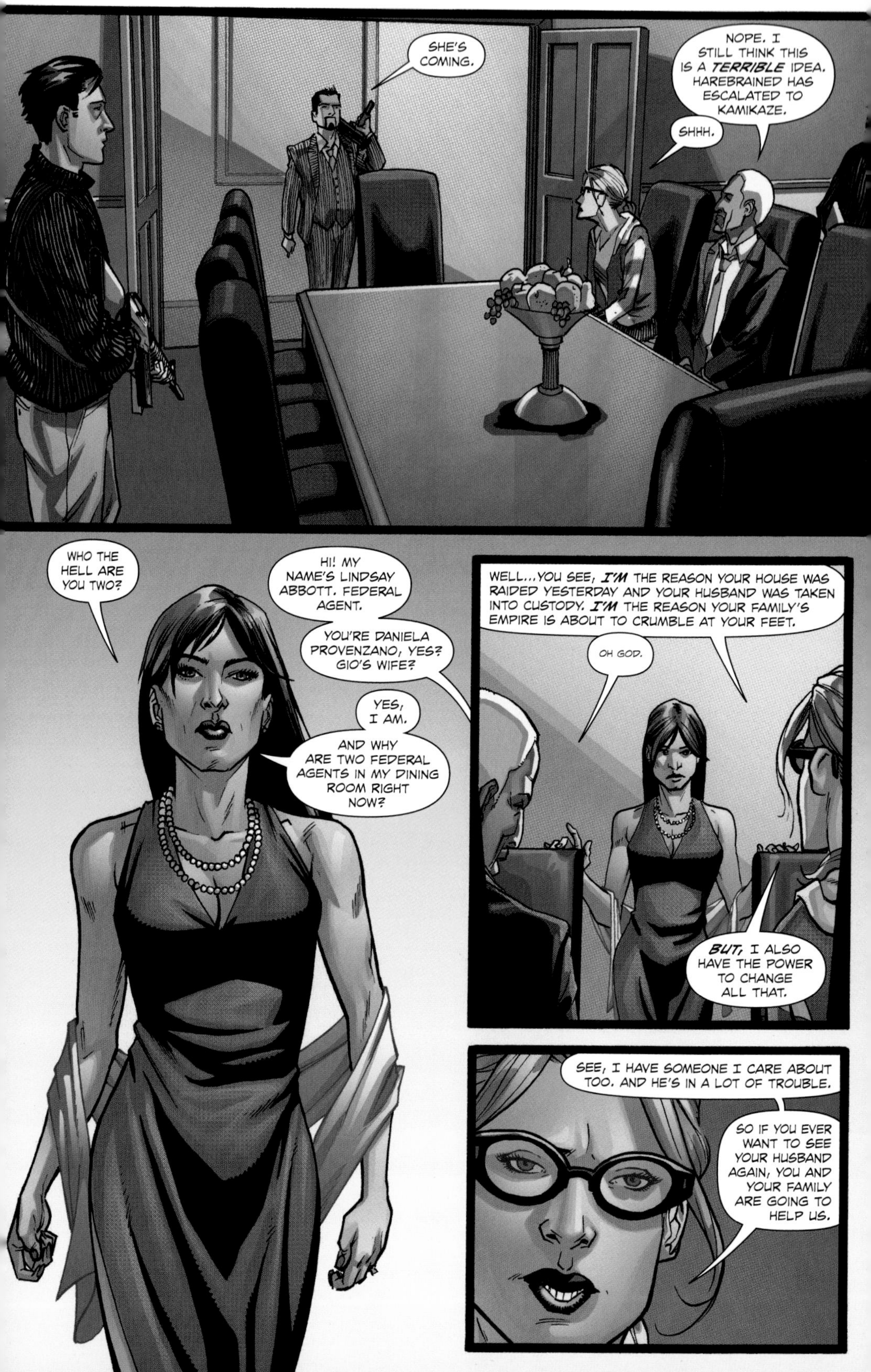
SHE'S COMING.
NOPE. I STILL THINK THIS IS A TERRIBLE IDEA. HAREBRAINED HAS ESCALATED TO KAMIKAZE.
SHHH.
WHO THE HELL ARE YOU TWO?
HI! MY NAME'S LINDSAY ABBOTT. FEDERAL AGENT.
YOU'RE DANIELA PROVENZANO, YES? GIO'S WIFE?
YES, I AM.
AND WHY ARE TWO FEDERAL AGENTS IN MY DINING ROOM RIGHT NOW?
WELL...YOU SEE, I'M THE REASON YOUR HOUSE WAS RAIDED YESTERDAY AND YOUR HUSBAND WAS TAKEN INTO CUSTODY. I'M THE REASON YOUR FAMILY'S EMPIRE IS ABOUT TO CRUMBLE AT YOUR FEET.
OH GOD.
BUT, I ALSO HAVE THE POWER TO CHANGE ALL THAT.
SEE, I HAVE SOMEONE I CARE ABOUT TOO. AND HE'S IN A LOT OF TROUBLE.
SO IF YOU EVER WANT TO SEE YOUR HUSBAND AGAIN, YOU AND YOUR FAMILY ARE GOING TO HELP US.

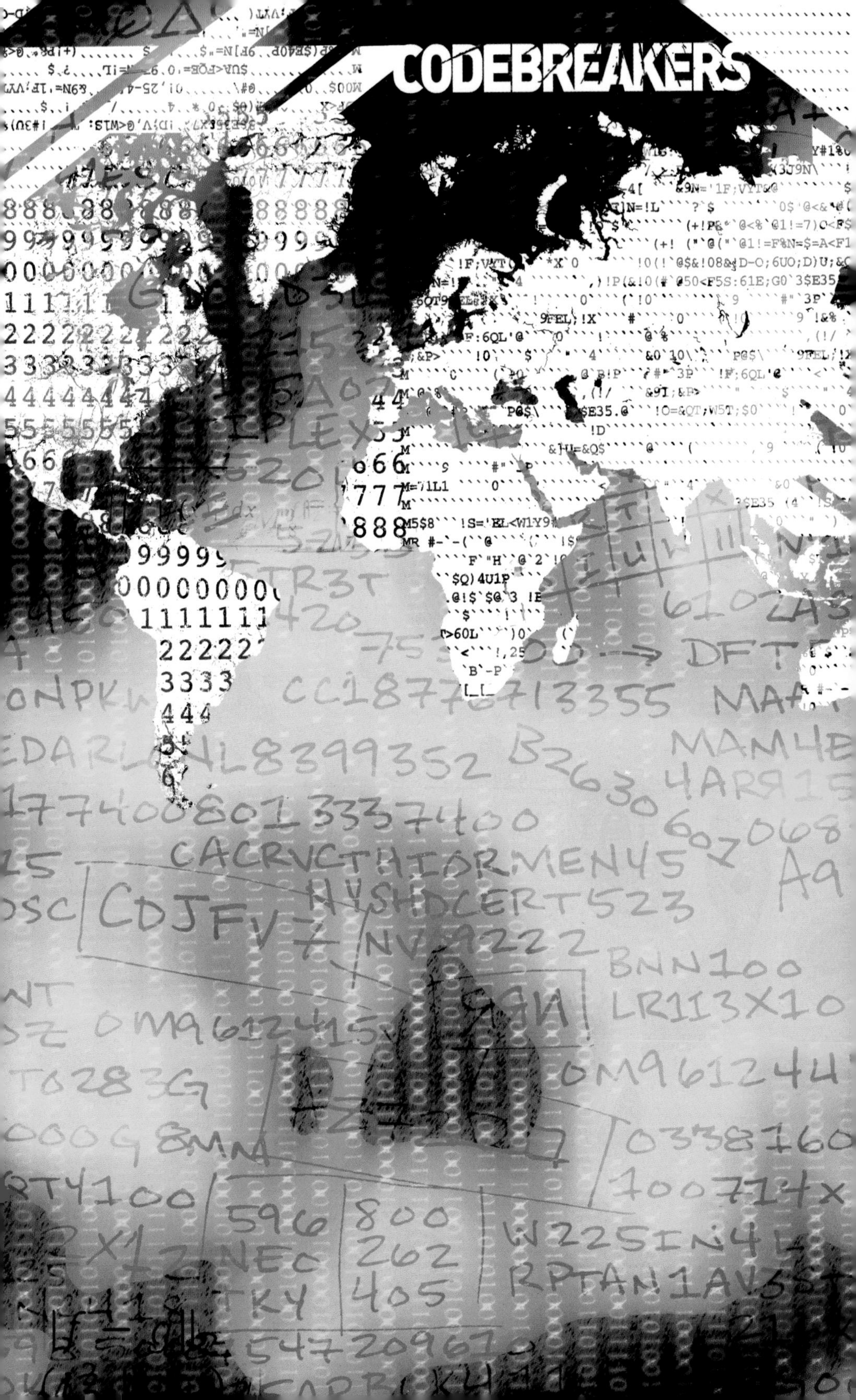
CODEBREAKERS

CHAPTER: THREE

CODE BREAKERS

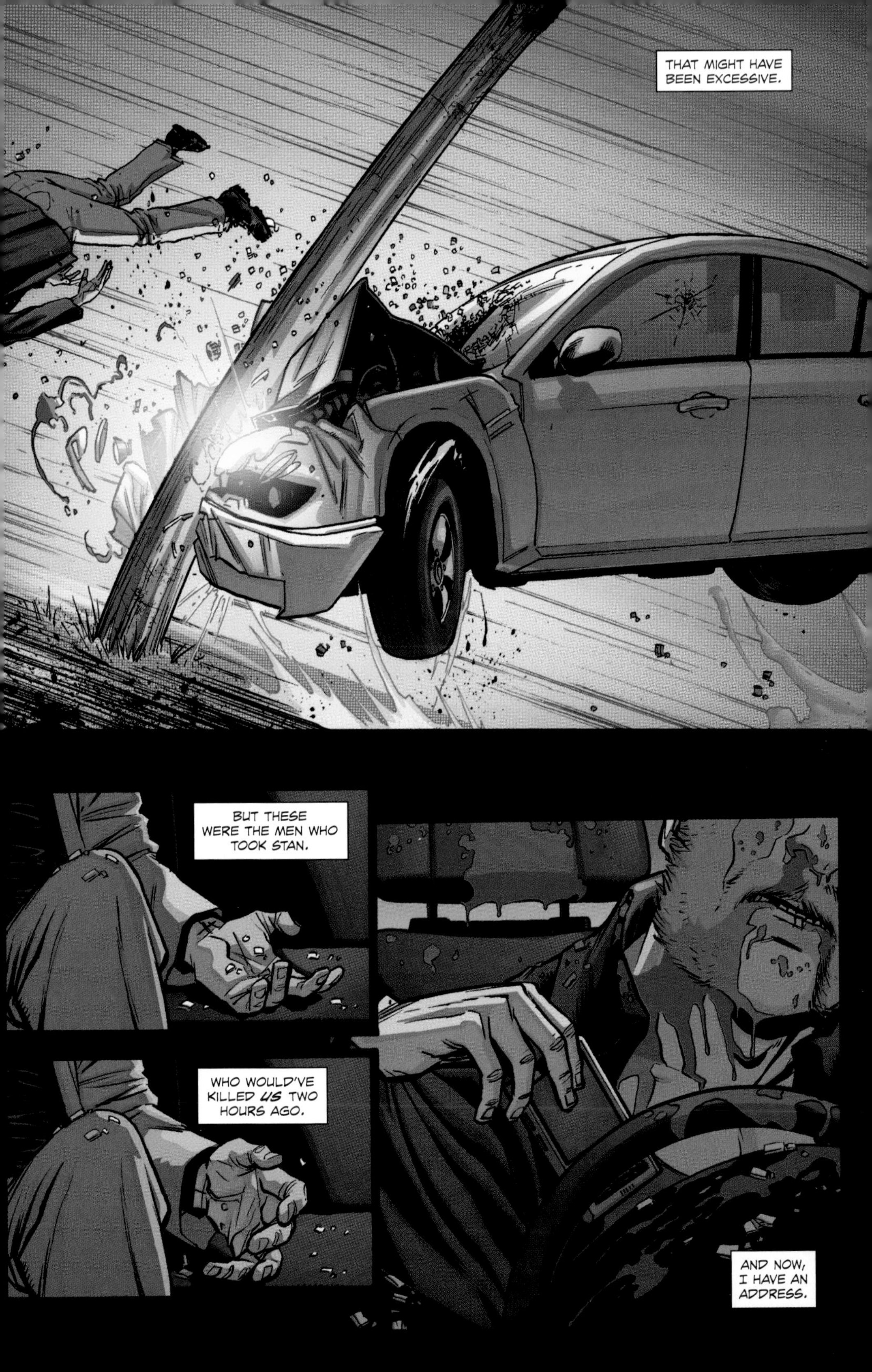
THAT MIGHT HAVE BEEN EXCESSIVE.
BUT THESE WERE THE MEN WHO TOOK STAN.
WHO WOULD'VE KILLED *US* TWO HOURS AGO.
AND NOW, I HAVE AN ADDRESS.

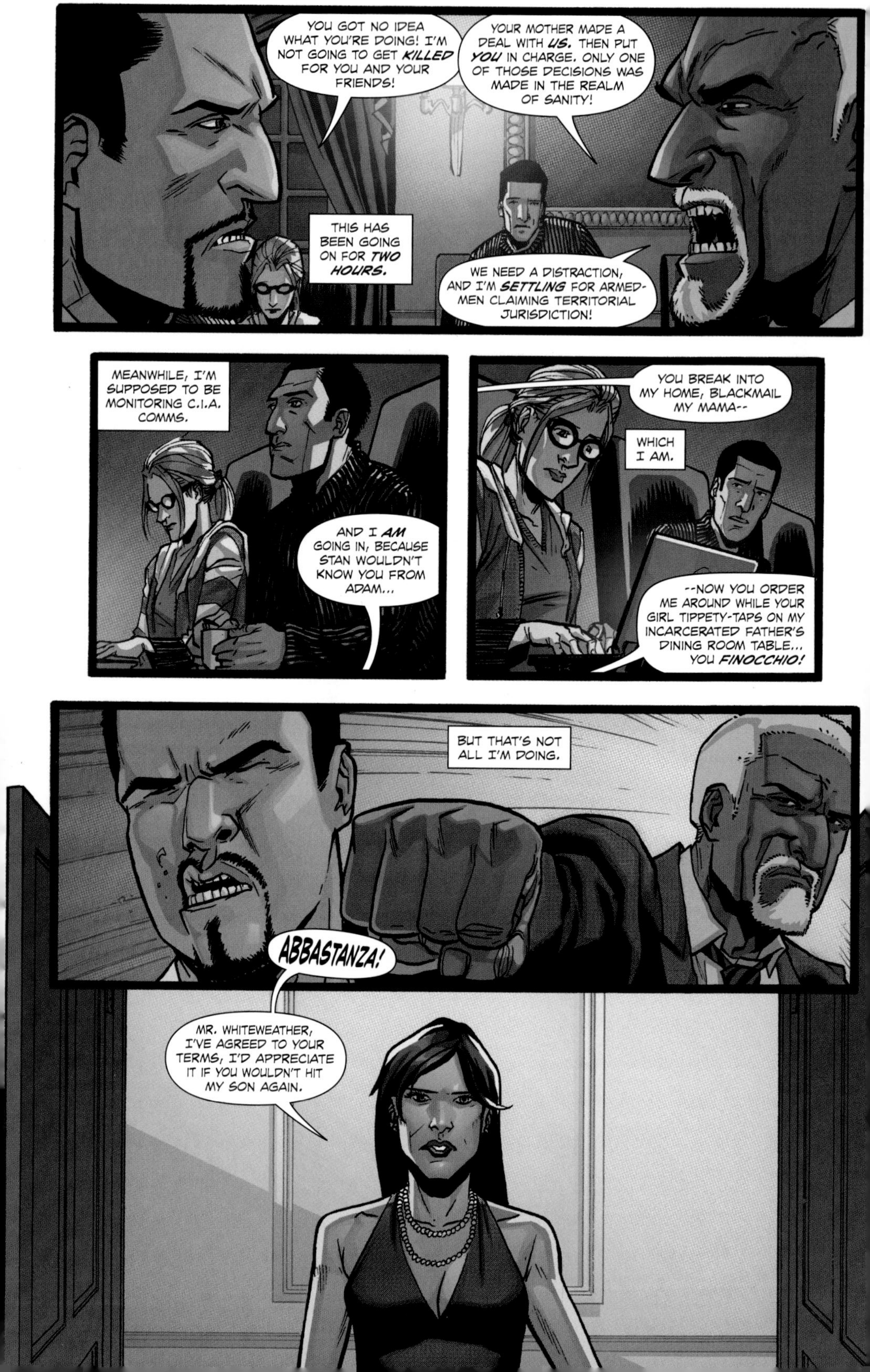
YOU GOT NO IDEA WHAT YOU'RE DOING! I'M NOT GOING TO GET KILLED FOR YOU AND YOUR FRIENDS!
YOUR MOTHER MADE A DEAL WITH US. THEN PUT YOU IN CHARGE. ONLY ONE OF THOSE DECISIONS WAS MADE IN THE REALM OF SANITY!
THIS HAS BEEN GOING ON FOR TWO HOURS.
WE NEED A DISTRACTION, AND I'M SETTLING FOR ARMED-MEN CLAIMING TERRITORIAL JURISDICTION!
MEANWHILE, I'M SUPPOSED TO BE MONITORING C.I.A. COMMS.
AND I AM GOING IN, BECAUSE STAN WOULDN'T KNOW YOU FROM ADAM...
YOU BREAK INTO MY HOME, BLACKMAIL MY MAMA--
WHICH I AM.
--NOW YOU ORDER ME AROUND WHILE YOUR GIRL TIPPETY-TAPS ON MY INCARCERATED FATHER'S DINING ROOM TABLE... YOU FINOCCHIO!
BUT THAT'S NOT ALL I'M DOING.
ABBASTANZA!
MR. WHITEWEATHER, I'VE AGREED TO YOUR TERMS, I'D APPRECIATE IT IF YOU WOULDN'T HIT MY SON AGAIN.

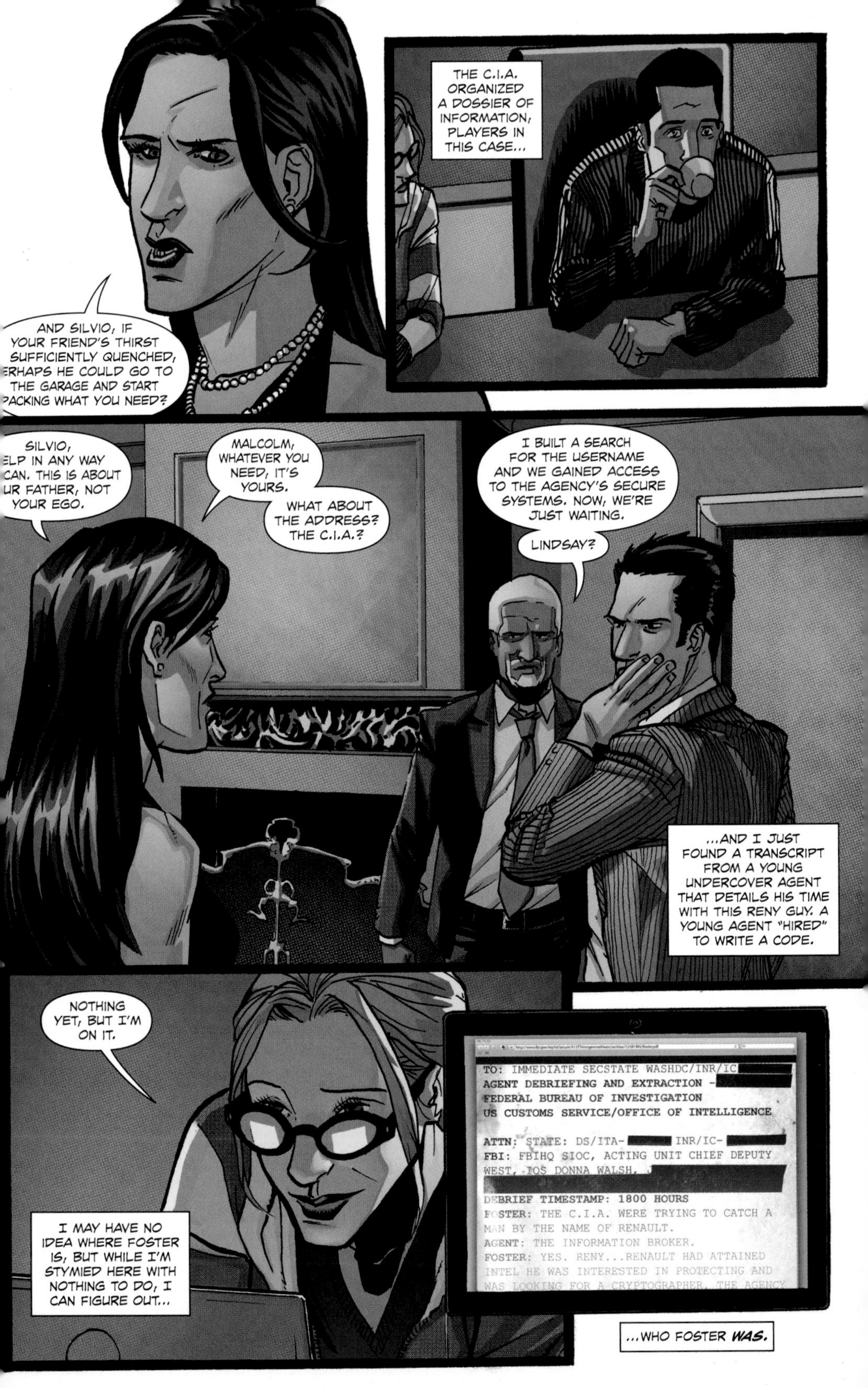
AND SILVIO, IF YOUR FRIEND'S THIRST SUFFICIENTLY QUENCHED, ERHAPS HE COULD GO TO THE GARAGE AND START PACKING WHAT YOU NEED?
THE C.I.A. ORGANIZED A DOSSIER OF INFORMATION, PLAYERS IN THIS CASE...
SILVIO, ELP IN ANY WAY CAN. THIS IS ABOUT UR FATHER, NOT YOUR EGO.
MALCOLM, WHATEVER YOU NEED, IT'S YOURS.
WHAT ABOUT THE ADDRESS? THE C.I.A.?
I BUILT A SEARCH FOR THE USERNAME AND WE GAINED ACCESS TO THE AGENCY'S SECURE SYSTEMS. NOW, WE'RE JUST WAITING.
LINDSAY?
...AND I JUST FOUND A TRANSCRIPT FROM A YOUNG UNDERCOVER AGENT THAT DETAILS HIS TIME WITH THIS RENY GUY. A YOUNG AGENT "HIRED" TO WRITE A CODE.
NOTHING YET, BUT I'M ON IT.
I MAY HAVE NO IDEA WHERE FOSTER IS, BUT WHILE I'M STYMIED HERE WITH NOTHING TO DO, I CAN FIGURE OUT...
TO: IMMEDIATE SECSTATE WASHDC/INR/IC [redacted]
AGENT DEBRIEFING AND EXTRACTION - [redacted]
FEDERAL BUREAU OF INVESTIGATION
US CUSTOMS SERVICE/OFFICE OF INTELLIGENCE
ATTN: STATE: DS/ITA- [redacted] INR/IC- [redacted]
FBI: FBIHQ SIOC, ACTING UNIT CHIEF DEPUTY
WEST, IOS DONNA WALSH, [redacted]
DEBRIEF TIMESTAMP: 1800 HOURS
FOSTER: THE C.I.A. WERE TRYING TO CATCH A
MAN BY THE NAME OF RENAULT.
AGENT: THE INFORMATION BROKER.
FOSTER: YES. RENY...RENAULT HAD ATTAINED
INTEL HE WAS INTERESTED IN PROTECTING AND
WAS LOOKING FOR A CRYPTOGRAPHER. THE AGENCY
...WHO FOSTER WAS.

THE C.I.A. WERE TRYING TO CATCH A MAN BY THE NAME OF RENAULT.

THE INFORMATION BROKER.

I TOOK DOZENS OF TESTS, I WAS INTERVIEWED DOZENS OF TIMES BY COUNTLESS PEOPLE, **NONE** OF THEM THE TARGET. THEN FINALLY...HE SUMMONED ME.

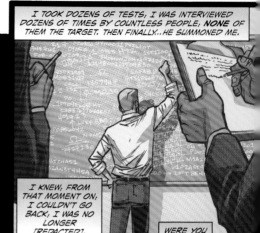

YES. RENY...**RENAULT** HAD ATTAINED INTEL HE WAS INTERESTED IN PROTECTING AND WAS LOOKING FOR A CRYPTOGRAPHER. THE AGENCY CAME TO ME; THEY NEEDED SOMEONE ADEPT ENOUGH AT CODE TO PASS.

I KNEW, FROM THAT MOMENT ON, I COULDN'T GO BACK, I WAS NO LONGER [REDACTED].

WERE YOU NERVOUS?

I WAS TERRIFIED.

LOOKING BACK ON EVERYTHING THAT HAPPENED, DO YOU FEEL YOU WERE ULTIMATELY UNPREPARED FOR THE JOB?

YES.

BUT WHAT SECOND YEAR EVER GETS AN OPPORTUNITY LIKE THIS? THE AGENCY BELIEVED IN ME, BACKED ME, AND AT THE TIME, THE AGENCY WAS THE CLOSEST THING I'D EVER HAD TO--

LET'S GO BACK TO THE FIRST DAY. TELL ME ABOUT MEETING RENAULT.

HE MADE YOU FEEL ON EDGE AND AT EASE ALL AT ONCE. INTEL DIDN'T SCRATCH THE SURFACE. I'D NEVER MET ANYONE LIKE HIM.

THERE'S MY KID GENIUS. PLEASED TO MEET YOU. I'VE HEARD GREAT THINGS.

GOOD TO MEET YOU. I--

LET'S HURDLE OVER THE SMALL TALK. I'M DRUNK AND PREPARED TO BE IMPRESSED. WHAT SAY WE GET STARTED?

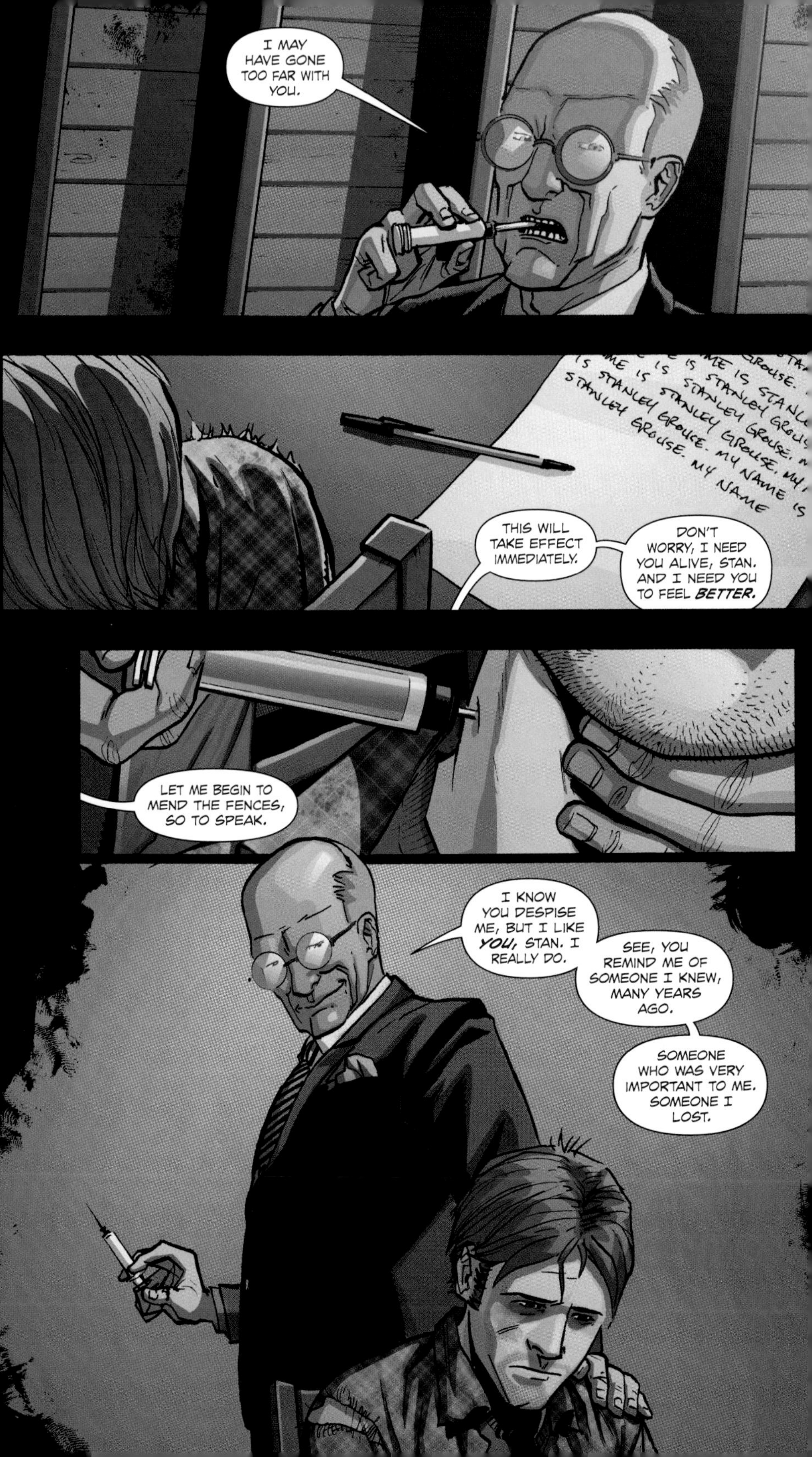
I MAY HAVE GONE TOO FAR WITH YOU.
THIS WILL TAKE EFFECT IMMEDIATELY.
DON'T WORRY, I NEED YOU ALIVE, STAN. AND I NEED YOU TO FEEL BETTER.
LET ME BEGIN TO MEND THE FENCES, SO TO SPEAK.
I KNOW YOU DESPISE ME, BUT I LIKE YOU, STAN. I REALLY DO.
SEE, YOU REMIND ME OF SOMEONE I KNEW, MANY YEARS AGO.
SOMEONE WHO WAS VERY IMPORTANT TO ME. SOMEONE I LOST.

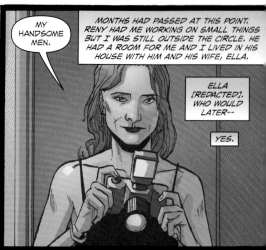

MY HANDSOME MEN.

MONTHS HAD PASSED AT THIS POINT. RENY HAD ME WORKING ON SMALL THINGS BUT I WAS STILL OUTSIDE THE CIRCLE. HE HAD A ROOM FOR ME AND I LIVED IN HIS HOUSE WITH HIM AND HIS WIFE, ELLA.

ELLA [REDACTED]. WHO WOULD LATER--

YES.

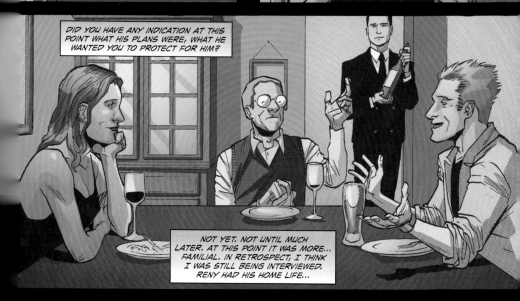

DID YOU HAVE ANY INDICATION AT THIS POINT WHAT HIS PLANS WERE, WHAT HE WANTED YOU TO PROTECT FOR HIM?

NOT YET. NOT UNTIL MUCH LATER. AT THIS POINT IT WAS MORE... FAMILIAL. IN RETROSPECT, I THINK I WAS STILL BEING INTERVIEWED. RENY HAD HIS HOME LIFE...

...AND THEN HE HAD "THE WAREHOUSE." THAT'S WHAT HE CALLED IT. HE SPENT MOST OF HIS DAYS THERE, WHILE ELLA AND I STAYED AT THE ESTATE.

HOW MUCH DID ELLA KNOW ABOUT RENAULT?

I DON'T KNOW. ENOUGH.

ENOUGH?

YES. ENOUGH TO FEAR HIM.

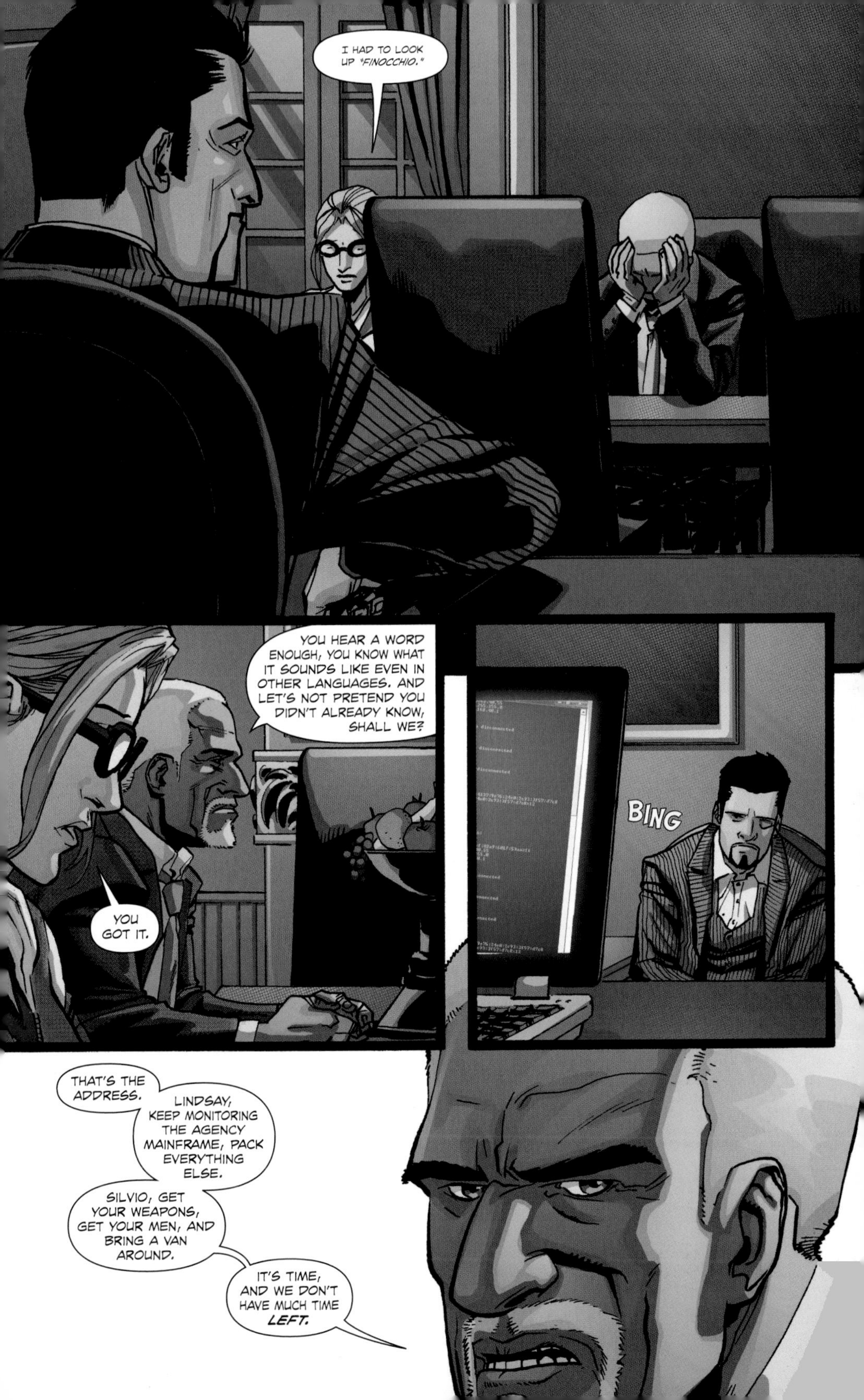
I HAD TO LOOK UP "FINOCCHIO."
YOU HEAR A WORD ENOUGH, YOU KNOW WHAT IT SOUNDS LIKE EVEN IN OTHER LANGUAGES. AND LET'S NOT PRETEND YOU DIDN'T ALREADY KNOW, SHALL WE?
YOU GOT IT.
BING
THAT'S THE ADDRESS.
LINDSAY, KEEP MONITORING THE AGENCY MAINFRAME, PACK EVERYTHING ELSE.
SILVIO, GET YOUR WEAPONS, GET YOUR MEN, AND BRING A VAN AROUND.
IT'S TIME, AND WE DON'T HAVE MUCH TIME LEFT.

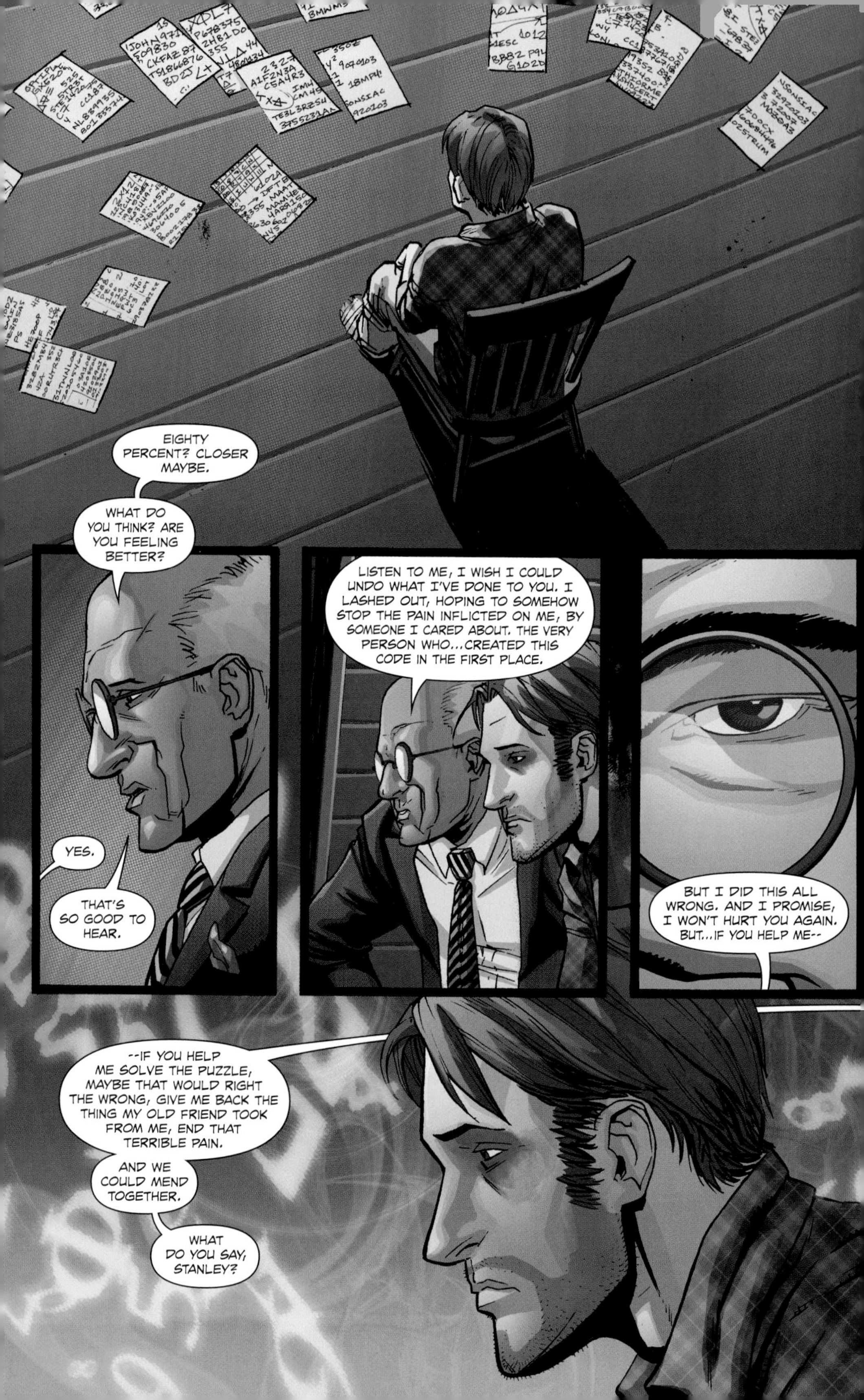

EIGHTY PERCENT? CLOSER MAYBE.
WHAT DO YOU THINK? ARE YOU FEELING BETTER?
YES.
THAT'S SO GOOD TO HEAR.
LISTEN TO ME, I WISH I COULD UNDO WHAT I'VE DONE TO YOU. I LASHED OUT, HOPING TO SOMEHOW STOP THE PAIN INFLICTED ON ME, BY SOMEONE I CARED ABOUT. THE VERY PERSON WHO...CREATED THIS CODE IN THE FIRST PLACE.
BUT I DID THIS ALL WRONG. AND I PROMISE, I WON'T HURT YOU AGAIN. BUT...IF YOU HELP ME--
--IF YOU HELP ME SOLVE THE PUZZLE, MAYBE THAT WOULD RIGHT THE WRONG, GIVE ME BACK THE THING MY OLD FRIEND TOOK FROM ME, END THAT TERRIBLE PAIN.
AND WE COULD MEND TOGETHER.
WHAT DO YOU SAY, STANLEY?

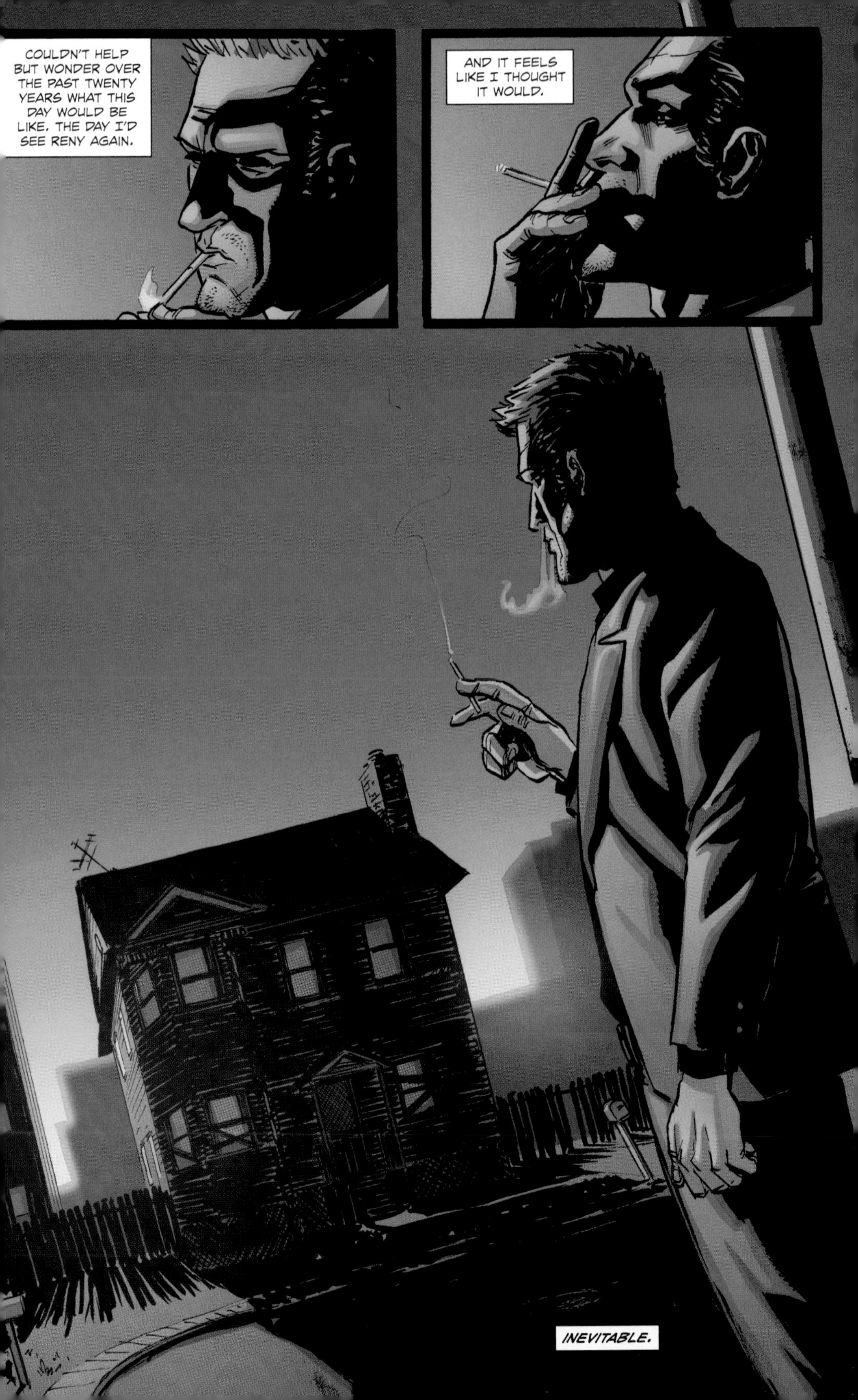
COULDN'T HELP BUT WONDER OVER THE PAST TWENTY YEARS WHAT THIS DAY WOULD BE LIKE. THE DAY I'D SEE RENY AGAIN.
AND IT FEELS LIKE I THOUGHT IT WOULD.
INEVITABLE.

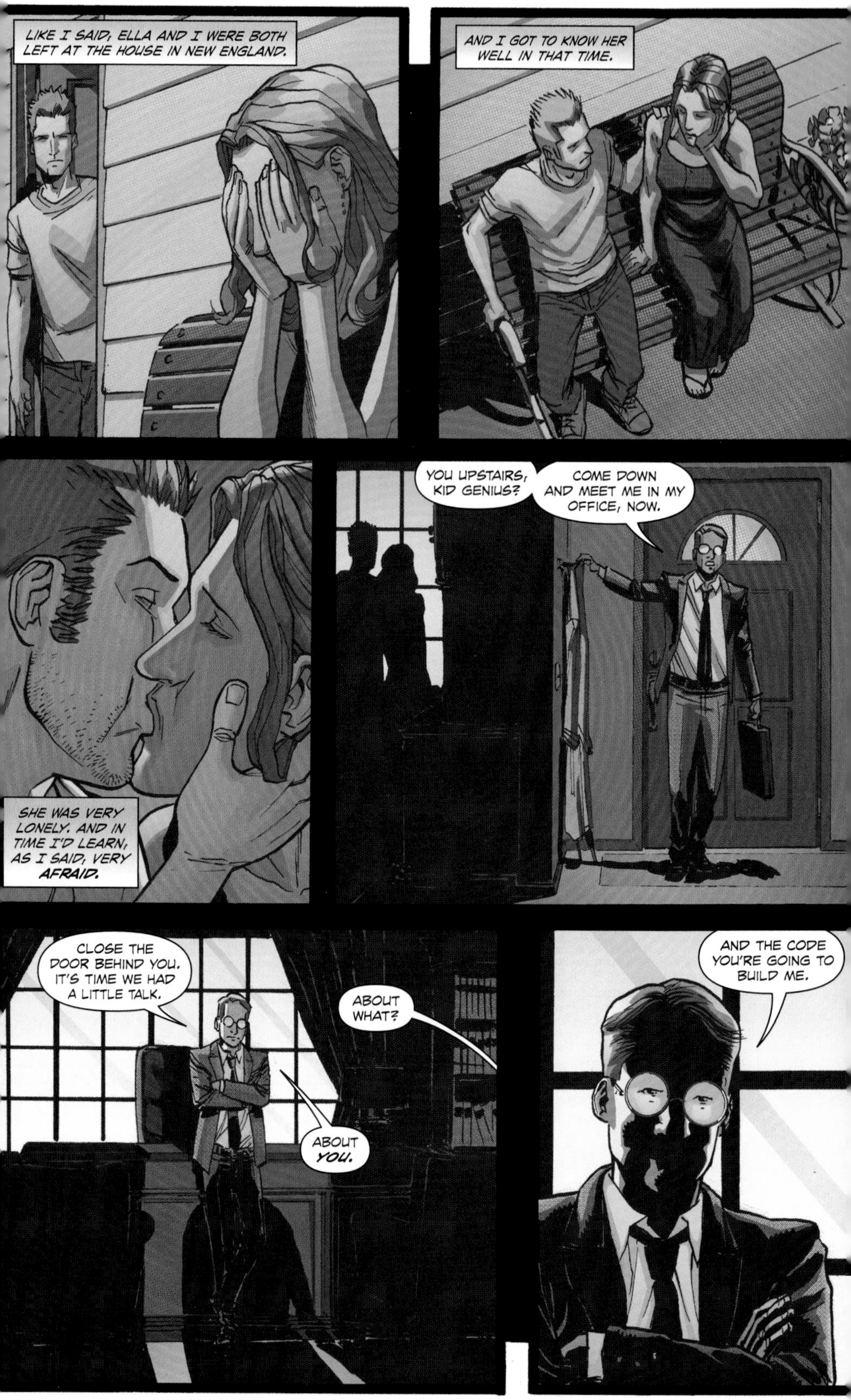

LIKE I SAID, ELLA AND I WERE BOTH LEFT AT THE HOUSE IN NEW ENGLAND.
AND I GOT TO KNOW HER WELL IN THAT TIME.
SHE WAS VERY LONELY. AND IN TIME I'D LEARN, AS I SAID, VERY **AFRAID.**
YOU UPSTAIRS, KID GENIUS?
COME DOWN AND MEET ME IN MY OFFICE, NOW.
CLOSE THE DOOR BEHIND YOU. IT'S TIME WE HAD A LITTLE TALK.
ABOUT WHAT?
ABOUT **YOU.**
AND THE CODE YOU'RE GOING TO BUILD ME.

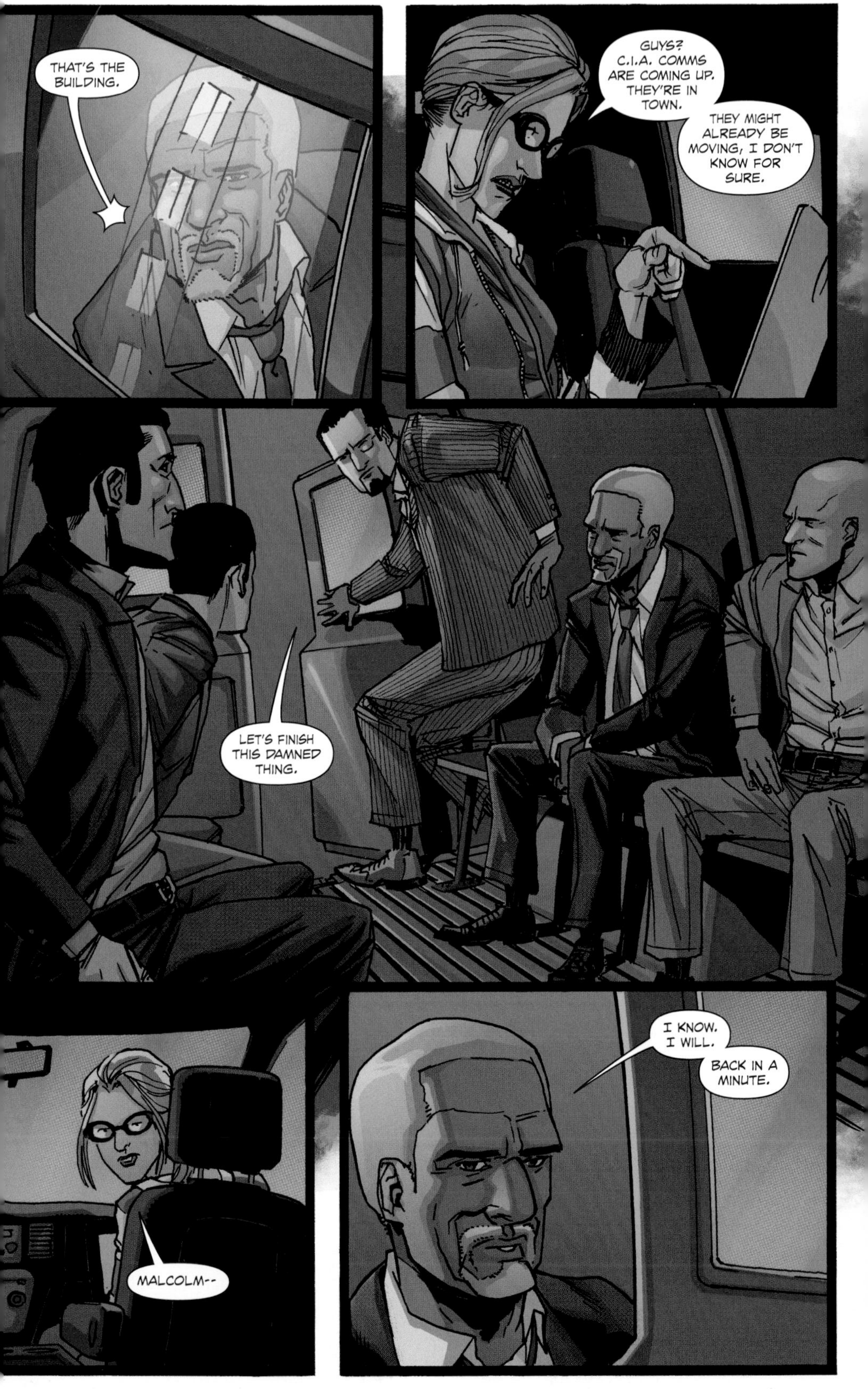
THAT'S THE BUILDING.
GUYS? C.I.A. COMMS ARE COMING UP. THEY'RE IN TOWN.
THEY MIGHT ALREADY BE MOVING, I DON'T KNOW FOR SURE.
LET'S FINISH THIS DAMNED THING.
MALCOLM--
I KNOW. I WILL.
BACK IN A MINUTE.

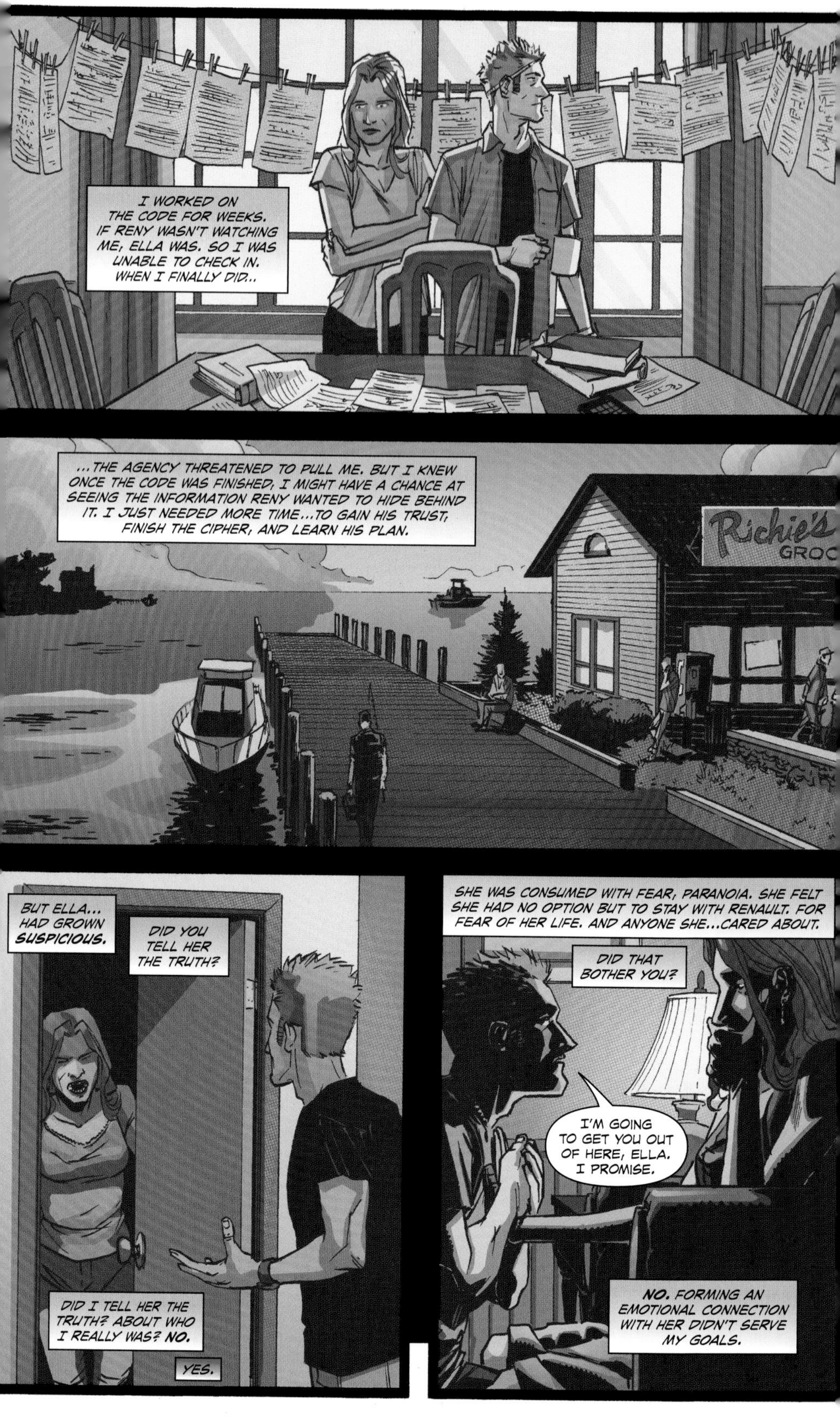
I WORKED ON THE CODE FOR WEEKS. IF RENY WASN'T WATCHING ME, ELLA WAS. SO I WAS UNABLE TO CHECK IN. WHEN I FINALLY DID...
...THE AGENCY THREATENED TO PULL ME. BUT I KNEW ONCE THE CODE WAS FINISHED, I MIGHT HAVE A CHANCE AT SEEING THE INFORMATION RENY WANTED TO HIDE BEHIND IT. I JUST NEEDED MORE TIME...TO GAIN HIS TRUST, FINISH THE CIPHER, AND LEARN HIS PLAN.
Richie's
GROC
BUT ELLA... HAD GROWN **SUSPICIOUS.**
DID YOU TELL HER THE TRUTH?
DID I TELL HER THE TRUTH? ABOUT WHO I REALLY WAS? **NO.**
YES.
SHE WAS CONSUMED WITH FEAR, PARANOIA. SHE FELT SHE HAD NO OPTION BUT TO STAY WITH RENAULT. FOR FEAR OF HER LIFE. AND ANYONE SHE...CARED ABOUT.
DID THAT BOTHER YOU?
I'M GOING TO GET YOU OUT OF HERE, ELLA. I PROMISE.
NO. FORMING AN EMOTIONAL CONNECTION WITH HER DIDN'T SERVE MY GOALS.

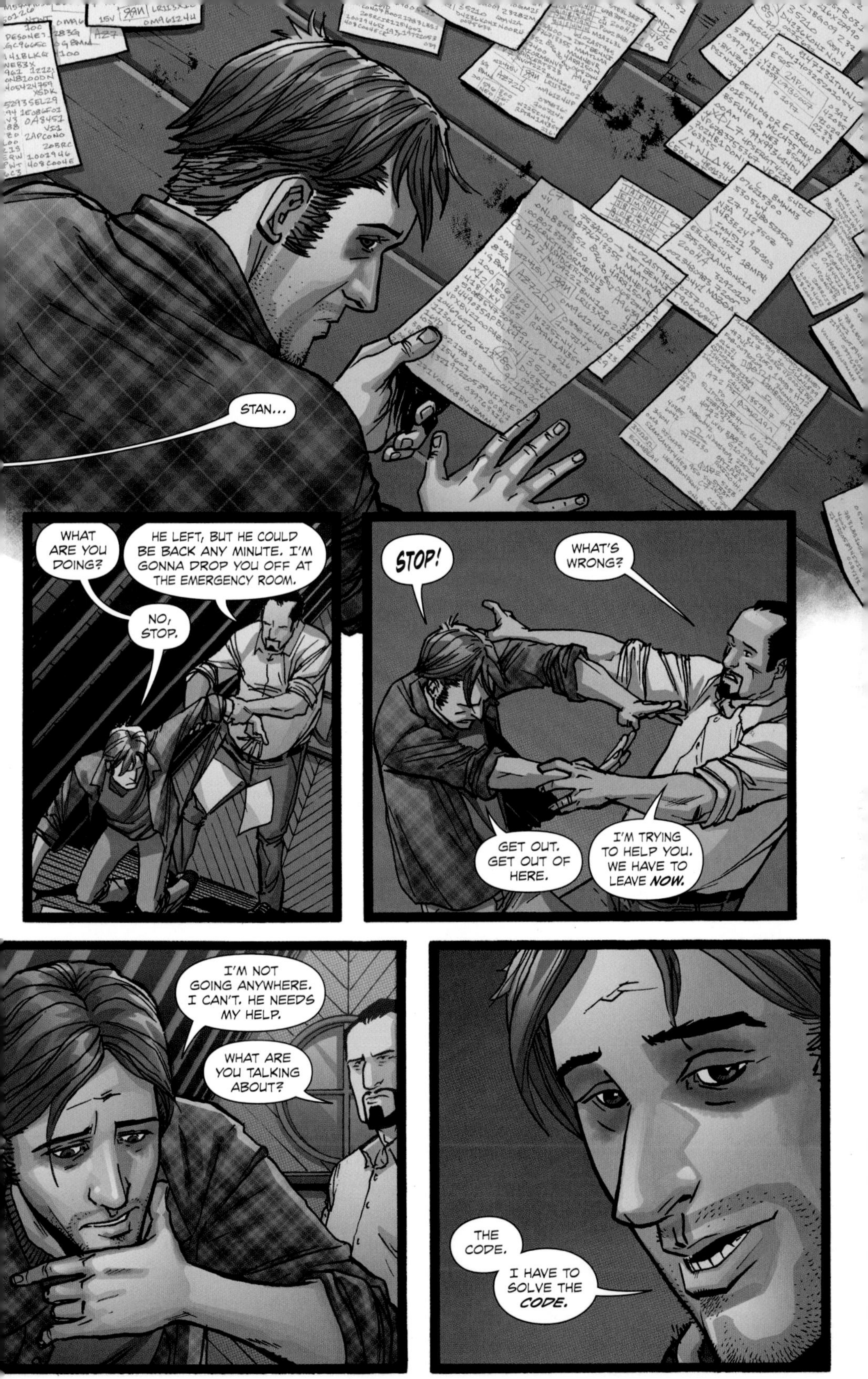
STAN...
WHAT ARE YOU DOING?
HE LEFT, BUT HE COULD BE BACK ANY MINUTE. I'M GONNA DROP YOU OFF AT THE EMERGENCY ROOM.
NO, STOP.
STOP!
WHAT'S WRONG?
GET OUT. GET OUT OF HERE.
I'M TRYING TO HELP YOU. WE HAVE TO LEAVE NOW.
I'M NOT GOING ANYWHERE. I CAN'T. HE NEEDS MY HELP.
WHAT ARE YOU TALKING ABOUT?
THE CODE.
I HAVE TO SOLVE THE CODE.

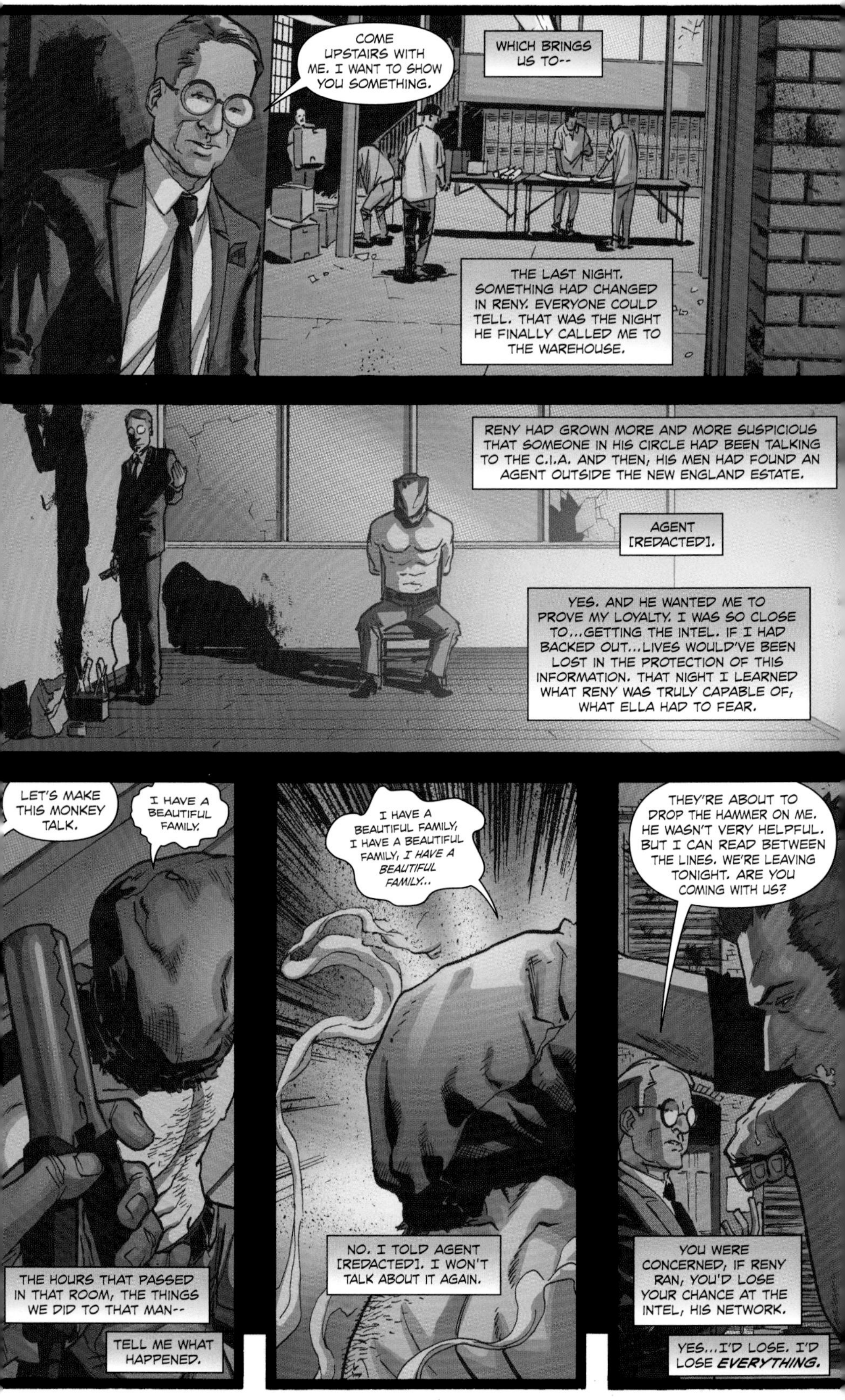
COME UPSTAIRS WITH ME. I WANT TO SHOW YOU SOMETHING.
WHICH BRINGS US TO--
THE LAST NIGHT. SOMETHING HAD CHANGED IN RENY. EVERYONE COULD TELL. THAT WAS THE NIGHT HE FINALLY CALLED ME TO THE WAREHOUSE.
RENY HAD GROWN MORE AND MORE SUSPICIOUS THAT SOMEONE IN HIS CIRCLE HAD BEEN TALKING TO THE C.I.A. AND THEN, HIS MEN HAD FOUND AN AGENT OUTSIDE THE NEW ENGLAND ESTATE.
AGENT [REDACTED].
YES. AND HE WANTED ME TO PROVE MY LOYALTY. I WAS SO CLOSE TO...GETTING THE INTEL. IF I HAD BACKED OUT...LIVES WOULD'VE BEEN LOST IN THE PROTECTION OF THIS INFORMATION. THAT NIGHT I LEARNED WHAT RENY WAS TRULY CAPABLE OF, WHAT ELLA HAD TO FEAR.
LET'S MAKE THIS MONKEY TALK.
I HAVE A BEAUTIFUL FAMILY.
THE HOURS THAT PASSED IN THAT ROOM, THE THINGS WE DID TO THAT MAN--
TELL ME WHAT HAPPENED.
I HAVE A BEAUTIFUL FAMILY, I HAVE A BEAUTIFUL FAMILY, *I HAVE A BEAUTIFUL FAMILY...*
NO. I TOLD AGENT [REDACTED]. I WON'T TALK ABOUT IT AGAIN.
THEY'RE ABOUT TO DROP THE HAMMER ON ME. HE WASN'T VERY HELPFUL. BUT I CAN READ BETWEEN THE LINES. WE'RE LEAVING TONIGHT. ARE YOU COMING WITH US?
YOU WERE CONCERNED, IF RENY RAN, YOU'D LOSE YOUR CHANCE AT THE INTEL, HIS NETWORK.
YES...I'D LOSE. I'D LOSE ***EVERYTHING.***

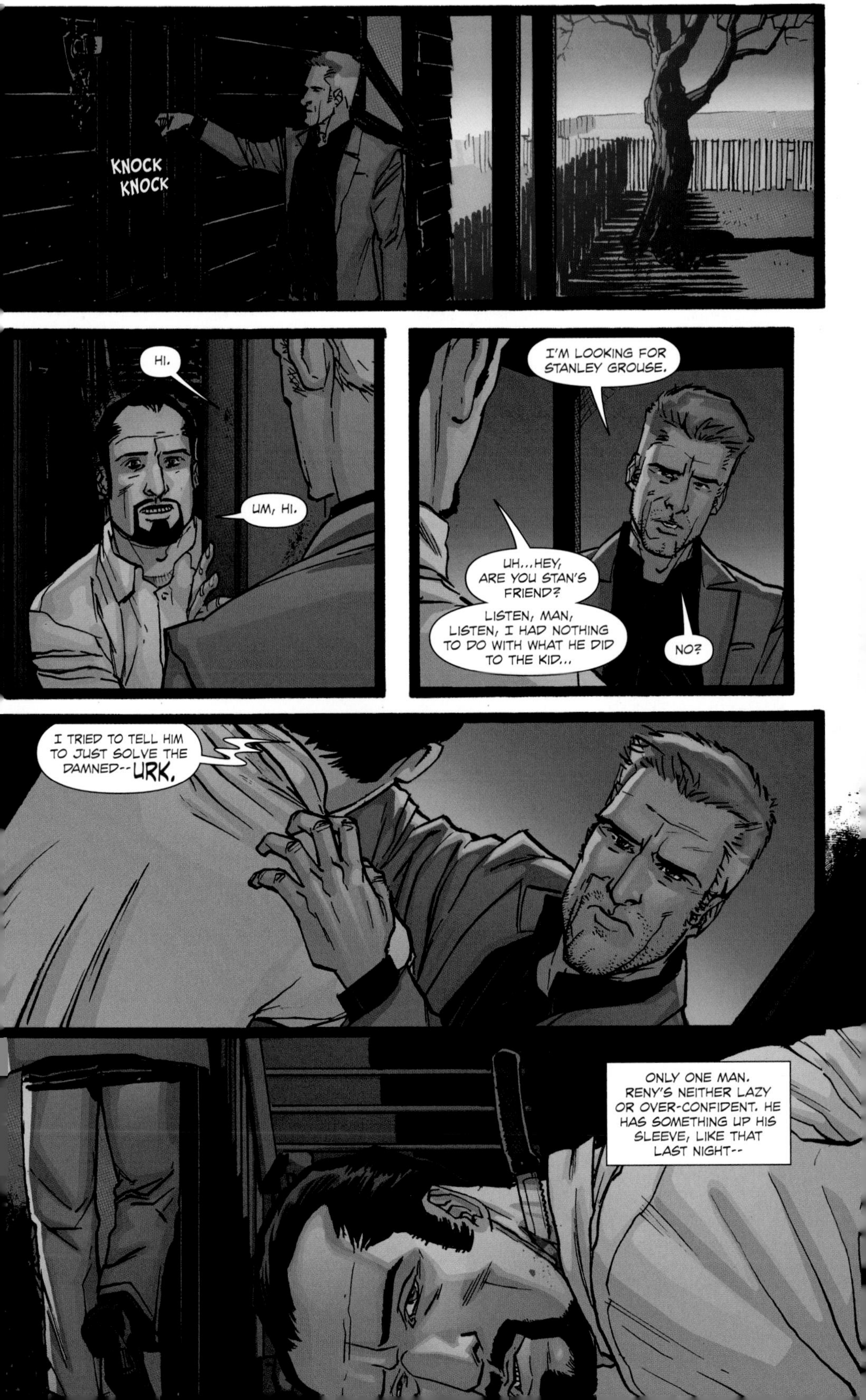
KNOCK KNOCK
HI.
UM, HI.
I'M LOOKING FOR STANLEY GROUSE.
UH...HEY, ARE YOU STAN'S FRIEND?
LISTEN, MAN, LISTEN, I HAD NOTHING TO DO WITH WHAT HE DID TO THE KID...
NO?
I TRIED TO TELL HIM TO JUST SOLVE THE DAMNED--URK.
ONLY ONE MAN. RENY'S NEITHER LAZY OR OVER-CONFIDENT. HE HAS SOMETHING UP HIS SLEEVE, LIKE THAT LAST NIGHT--

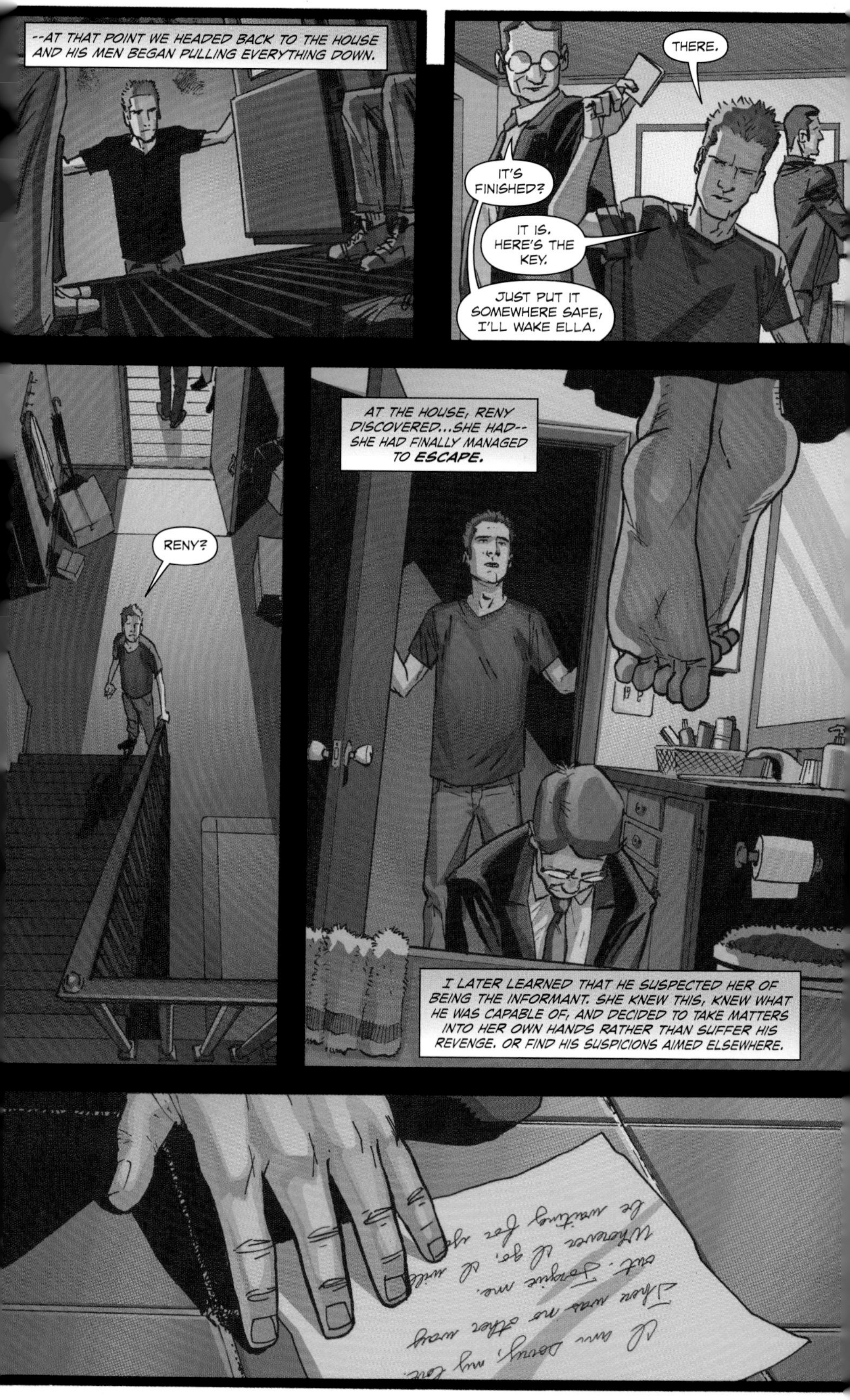
--AT THAT POINT WE HEADED BACK TO THE HOUSE AND HIS MEN BEGAN PULLING EVERYTHING DOWN.
THERE.
IT'S FINISHED?
IT IS. HERE'S THE KEY.
JUST PUT IT SOMEWHERE SAFE, I'LL WAKE ELLA.
RENY?
AT THE HOUSE, RENY DISCOVERED...SHE HAD--SHE HAD FINALLY MANAGED TO ESCAPE.
I LATER LEARNED THAT HE SUSPECTED HER OF BEING THE INFORMANT. SHE KNEW THIS, KNEW WHAT HE WAS CAPABLE OF, AND DECIDED TO TAKE MATTERS INTO HER OWN HANDS RATHER THAN SUFFER HIS REVENGE. OR FIND HIS SUSPICIONS AIMED ELSEWHERE.

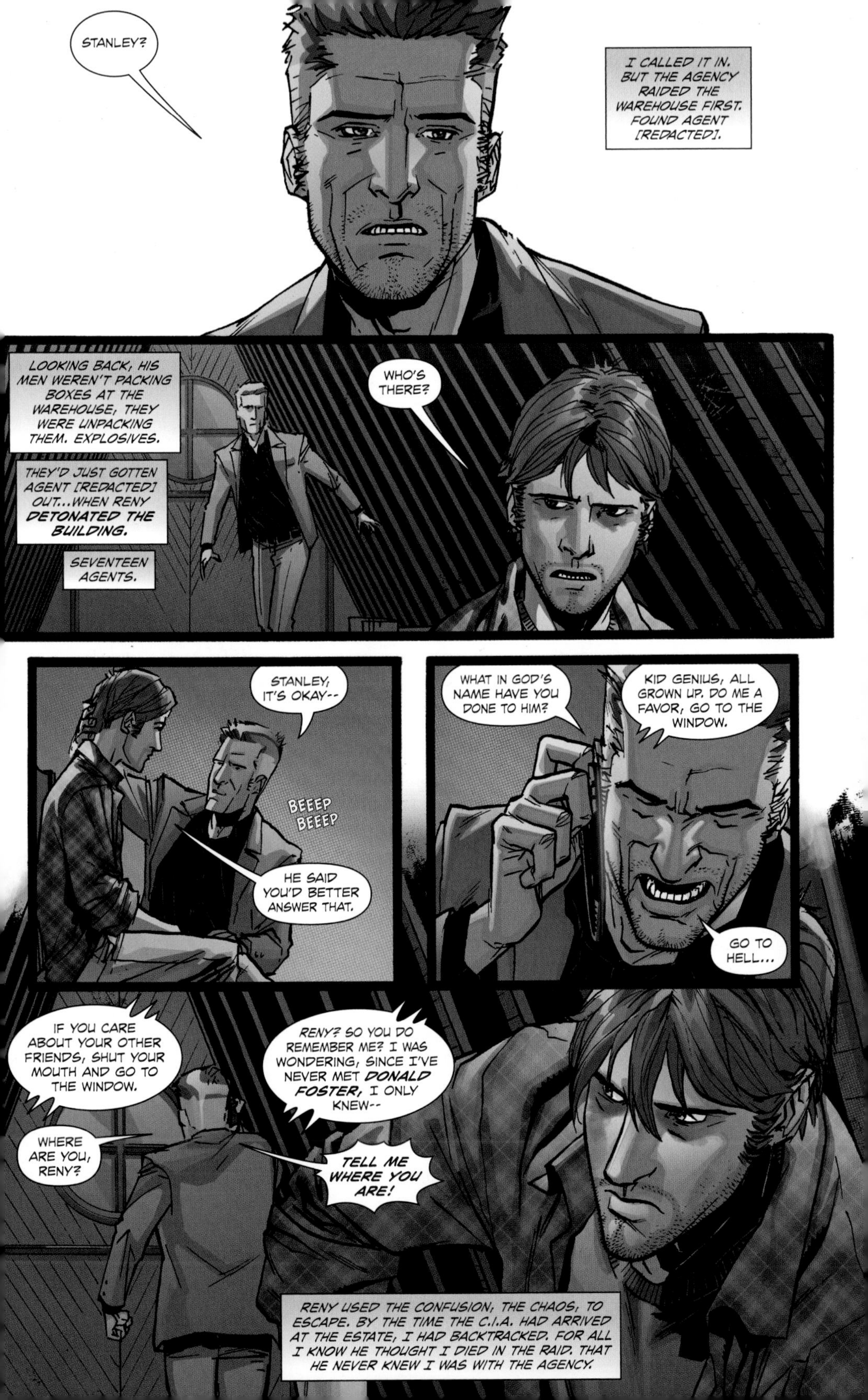
STANLEY?
I CALLED IT IN. BUT THE AGENCY RAIDED THE WAREHOUSE FIRST. FOUND AGENT [REDACTED].
LOOKING BACK, HIS MEN WEREN'T PACKING BOXES AT THE WAREHOUSE, THEY WERE UNPACKING THEM. EXPLOSIVES.
THEY'D JUST GOTTEN AGENT [REDACTED] OUT...WHEN RENY DETONATED THE BUILDING.
SEVENTEEN AGENTS.
WHO'S THERE?
STANLEY, IT'S OKAY--
BEEEP BEEEP
HE SAID YOU'D BETTER ANSWER THAT.
WHAT IN GOD'S NAME HAVE YOU DONE TO HIM?
KID GENIUS, ALL GROWN UP. DO ME A FAVOR, GO TO THE WINDOW.
GO TO HELL...
IF YOU CARE ABOUT YOUR OTHER FRIENDS, SHUT YOUR MOUTH AND GO TO THE WINDOW.
RENY? SO YOU DO REMEMBER ME? I WAS WONDERING, SINCE I'VE NEVER MET DONALD FOSTER, I ONLY KNEW--
WHERE ARE YOU, RENY?
TELL ME WHERE YOU ARE!
RENY USED THE CONFUSION, THE CHAOS, TO ESCAPE. BY THE TIME THE C.I.A. HAD ARRIVED AT THE ESTATE, I HAD BACKTRACKED. FOR ALL I KNOW HE THOUGHT I DIED IN THE RAID. THAT HE NEVER KNEW I WAS WITH THE AGENCY.

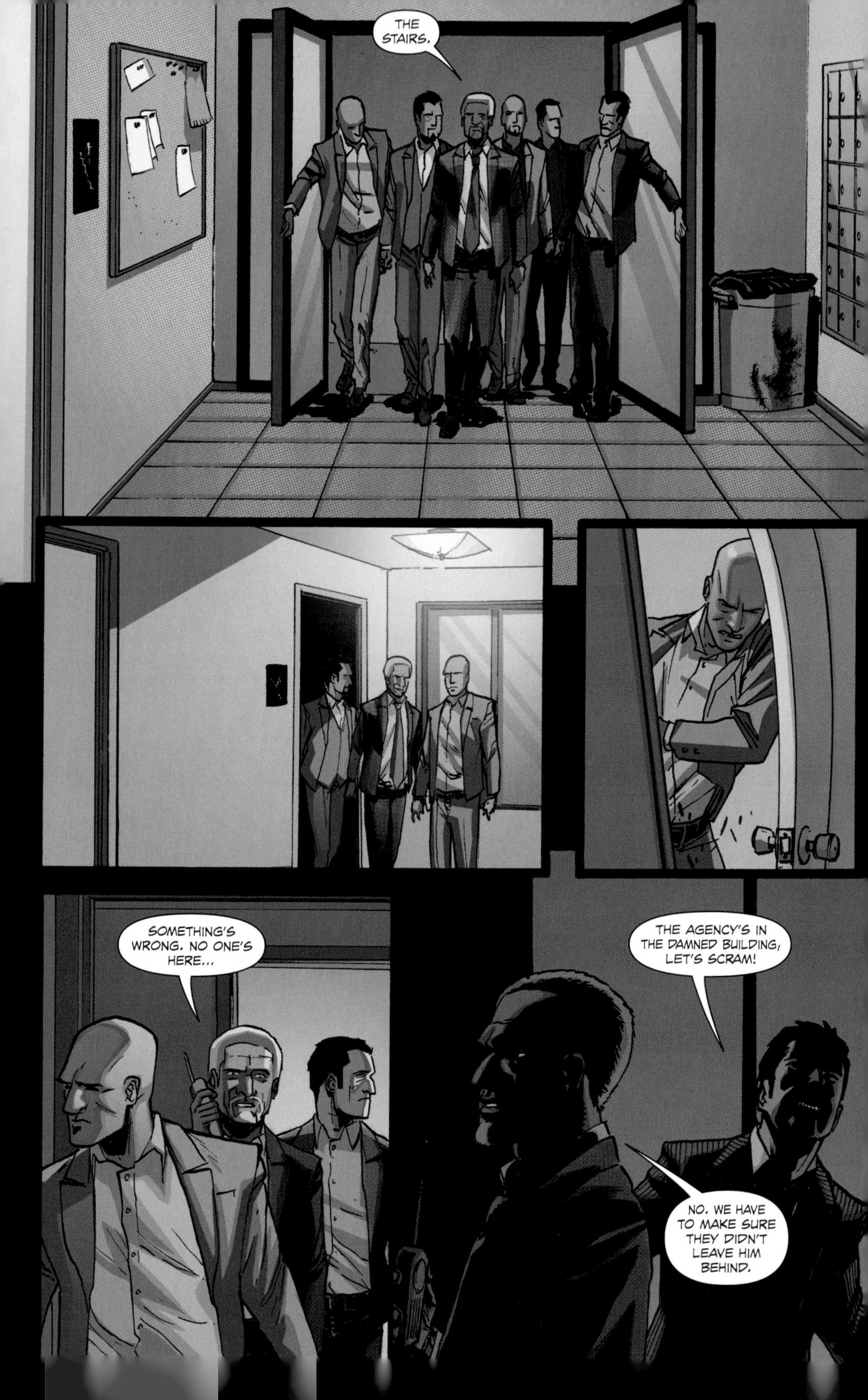
THE STAIRS.
SOMETHING'S WRONG. NO ONE'S HERE...
THE AGENCY'S IN THE DAMNED BUILDING, LET'S SCRAM!
NO. WE HAVE TO MAKE SURE THEY DIDN'T LEAVE HIM BEHIND.

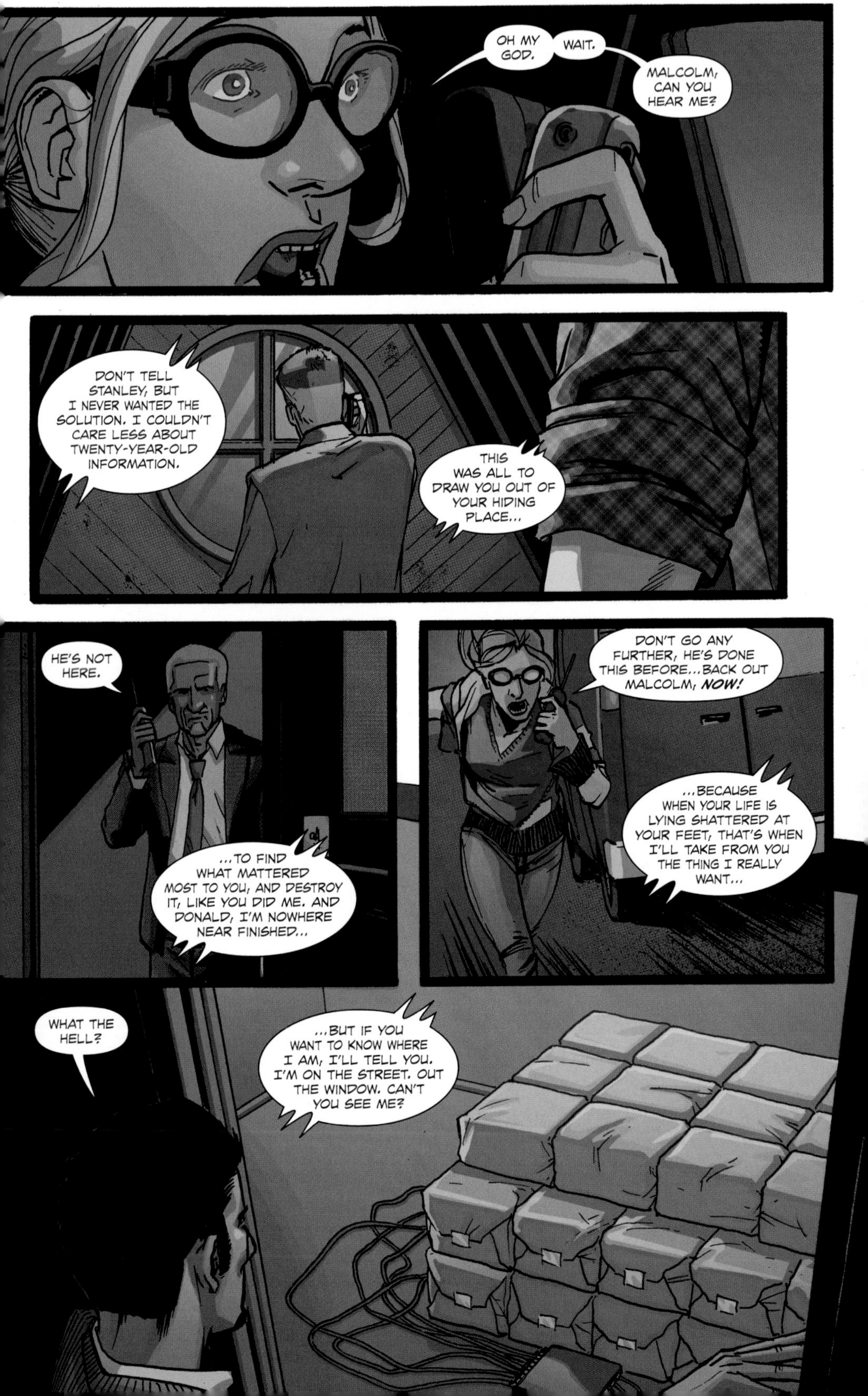
OH MY GOD.
WAIT.
MALCOLM, CAN YOU HEAR ME?
DON'T TELL STANLEY, BUT I NEVER WANTED THE SOLUTION. I COULDN'T CARE LESS ABOUT TWENTY-YEAR-OLD INFORMATION.
THIS WAS ALL TO DRAW YOU OUT OF YOUR HIDING PLACE...
HE'S NOT HERE.
...TO FIND WHAT MATTERED MOST TO YOU, AND DESTROY IT, LIKE YOU DID ME. AND DONALD, I'M NOWHERE NEAR FINISHED...
DON'T GO ANY FURTHER, HE'S DONE THIS BEFORE...BACK OUT MALCOLM, ***NOW!***
...BECAUSE WHEN YOUR LIFE IS LYING SHATTERED AT YOUR FEET, THAT'S WHEN I'LL TAKE FROM YOU THE THING I REALLY WANT...
WHAT THE HELL?
...BUT IF YOU WANT TO KNOW WHERE I AM, I'LL TELL YOU. I'M ON THE STREET. OUT THE WINDOW. CAN'T YOU SEE ME?

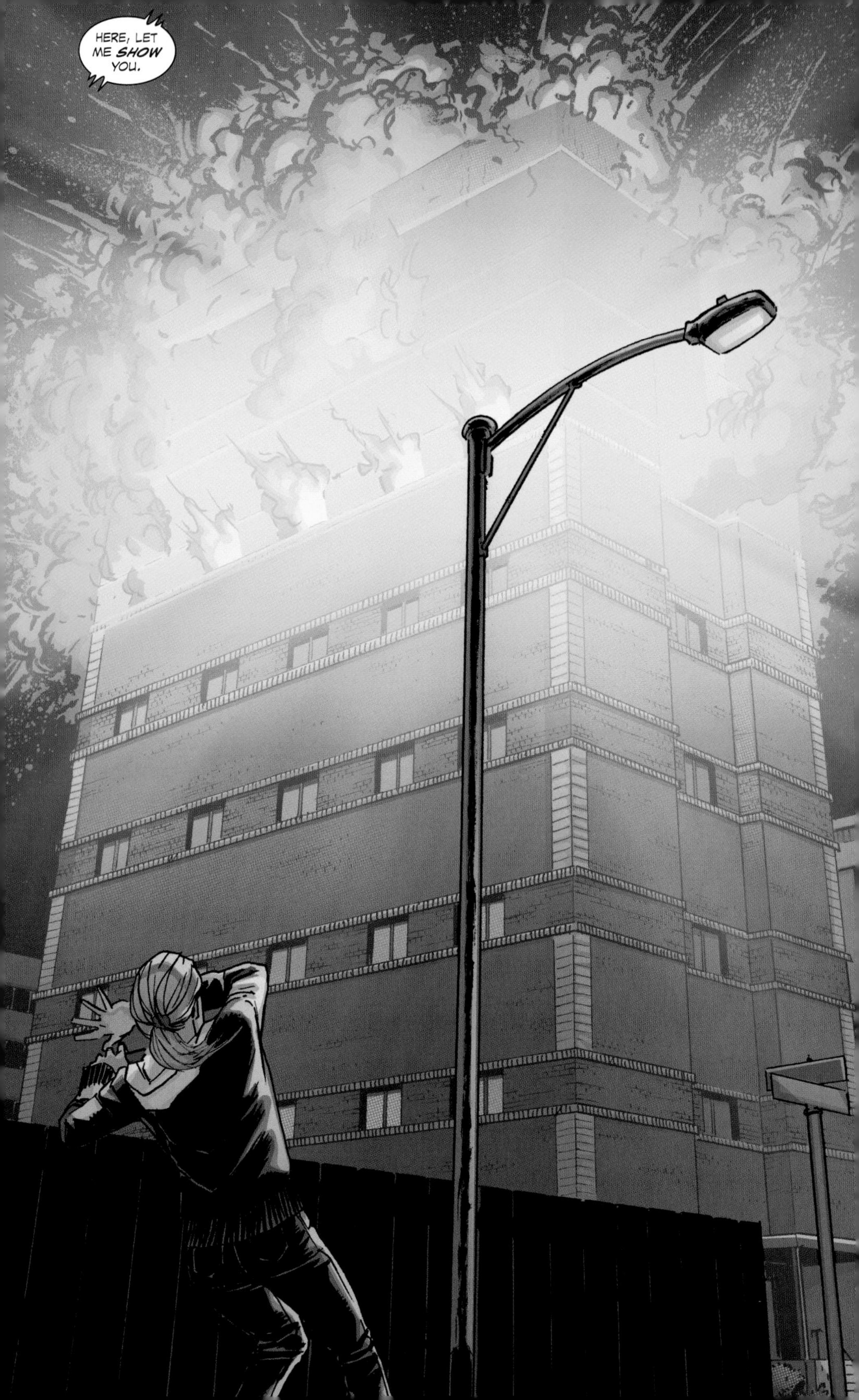
HERE, LET ME **SHOW** YOU.

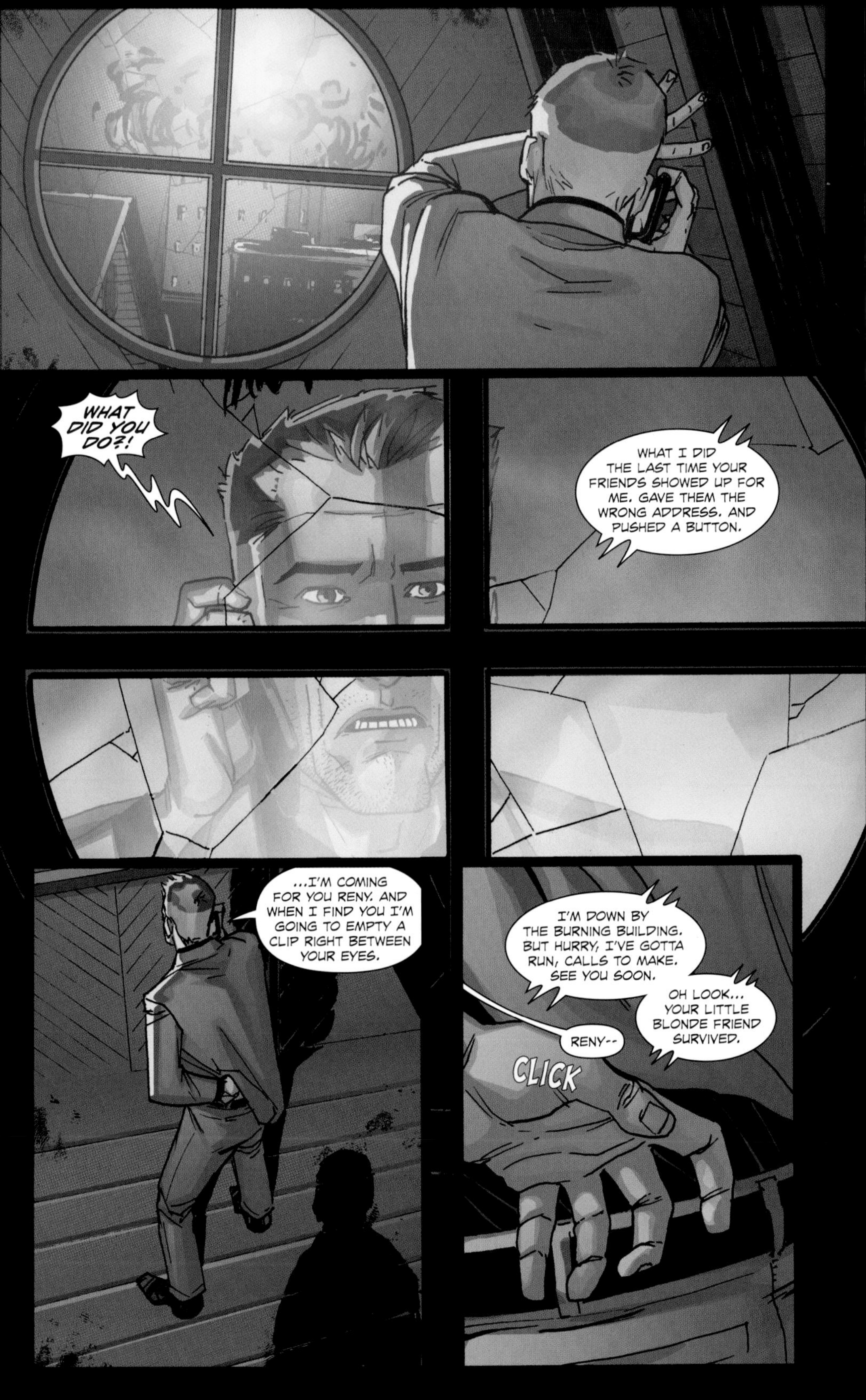
WHAT DID YOU DO?!
WHAT I DID THE LAST TIME YOUR FRIENDS SHOWED UP FOR ME. GAVE THEM THE WRONG ADDRESS. AND PUSHED A BUTTON.
...I'M COMING FOR YOU RENY. AND WHEN I FIND YOU I'M GOING TO EMPTY A CLIP RIGHT BETWEEN YOUR EYES.
I'M DOWN BY THE BURNING BUILDING. BUT HURRY, I'VE GOTTA RUN, CALLS TO MAKE. SEE YOU SOON.
OH LOOK... YOUR LITTLE BLONDE FRIEND SURVIVED.
RENY--
CLICK

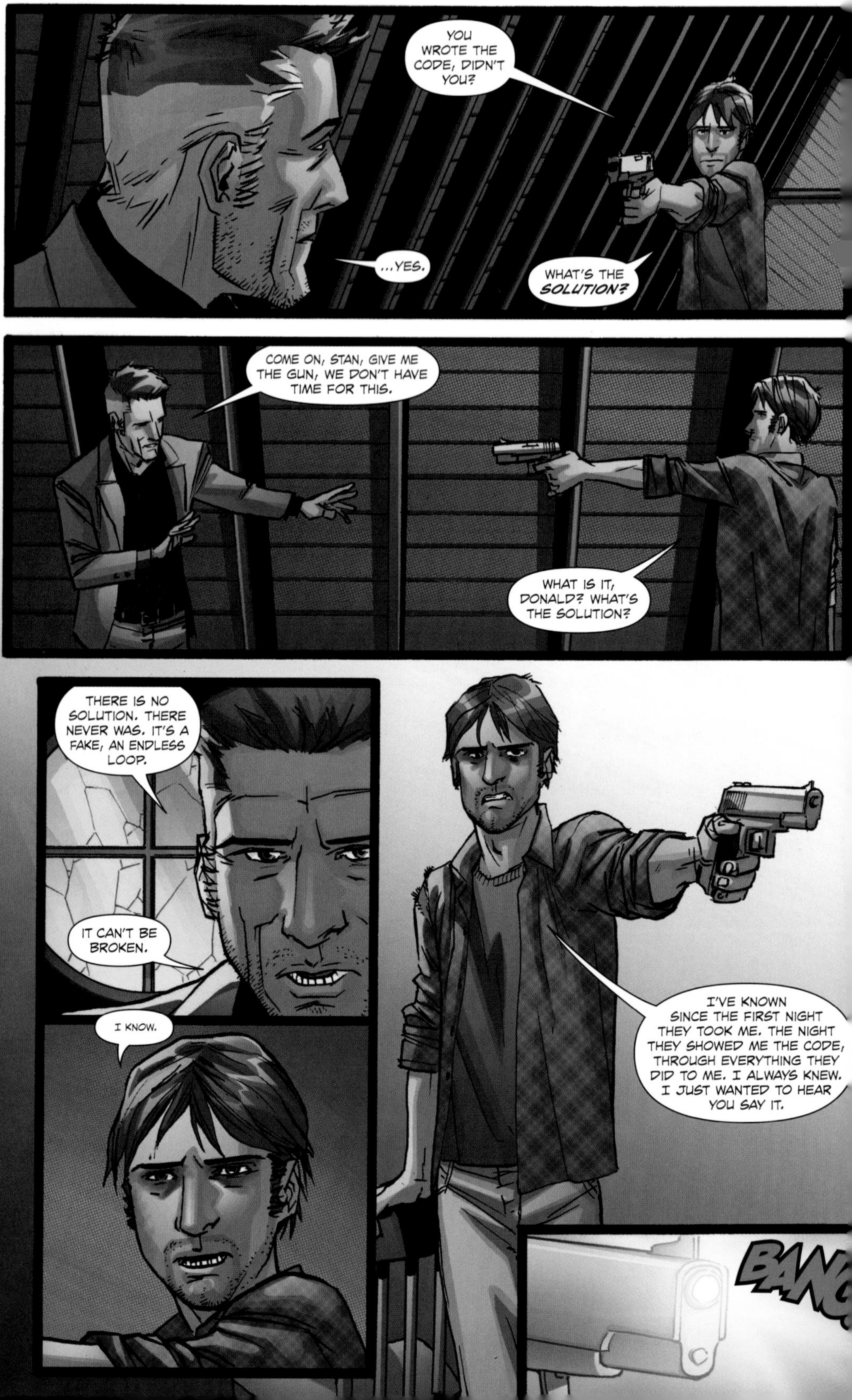
YOU WROTE THE CODE, DIDN'T YOU?
...YES.
WHAT'S THE SOLUTION?
COME ON, STAN, GIVE ME THE GUN, WE DON'T HAVE TIME FOR THIS.
WHAT IS IT, DONALD? WHAT'S THE SOLUTION?
THERE IS NO SOLUTION. THERE NEVER WAS. IT'S A FAKE, AN ENDLESS LOOP.
IT CAN'T BE BROKEN.
I KNOW.
I'VE KNOWN SINCE THE FIRST NIGHT THEY TOOK ME. THE NIGHT THEY SHOWED ME THE CODE, THROUGH EVERYTHING THEY DID TO ME. I ALWAYS KNEW. I JUST WANTED TO HEAR YOU SAY IT.
BANG

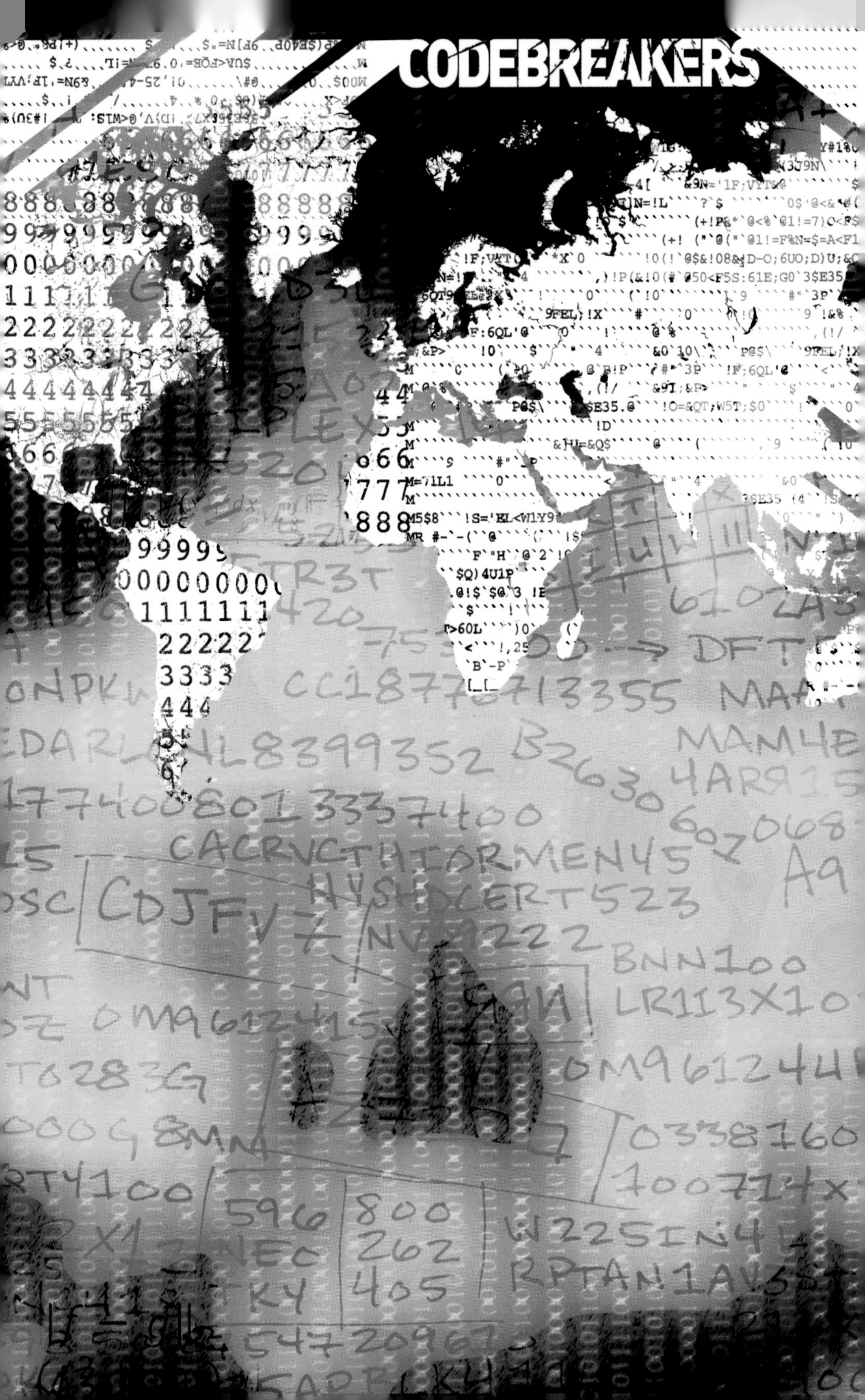
CODEBREAKERS

CHAPTER: FOUR

C O D E B R E A K E R S

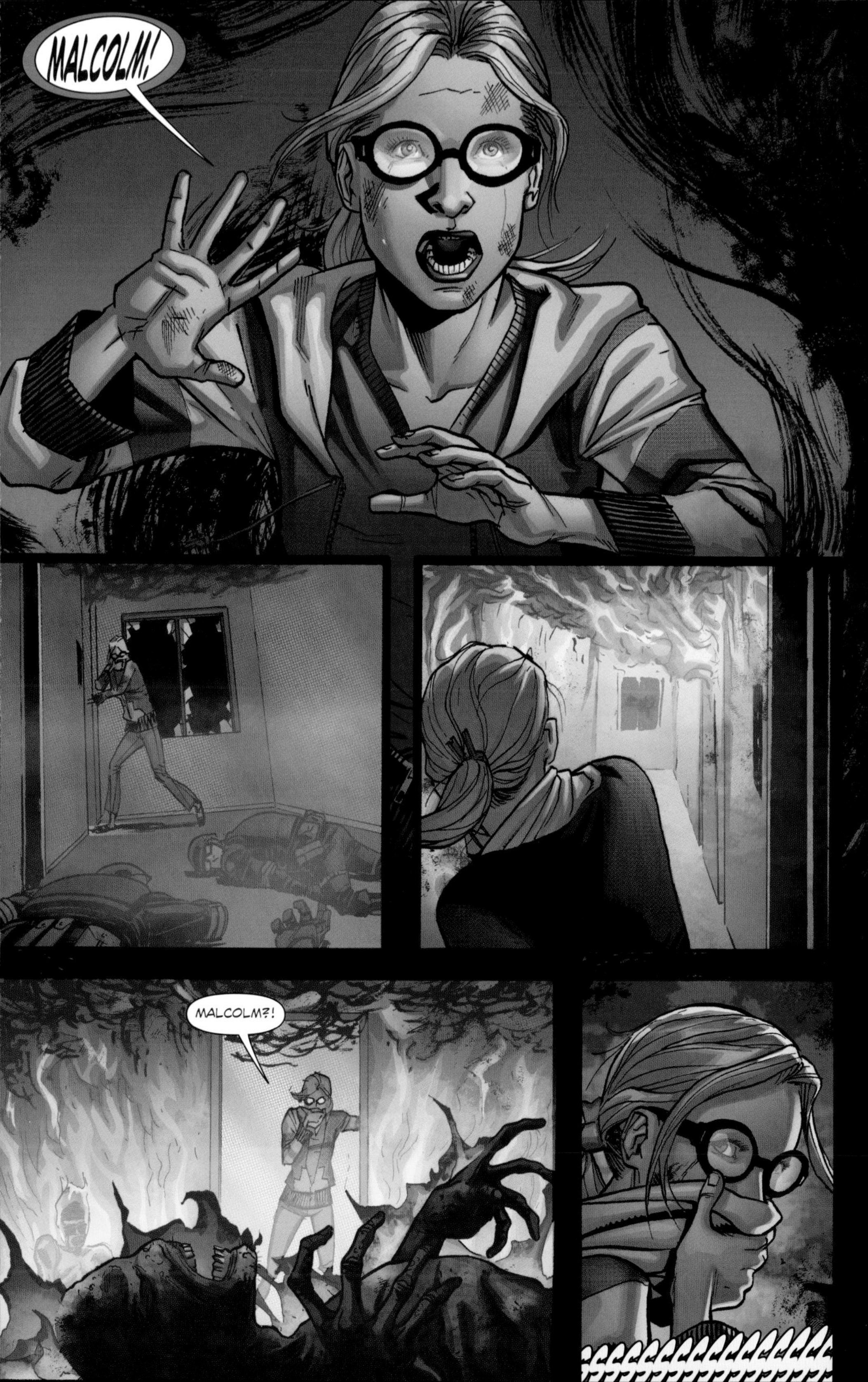
MALCOLM!
MALCOLM?!
SSSSSSSSSSSSSSSSSSS

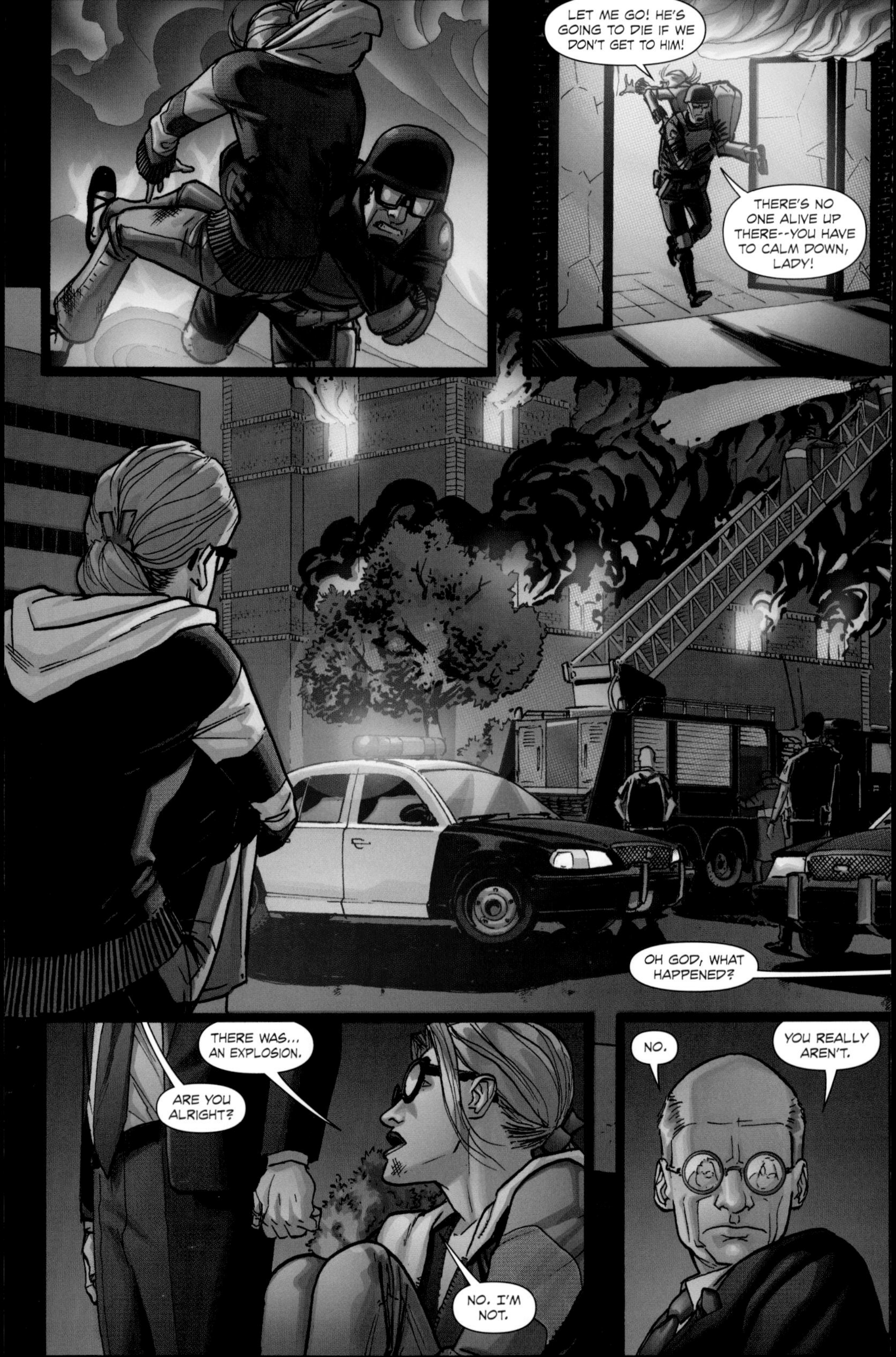
LET ME GO! HE'S GOING TO DIE IF WE DON'T GET TO HIM!
THERE'S NO ONE ALIVE UP THERE--YOU HAVE TO CALM DOWN, LADY!
OH GOD, WHAT HAPPENED?
ARE YOU ALRIGHT?
THERE WAS... AN EXPLOSION.
NO. I'M NOT.
NO.
YOU REALLY AREN'T.

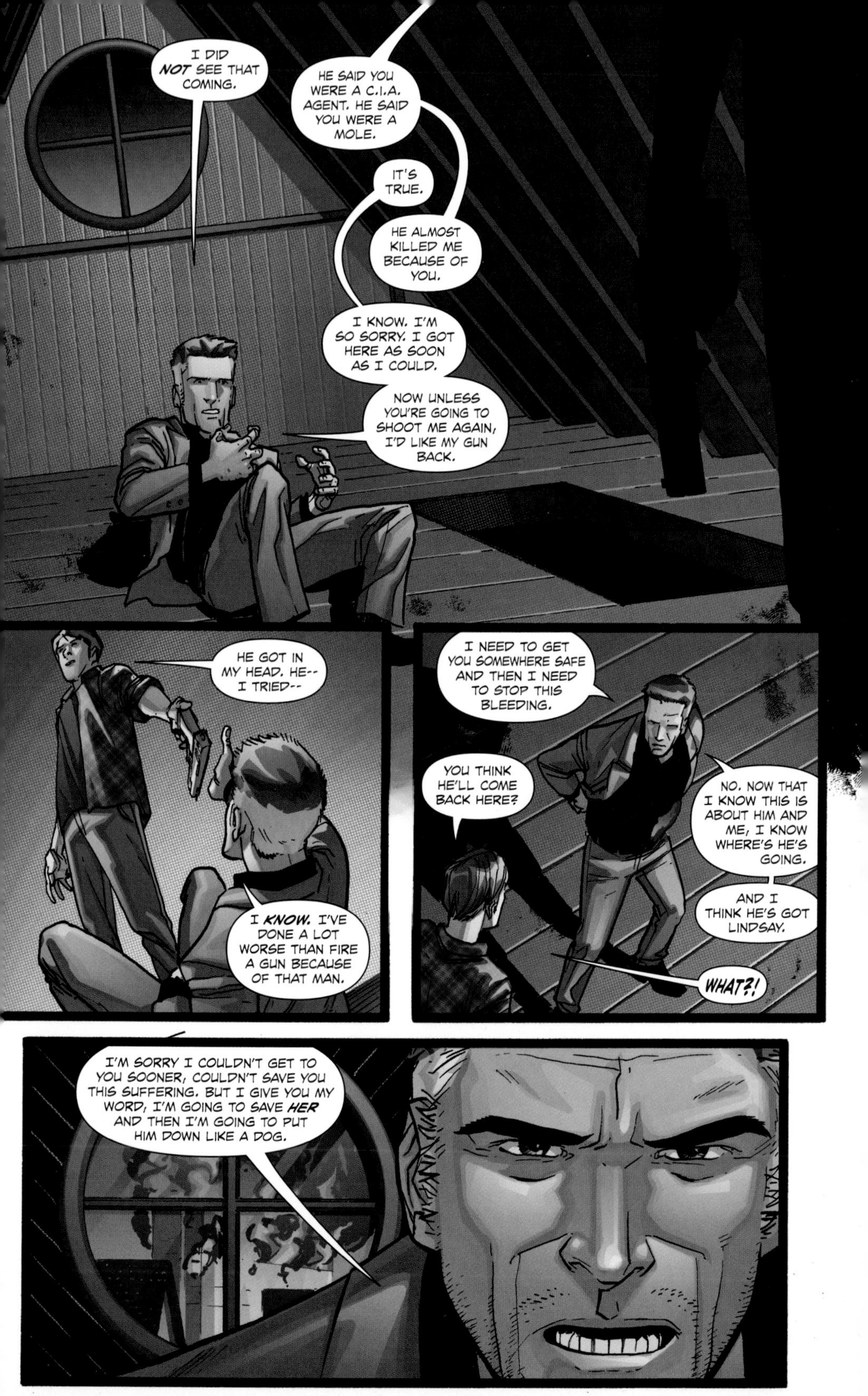
I DID *NOT* SEE THAT COMING.
HE SAID YOU WERE A C.I.A. AGENT. HE SAID YOU WERE A MOLE.
IT'S TRUE.
HE ALMOST KILLED ME BECAUSE OF YOU.
I KNOW. I'M SO SORRY. I GOT HERE AS SOON AS I COULD.
NOW UNLESS YOU'RE GOING TO SHOOT ME AGAIN, I'D LIKE MY GUN BACK.
HE GOT IN MY HEAD. HE-- I TRIED--
I *KNOW.* I'VE DONE A LOT WORSE THAN FIRE A GUN BECAUSE OF THAT MAN.
I NEED TO GET YOU SOMEWHERE SAFE AND THEN I NEED TO STOP THIS BLEEDING.
YOU THINK HE'LL COME BACK HERE?
NO. NOW THAT I KNOW THIS IS ABOUT HIM AND ME, I KNOW WHERE'S HE'S GOING.
AND I THINK HE'S GOT LINDSAY.
WHAT?!
I'M SORRY I COULDN'T GET TO YOU SOONER, COULDN'T SAVE YOU THIS SUFFERING. BUT I GIVE YOU MY WORD, I'M GOING TO SAVE *HER* AND THEN I'M GOING TO PUT HIM DOWN LIKE A DOG.

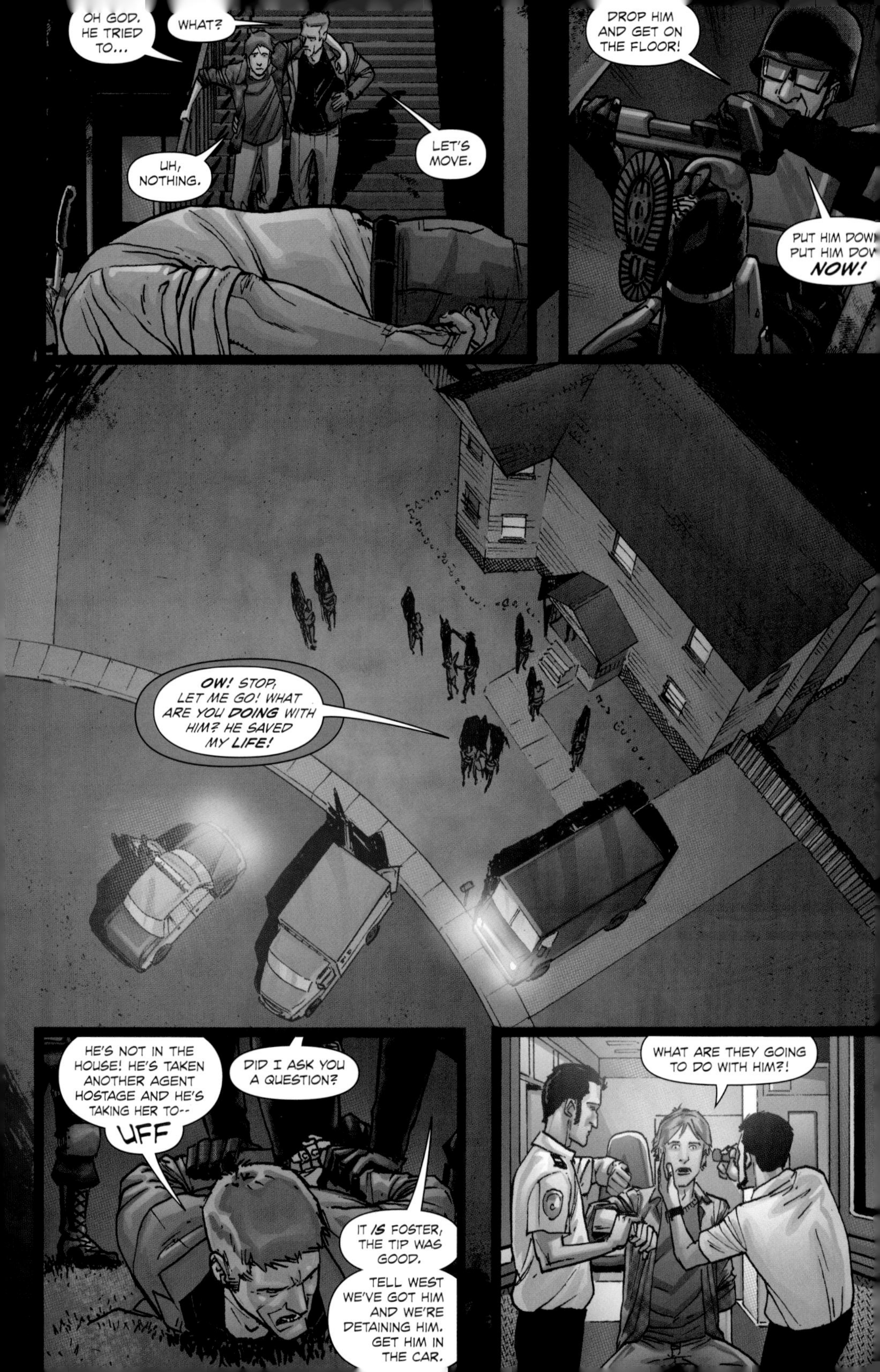
OH GOD. HE TRIED TO...
WHAT?
UH, NOTHING.
LET'S MOVE.
DROP HIM AND GET ON THE FLOOR!
PUT HIM DOW
PUT HIM DOW
NOW!
OW! STOP, LET ME GO! WHAT ARE YOU DOING WITH HIM? HE SAVED MY LIFE!
HE'S NOT IN THE HOUSE! HE'S TAKEN ANOTHER AGENT HOSTAGE AND HE'S TAKING HER TO--
UFF
DID I ASK YOU A QUESTION?
IT IS FOSTER, THE TIP WAS GOOD.
TELL WEST WE'VE GOT HIM AND WE'RE DETAINING HIM. GET HIM IN THE CAR.
WHAT ARE THEY GOING TO DO WITH HIM?!

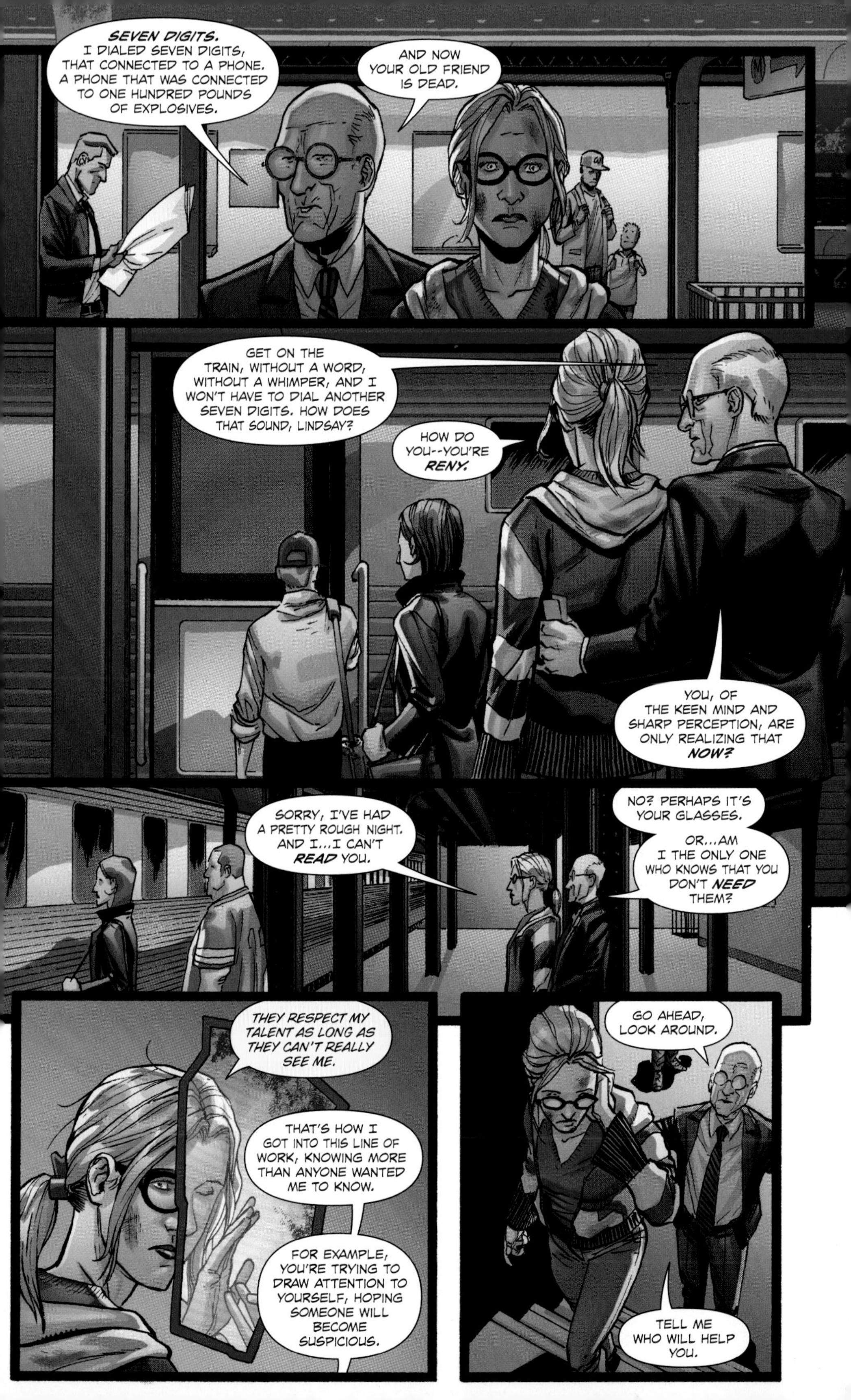
SEVEN DIGITS.
I DIALED SEVEN DIGITS, THAT CONNECTED TO A PHONE. A PHONE THAT WAS CONNECTED TO ONE HUNDRED POUNDS OF EXPLOSIVES.
AND NOW YOUR OLD FRIEND IS DEAD.
GET ON THE TRAIN, WITHOUT A WORD, WITHOUT A WHIMPER, AND I WON'T HAVE TO DIAL ANOTHER SEVEN DIGITS. HOW DOES THAT SOUND, LINDSAY?
HOW DO YOU--YOU'RE RENY.
YOU, OF THE KEEN MIND AND SHARP PERCEPTION, ARE ONLY REALIZING THAT NOW?
SORRY, I'VE HAD A PRETTY ROUGH NIGHT. AND I...I CAN'T READ YOU.
NO? PERHAPS IT'S YOUR GLASSES.
OR...AM I THE ONLY ONE WHO KNOWS THAT YOU DON'T NEED THEM?
THEY RESPECT MY TALENT AS LONG AS THEY CAN'T REALLY SEE ME.
THAT'S HOW I GOT INTO THIS LINE OF WORK, KNOWING MORE THAN ANYONE WANTED ME TO KNOW.
FOR EXAMPLE, YOU'RE TRYING TO DRAW ATTENTION TO YOURSELF, HOPING SOMEONE WILL BECOME SUSPICIOUS.
GO AHEAD, LOOK AROUND.
TELL ME WHO WILL HELP YOU.

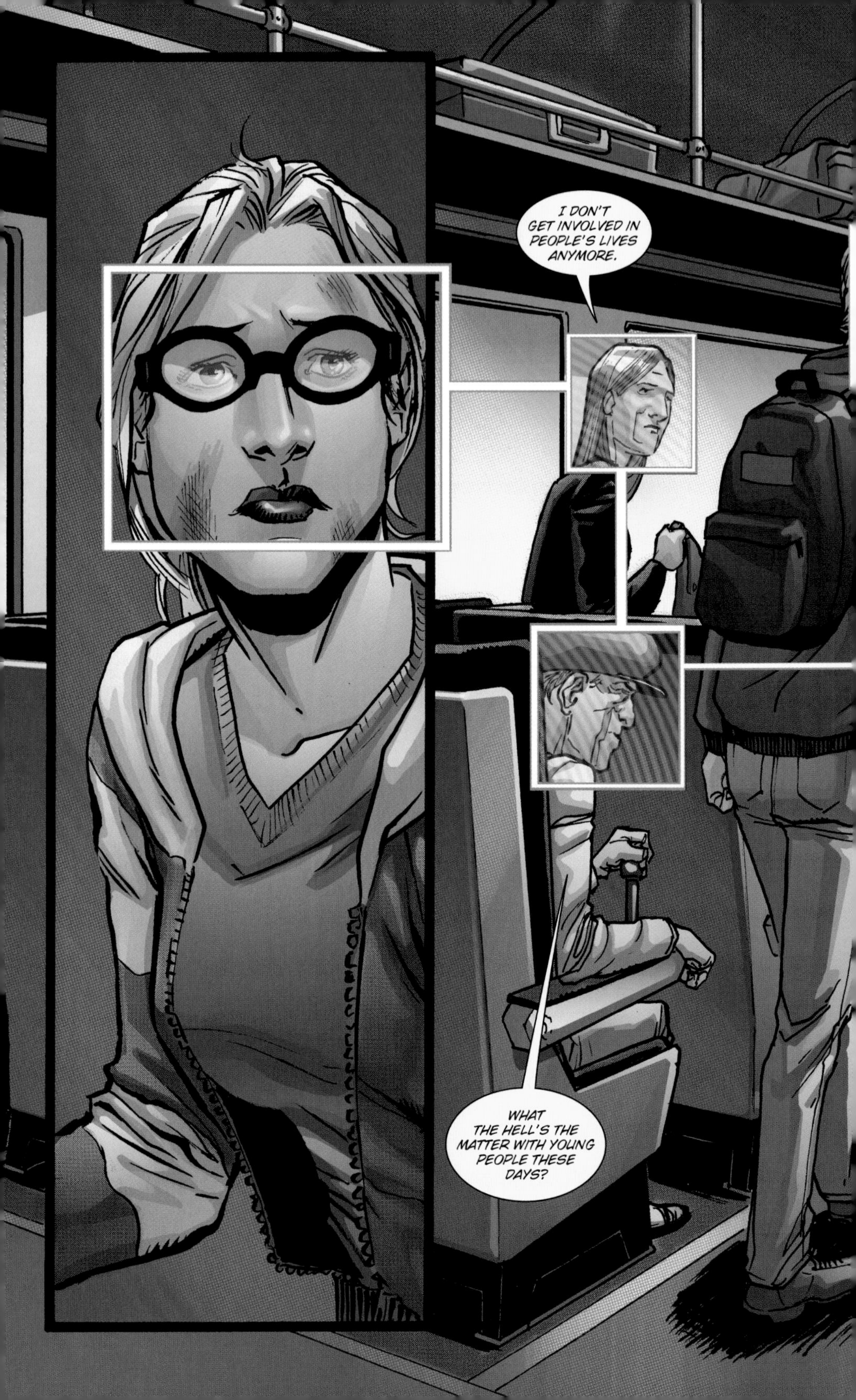
I DON'T GET INVOLVED IN PEOPLE'S LIVES ANYMORE.
WHAT THE HELL'S THE MATTER WITH YOUNG PEOPLE THESE DAYS?

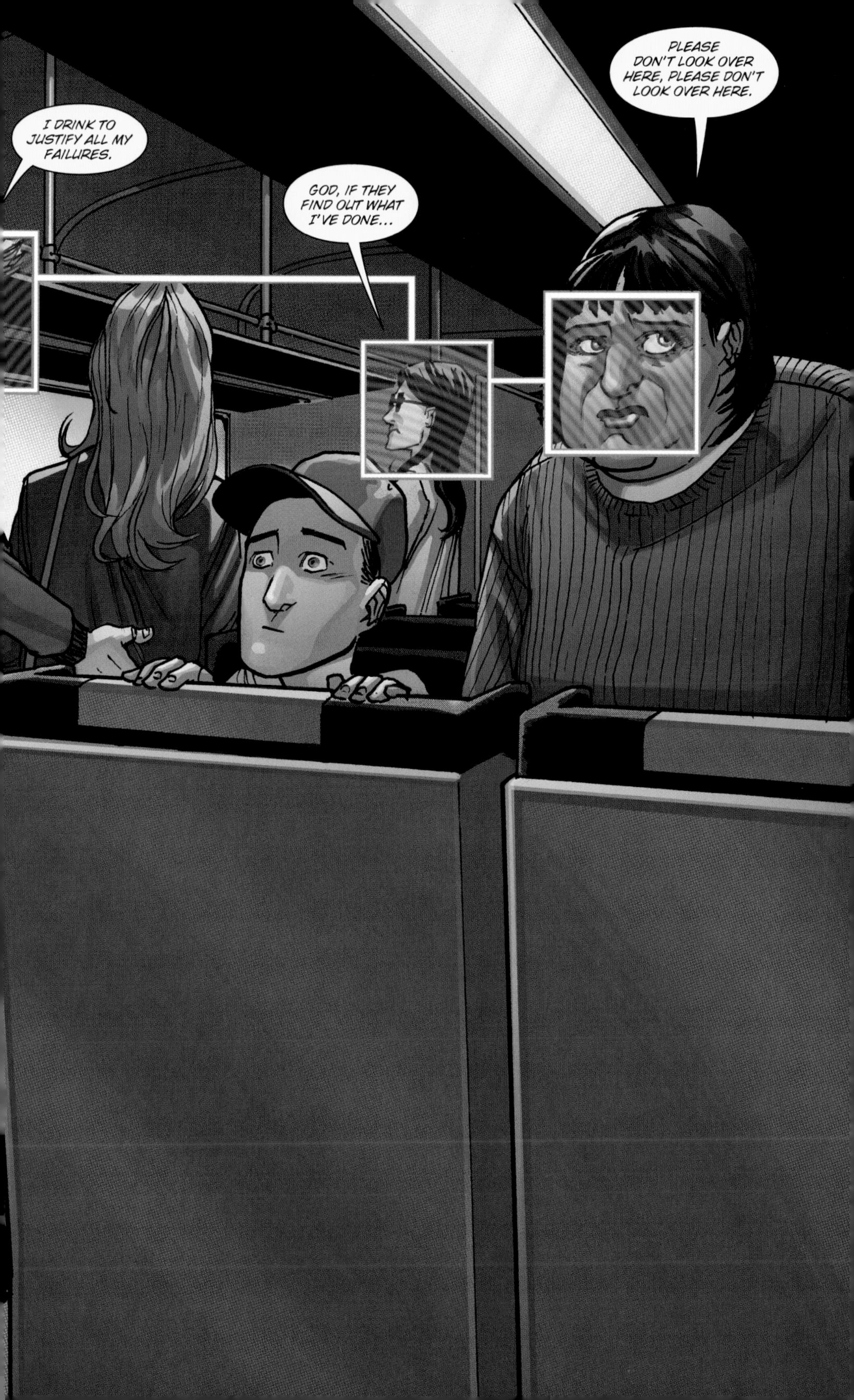
I DRINK TO JUSTIFY ALL MY FAILURES.
GOD, IF THEY FIND OUT WHAT I'VE DONE...
PLEASE DON'T LOOK OVER HERE, PLEASE DON'T LOOK OVER HERE.

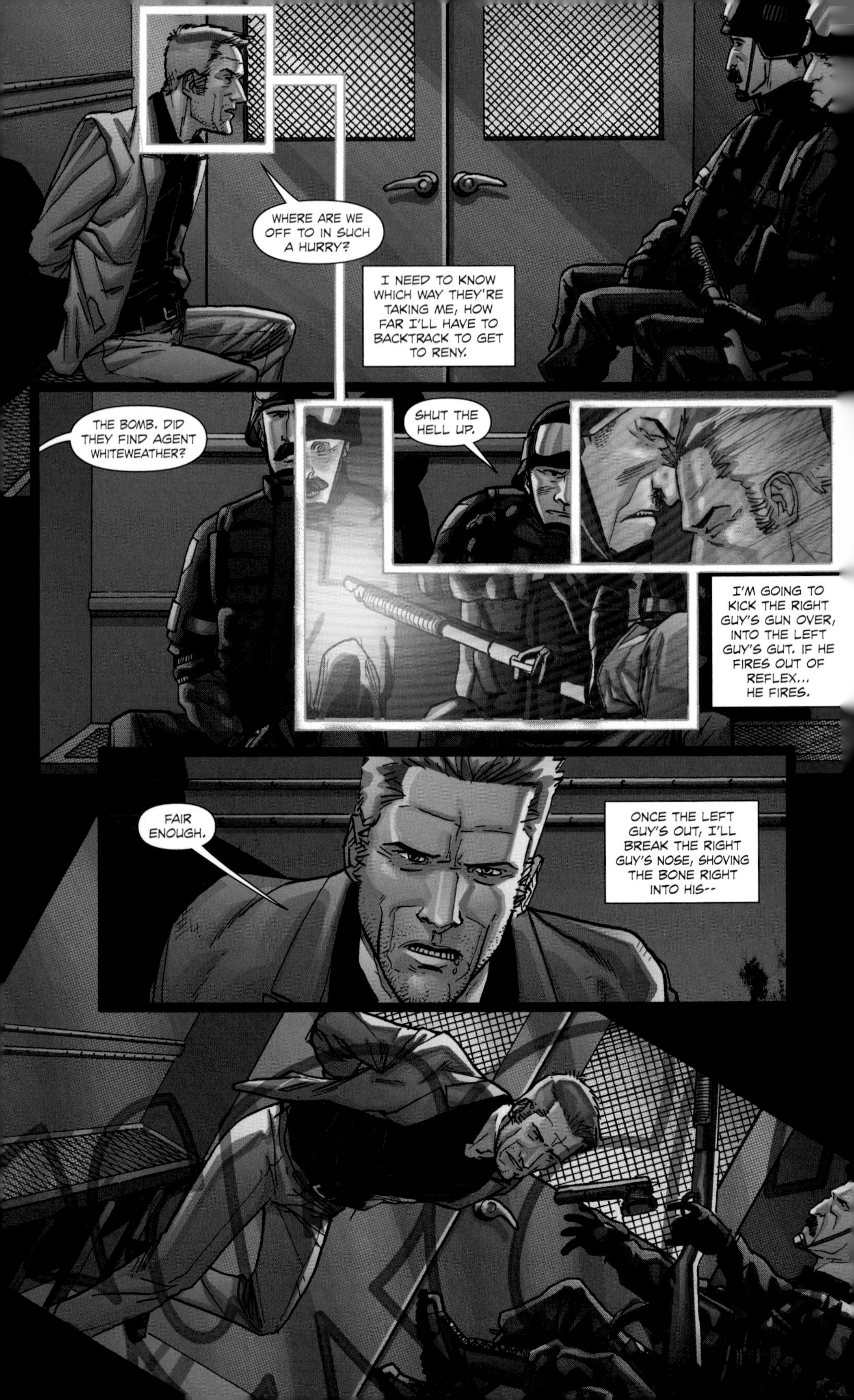
WHERE ARE WE OFF TO IN SUCH A HURRY?
I NEED TO KNOW WHICH WAY THEY'RE TAKING ME, HOW FAR I'LL HAVE TO BACKTRACK TO GET TO RENY.
THE BOMB. DID THEY FIND AGENT WHITEWEATHER?
SHUT THE HELL UP.
I'M GOING TO KICK THE RIGHT GUY'S GUN OVER, INTO THE LEFT GUY'S GUT. IF HE FIRES OUT OF REFLEX... HE FIRES.
FAIR ENOUGH.
ONCE THE LEFT GUY'S OUT, I'LL BREAK THE RIGHT GUY'S NOSE, SHOVING THE BONE RIGHT INTO HIS--

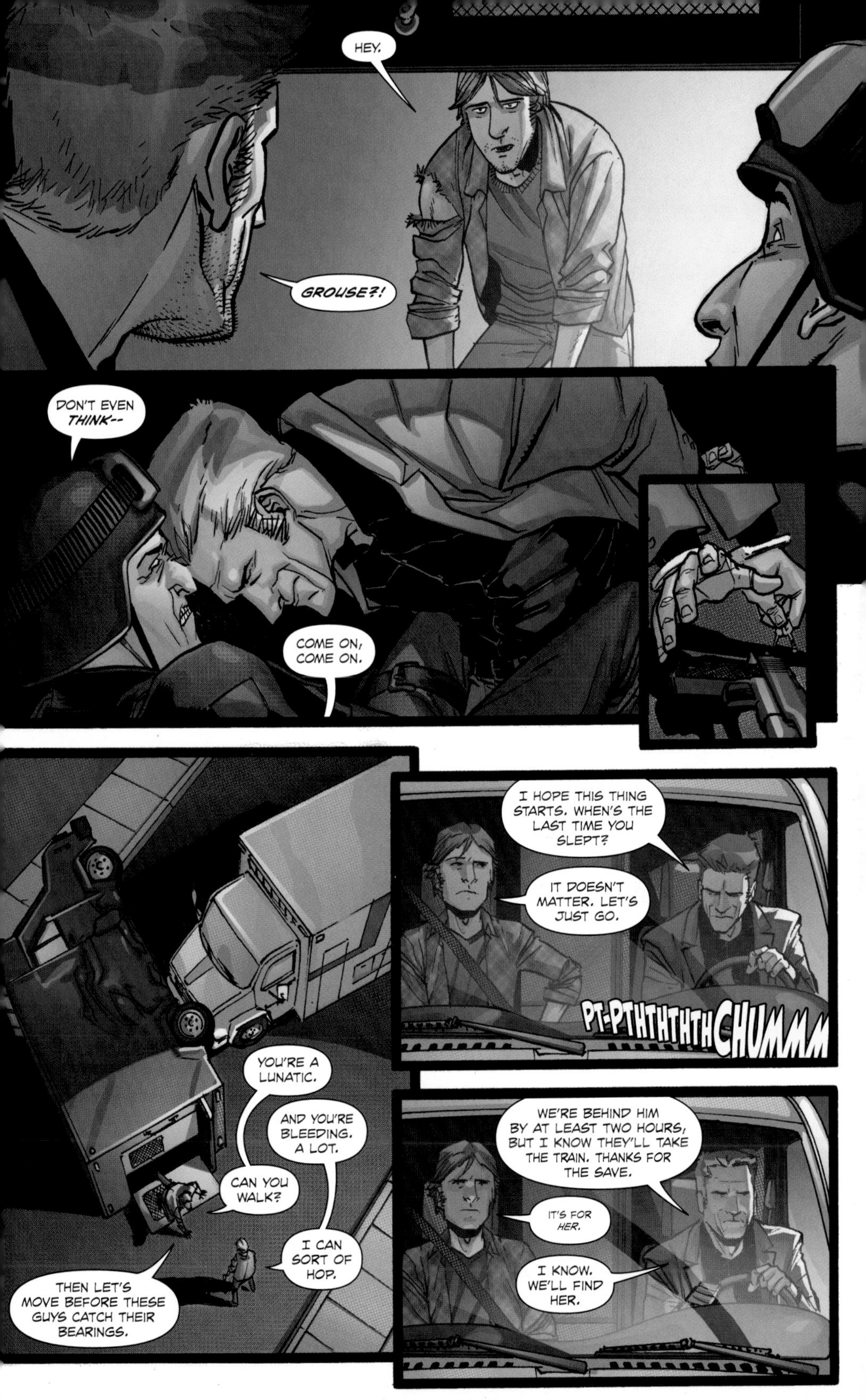
HEY.
GROUSE?!
DON'T EVEN THINK--
COME ON, COME ON.
I HOPE THIS THING STARTS. WHEN'S THE LAST TIME YOU SLEPT?
IT DOESN'T MATTER. LET'S JUST GO.
PT-PTHTHTHTHCHUMMM
YOU'RE A LUNATIC.
AND YOU'RE BLEEDING. A LOT.
CAN YOU WALK?
I CAN SORT OF HOP.
THEN LET'S MOVE BEFORE THESE GUYS CATCH THEIR BEARINGS.
WE'RE BEHIND HIM BY AT LEAST TWO HOURS, BUT I KNOW THEY'LL TAKE THE TRAIN. THANKS FOR THE SAVE.
IT'S FOR HER.
I KNOW. WE'LL FIND HER.

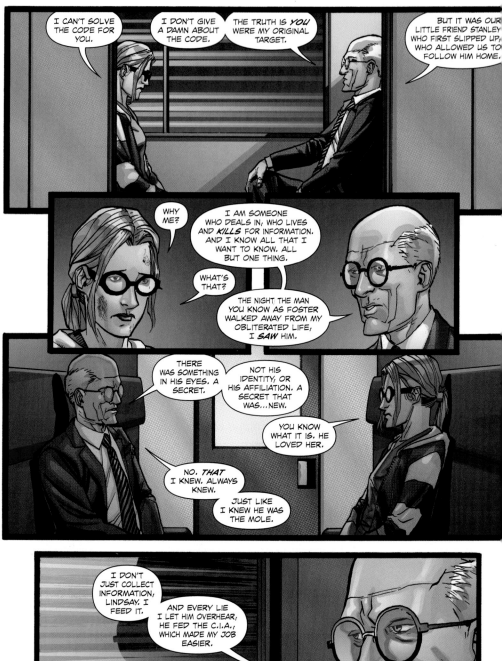

I CAN'T SOLVE THE CODE FOR YOU.

I DON'T GIVE A DAMN ABOUT THE CODE.

THE TRUTH IS *YOU* WERE MY ORIGINAL TARGET.

BUT IT WAS OUR LITTLE FRIEND STANLEY WHO FIRST SLIPPED UP, WHO ALLOWED US TO FOLLOW HIM HOME.

WHY ME?

I AM SOMEONE WHO DEALS IN, WHO LIVES AND *KILLS* FOR INFORMATION. AND I KNOW ALL THAT I WANT TO KNOW. ALL BUT ONE THING.

WHAT'S THAT?

THE NIGHT, THE MAN YOU KNOW AS FOSTER WALKED AWAY FROM MY OBLITERATED LIFE, I *SAW* HIM.

THERE WAS SOMETHING IN HIS EYES. A SECRET.

NOT HIS IDENTITY, OR HIS AFFILIATION. A SECRET THAT WAS...NEW.

YOU KNOW WHAT IT IS. HE LOVED HER.

NO. *THAT* I KNEW. ALWAYS KNEW.

JUST LIKE I KNEW HE WAS THE MOLE.

I DON'T JUST COLLECT INFORMATION, LINDSAY. I FEED IT.

AND EVERY LIE I LET HIM OVERHEAR, HE FED THE C.I.A., WHICH MADE MY JOB EASIER.

NO...

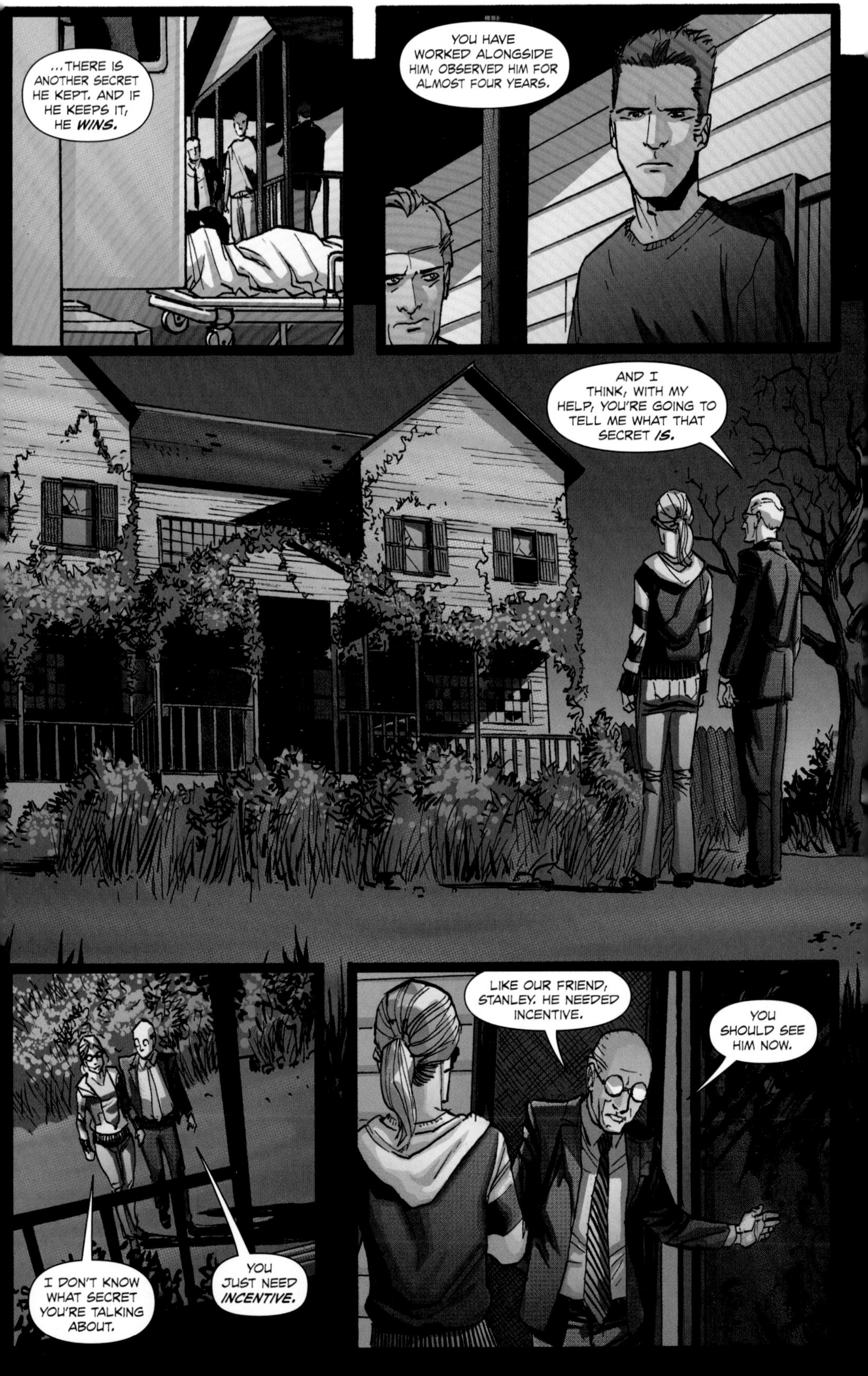
...THERE IS ANOTHER SECRET HE KEPT. AND IF HE KEEPS IT, HE *WINS.*
YOU HAVE WORKED ALONGSIDE HIM, OBSERVED HIM FOR ALMOST FOUR YEARS.
AND I THINK, WITH MY HELP, YOU'RE GOING TO TELL ME WHAT THAT SECRET *IS.*
I DON'T KNOW WHAT SECRET YOU'RE TALKING ABOUT.
YOU JUST NEED *INCENTIVE.*
LIKE OUR FRIEND, STANLEY. HE NEEDED INCENTIVE.
YOU SHOULD SEE HIM NOW.

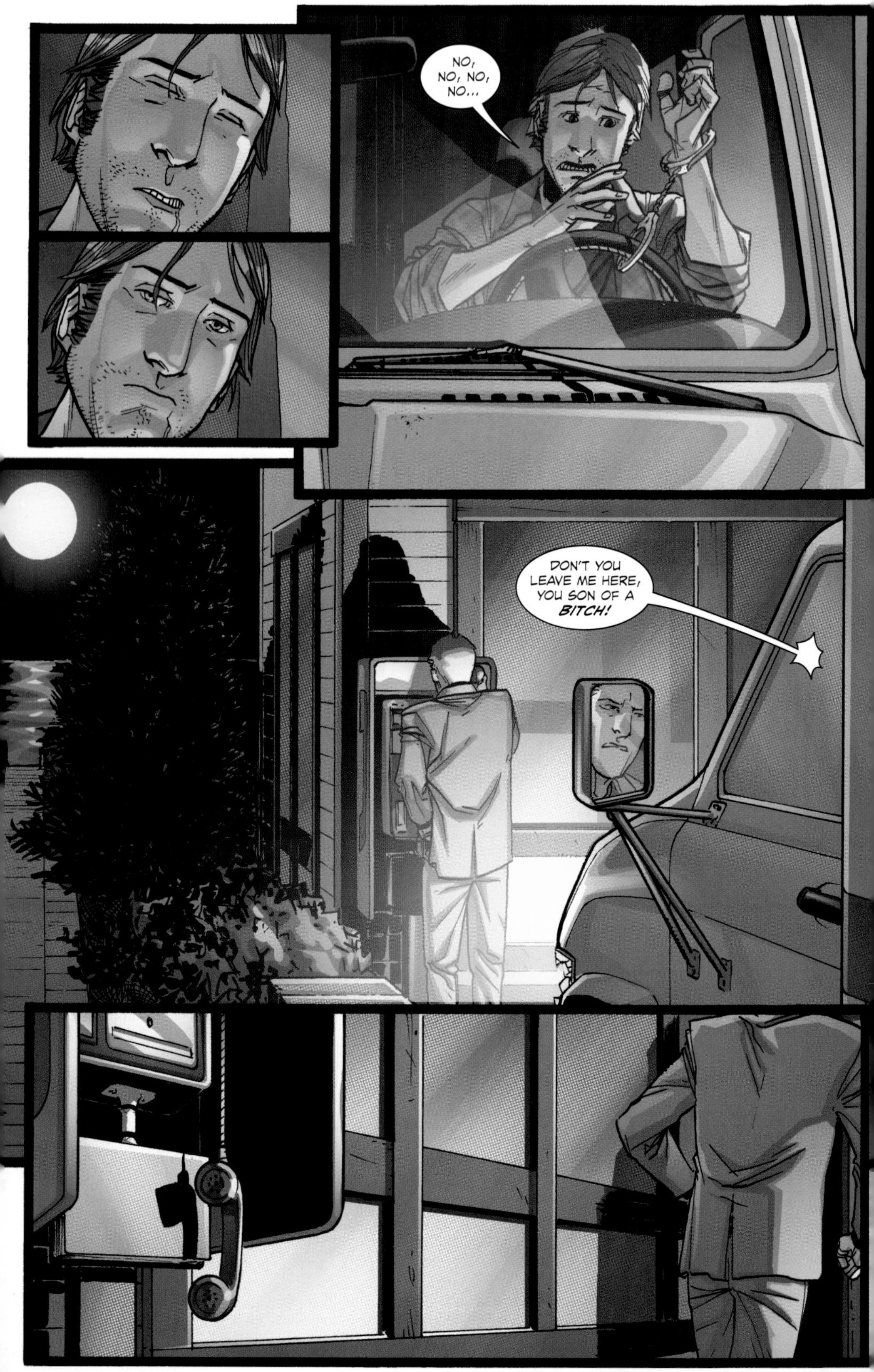
NO, NO, NO, NO...
DON'T YOU LEAVE ME HERE, YOU SON OF A *BITCH!*

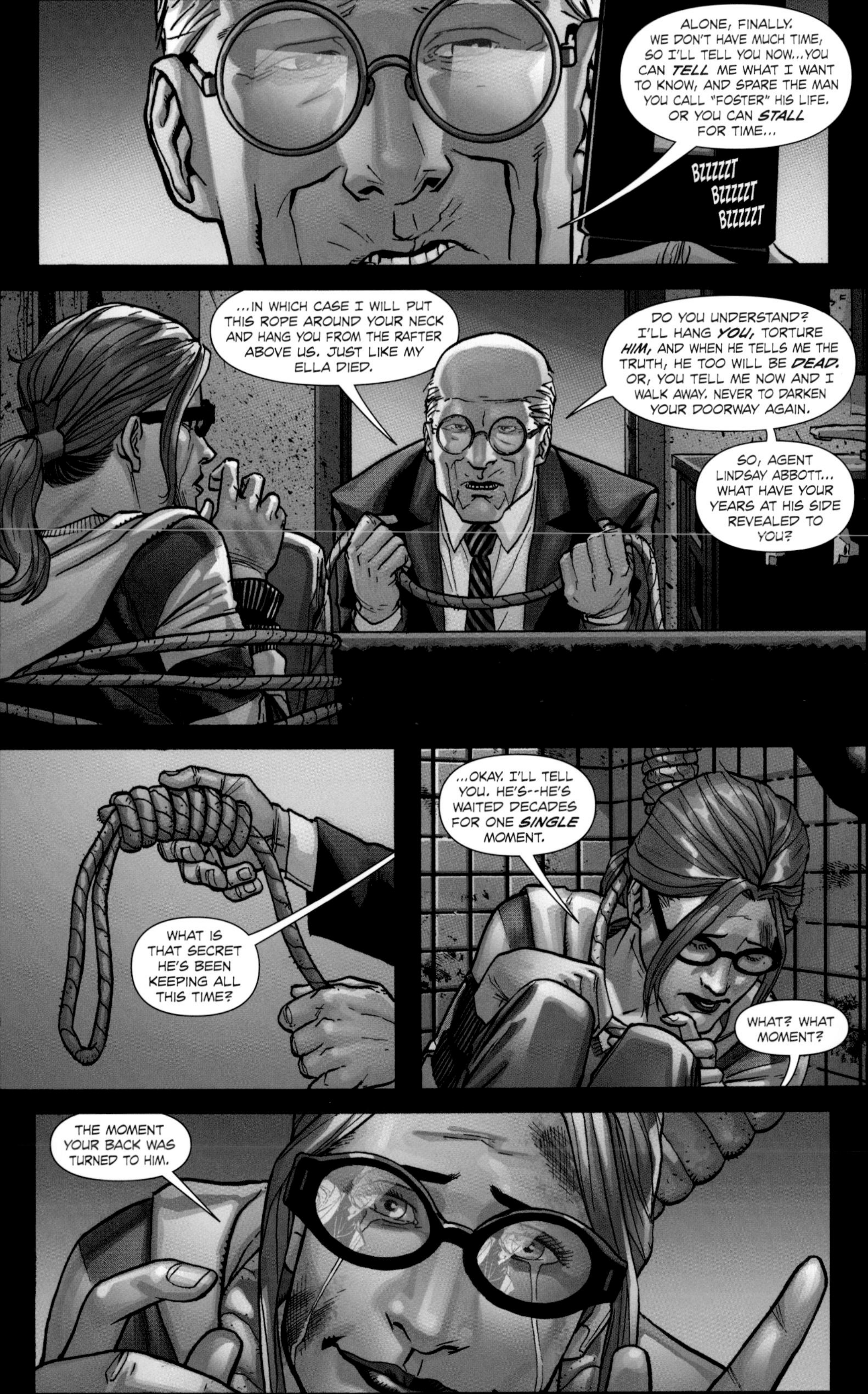
ALONE, FINALLY. WE DON'T HAVE MUCH TIME, SO I'LL TELL YOU NOW...YOU CAN TELL ME WHAT I WANT TO KNOW, AND SPARE THE MAN YOU CALL "FOSTER" HIS LIFE. OR YOU CAN STALL FOR TIME...
BZZZZZT BZZZZZT BZZZZZT
...IN WHICH CASE I WILL PUT THIS ROPE AROUND YOUR NECK AND HANG YOU FROM THE RAFTER ABOVE US. JUST LIKE MY ELLA DIED.
DO YOU UNDERSTAND? I'LL HANG YOU, TORTURE HIM, AND WHEN HE TELLS ME THE TRUTH, HE TOO WILL BE DEAD. OR, YOU TELL ME NOW AND I WALK AWAY. NEVER TO DARKEN YOUR DOORWAY AGAIN.
SO, AGENT LINDSAY ABBOTT... WHAT HAVE YOUR YEARS AT HIS SIDE REVEALED TO YOU?
WHAT IS THAT SECRET HE'S BEEN KEEPING ALL THIS TIME?
...OKAY. I'LL TELL YOU. HE'S--HE'S WAITED DECADES FOR ONE SINGLE MOMENT.
WHAT? WHAT MOMENT?
THE MOMENT YOUR BACK WAS TURNED TO HIM.

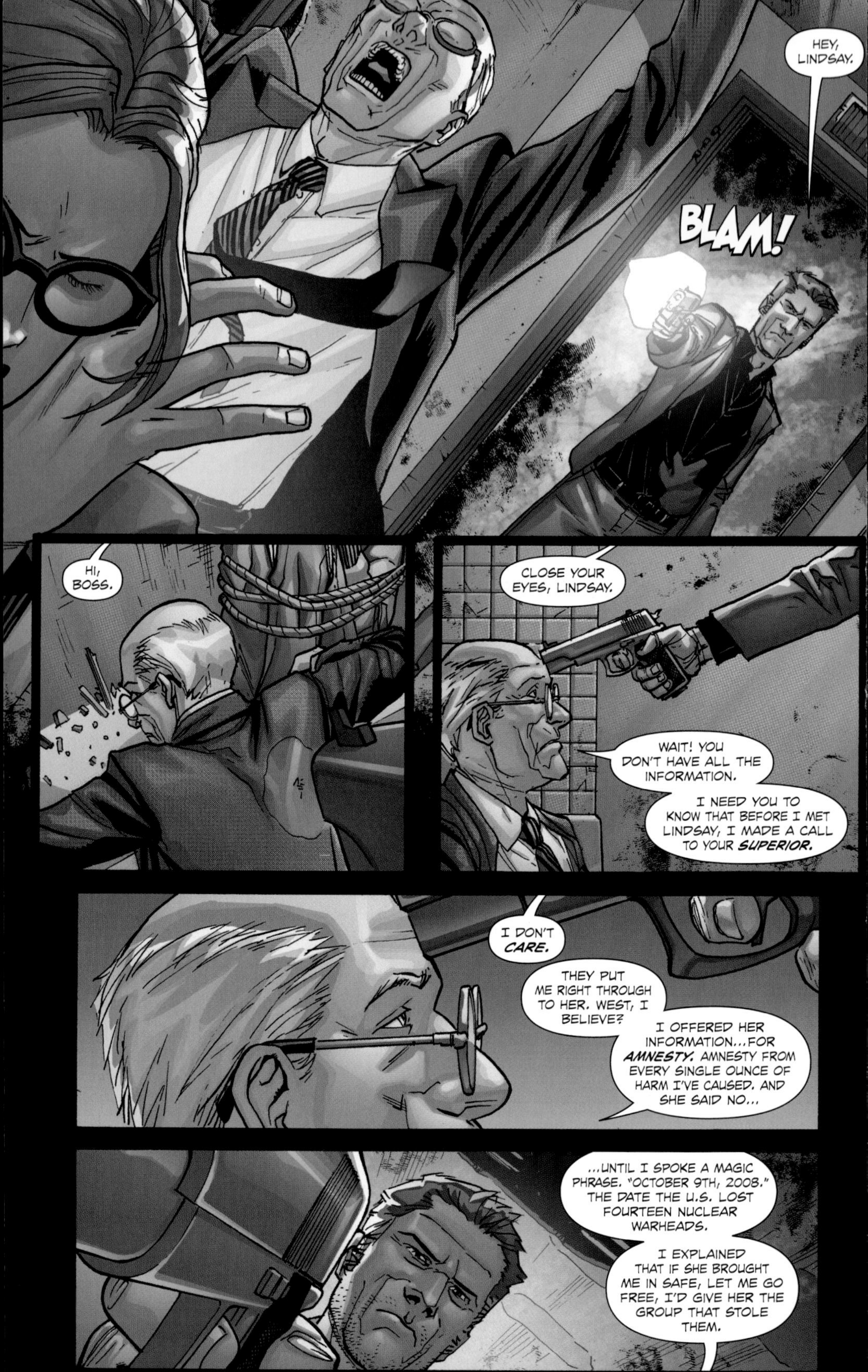
HEY, LINDSAY.
BLAM!
HI, BOSS.
CLOSE YOUR EYES, LINDSAY.
WAIT! YOU DON'T HAVE ALL THE INFORMATION.
I NEED YOU TO KNOW THAT BEFORE I MET LINDSAY, I MADE A CALL TO YOUR SUPERIOR.
I DON'T CARE.
THEY PUT ME RIGHT THROUGH TO HER. WEST, I BELIEVE?
I OFFERED HER INFORMATION...FOR AMNESTY. AMNESTY FROM EVERY SINGLE OUNCE OF HARM I'VE CAUSED. AND SHE SAID NO...
...UNTIL I SPOKE A MAGIC PHRASE. "OCTOBER 9TH, 2008." THE DATE THE U.S. LOST FOURTEEN NUCLEAR WARHEADS.
I EXPLAINED THAT IF SHE BROUGHT ME IN SAFE, LET ME GO FREE, I'D GIVE HER THE GROUP THAT STOLE THEM.

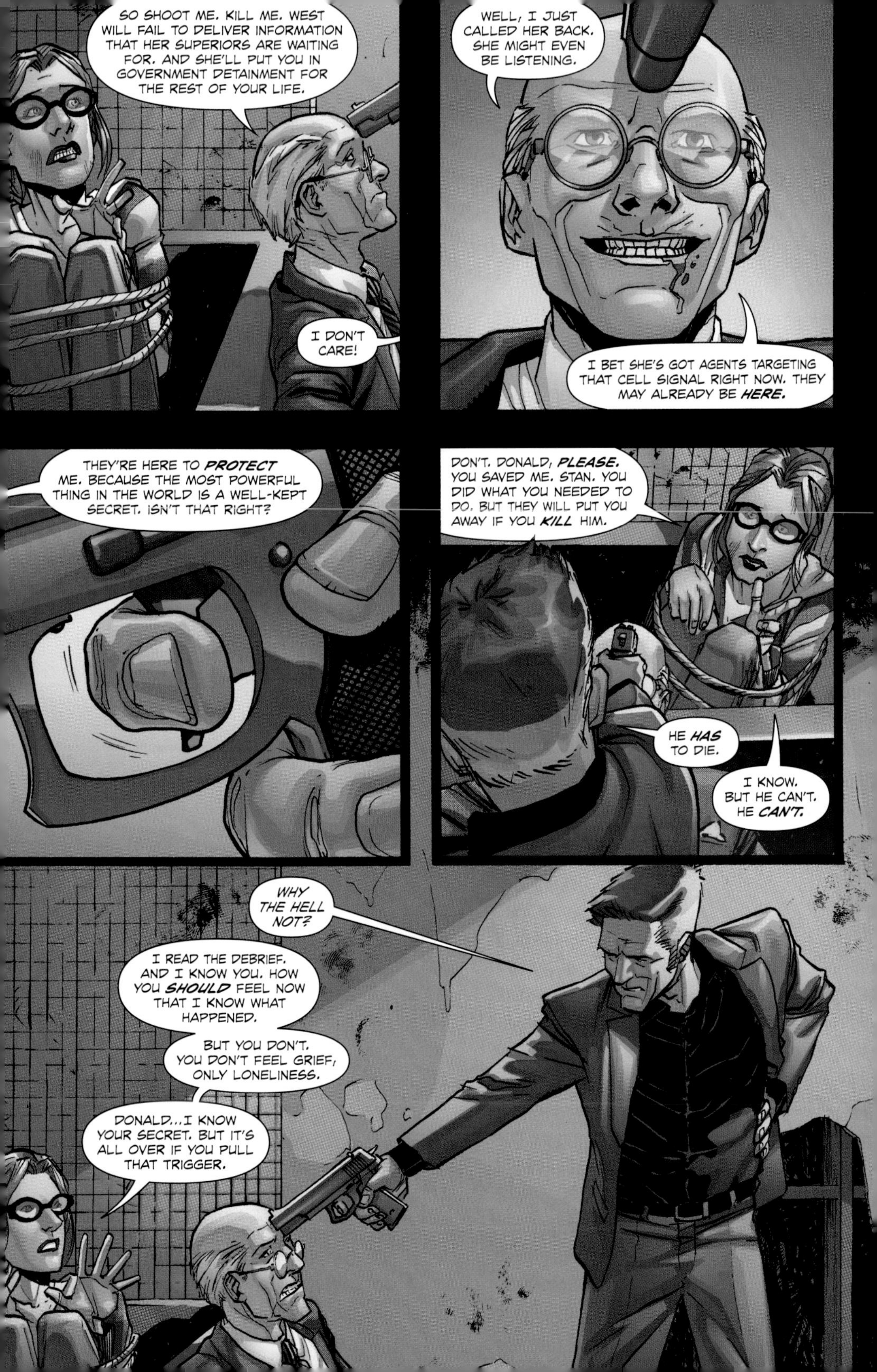
SO SHOOT ME. KILL ME. WEST WILL FAIL TO DELIVER INFORMATION THAT HER SUPERIORS ARE WAITING FOR. AND SHE'LL PUT YOU IN GOVERNMENT DETAINMENT FOR THE REST OF YOUR LIFE.
I DON'T CARE!
WELL, I JUST CALLED HER BACK. SHE MIGHT EVEN BE LISTENING.
I BET SHE'S GOT AGENTS TARGETING THAT CELL SIGNAL RIGHT NOW. THEY MAY ALREADY BE *HERE.*
THEY'RE HERE TO *PROTECT* ME. BECAUSE THE MOST POWERFUL THING IN THE WORLD IS A WELL-KEPT SECRET. ISN'T THAT RIGHT?
DON'T. DONALD, *PLEASE.* YOU SAVED ME. STAN. YOU DID WHAT YOU NEEDED TO DO. BUT THEY WILL PUT YOU AWAY IF YOU *KILL* HIM.
HE *HAS* TO DIE.
I KNOW. BUT HE CAN'T. HE *CAN'T.*
WHY THE HELL NOT?
I READ THE DEBRIEF. AND I KNOW YOU. HOW YOU *SHOULD* FEEL NOW THAT I KNOW WHAT HAPPENED.
BUT YOU DON'T. YOU DON'T FEEL GRIEF, ONLY LONELINESS.
DONALD...I KNOW YOUR SECRET. BUT IT'S ALL OVER IF YOU PULL THAT TRIGGER.

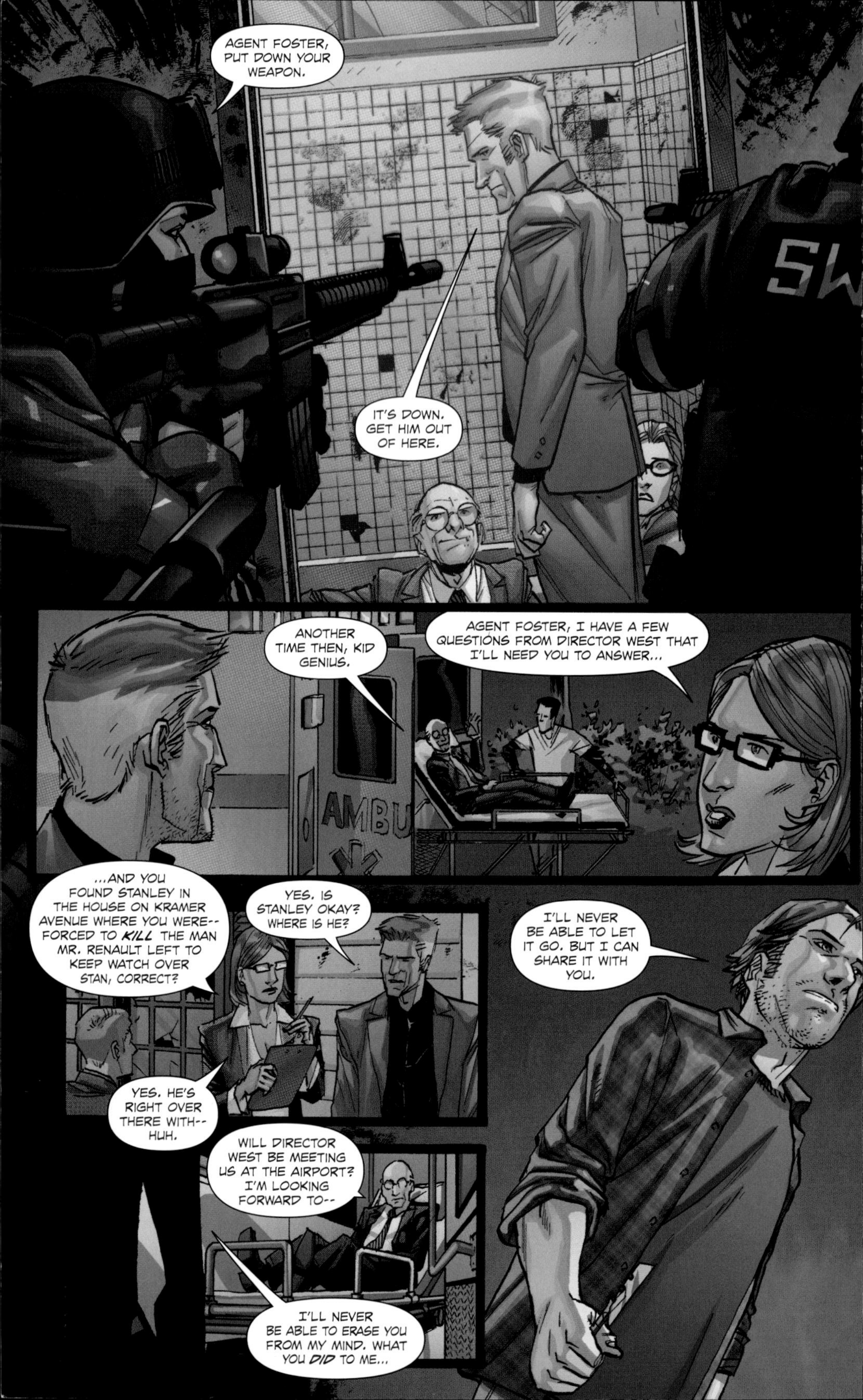
AGENT FOSTER, PUT DOWN YOUR WEAPON.
IT'S DOWN. GET HIM OUT OF HERE.
ANOTHER TIME THEN, KID GENIUS.
AGENT FOSTER, I HAVE A FEW QUESTIONS FROM DIRECTOR WEST THAT I'LL NEED YOU TO ANSWER...
AMBU
...AND YOU FOUND STANLEY IN THE HOUSE ON KRAMER AVENUE WHERE YOU WERE--FORCED TO KILL THE MAN MR. RENAULT LEFT TO KEEP WATCH OVER STAN, CORRECT?
YES. IS STANLEY OKAY? WHERE IS HE?
YES. HE'S RIGHT OVER THERE WITH--HUH.
WILL DIRECTOR WEST BE MEETING US AT THE AIRPORT? I'M LOOKING FORWARD TO--
I'LL NEVER BE ABLE TO ERASE YOU FROM MY MIND. WHAT YOU DID TO ME...
I'LL NEVER BE ABLE TO LET IT GO. BUT I CAN SHARE IT WITH YOU.

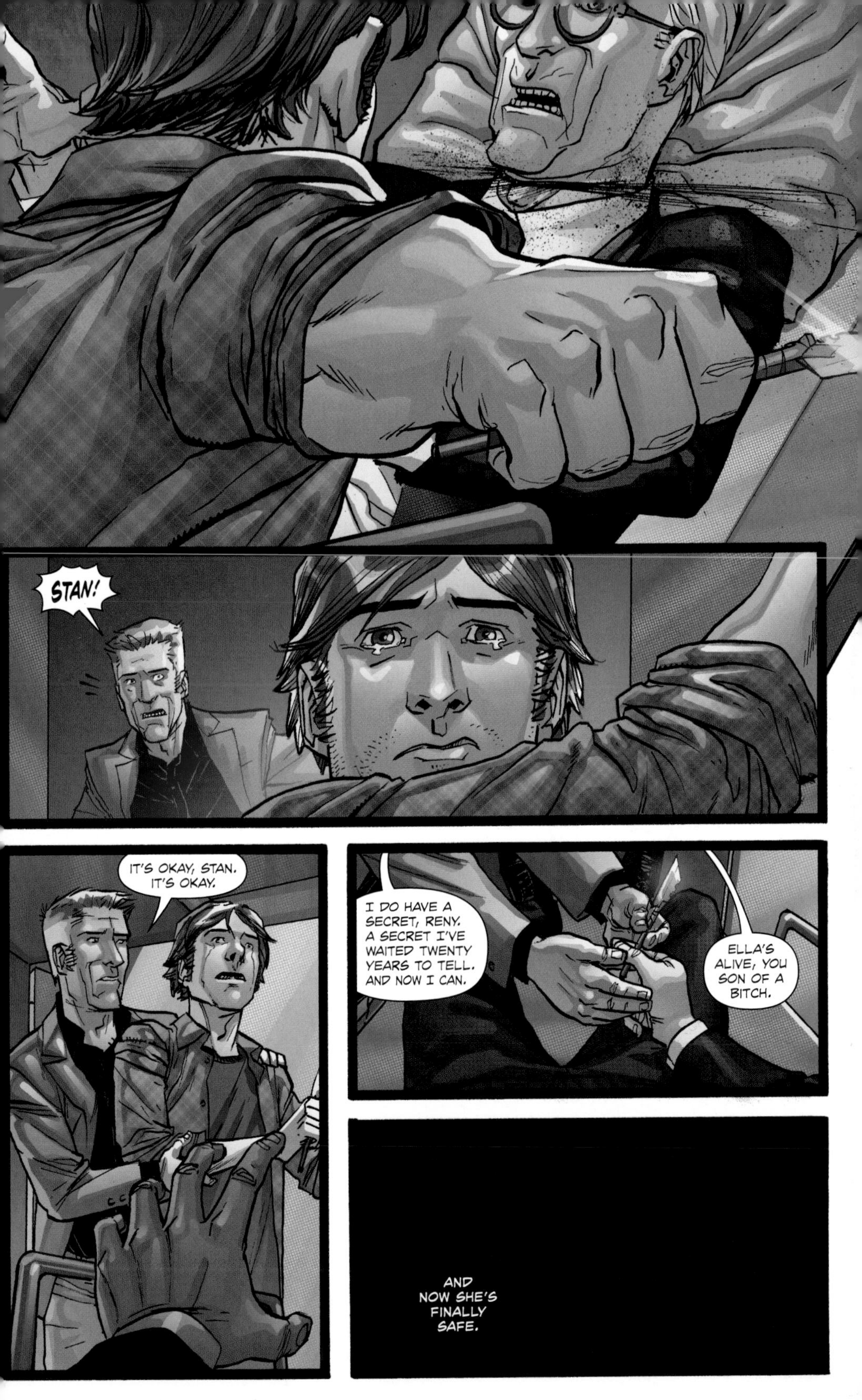
STAN!
IT'S OKAY, STAN. IT'S OKAY.
I DO HAVE A SECRET, RENY. A SECRET I'VE WAITED TWENTY YEARS TO TELL. AND NOW I CAN.
ELLA'S ALIVE, YOU SON OF A BITCH.
AND NOW SHE'S FINALLY SAFE.

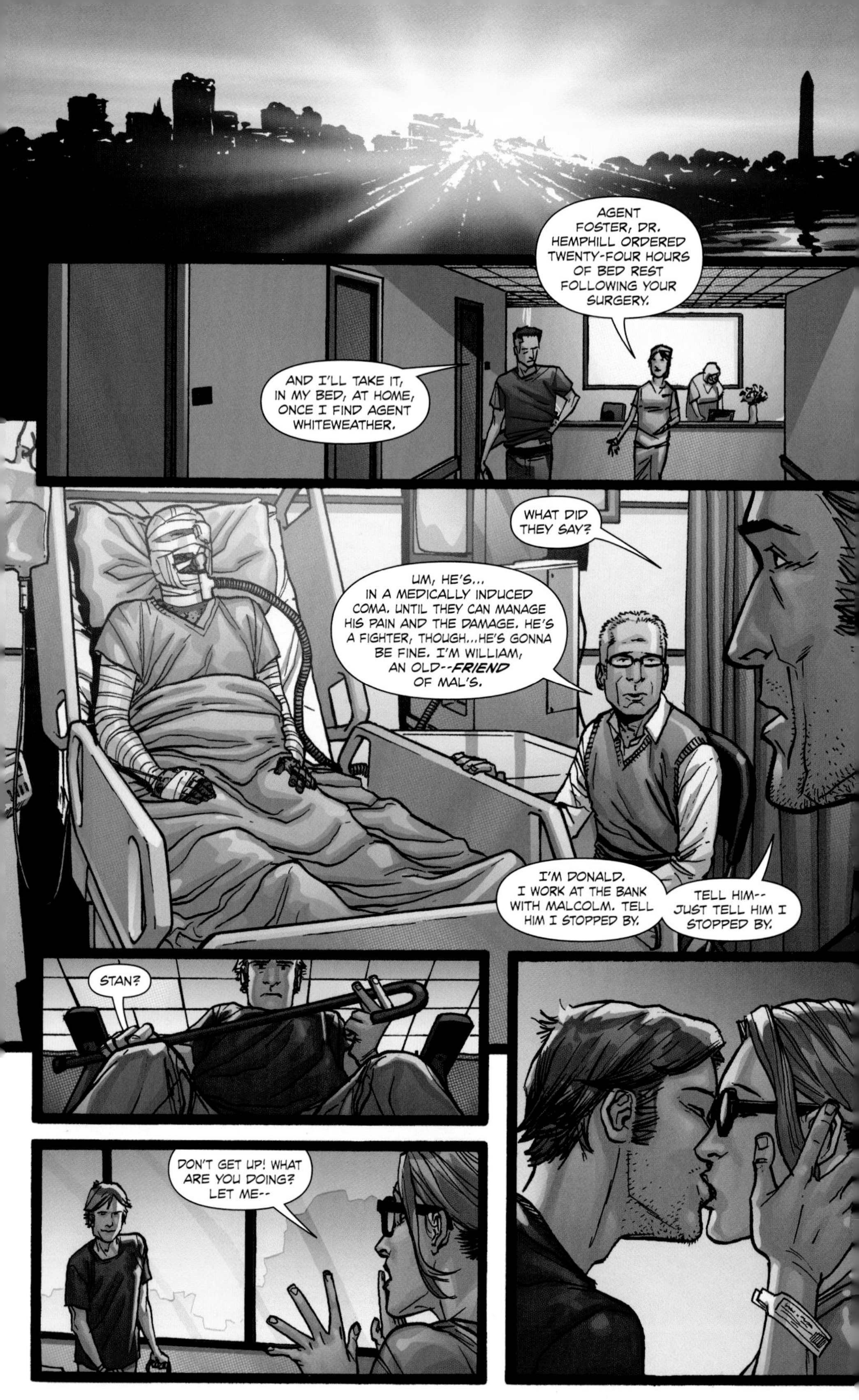
AGENT FOSTER, DR. HEMPHILL ORDERED TWENTY-FOUR HOURS OF BED REST FOLLOWING YOUR SURGERY.
AND I'LL TAKE IT, IN MY BED, AT HOME, ONCE I FIND AGENT WHITEWEATHER.
WHAT DID THEY SAY?
UM, HE'S... IN A MEDICALLY INDUCED COMA. UNTIL THEY CAN MANAGE HIS PAIN AND THE DAMAGE. HE'S A FIGHTER, THOUGH...HE'S GONNA BE FINE. I'M WILLIAM, AN OLD--FRIEND OF MAL'S.
I'M DONALD. I WORK AT THE BANK WITH MALCOLM. TELL HIM I STOPPED BY.
TELL HIM-- JUST TELL HIM I STOPPED BY.
STAN?
DON'T GET UP! WHAT ARE YOU DOING? LET ME--

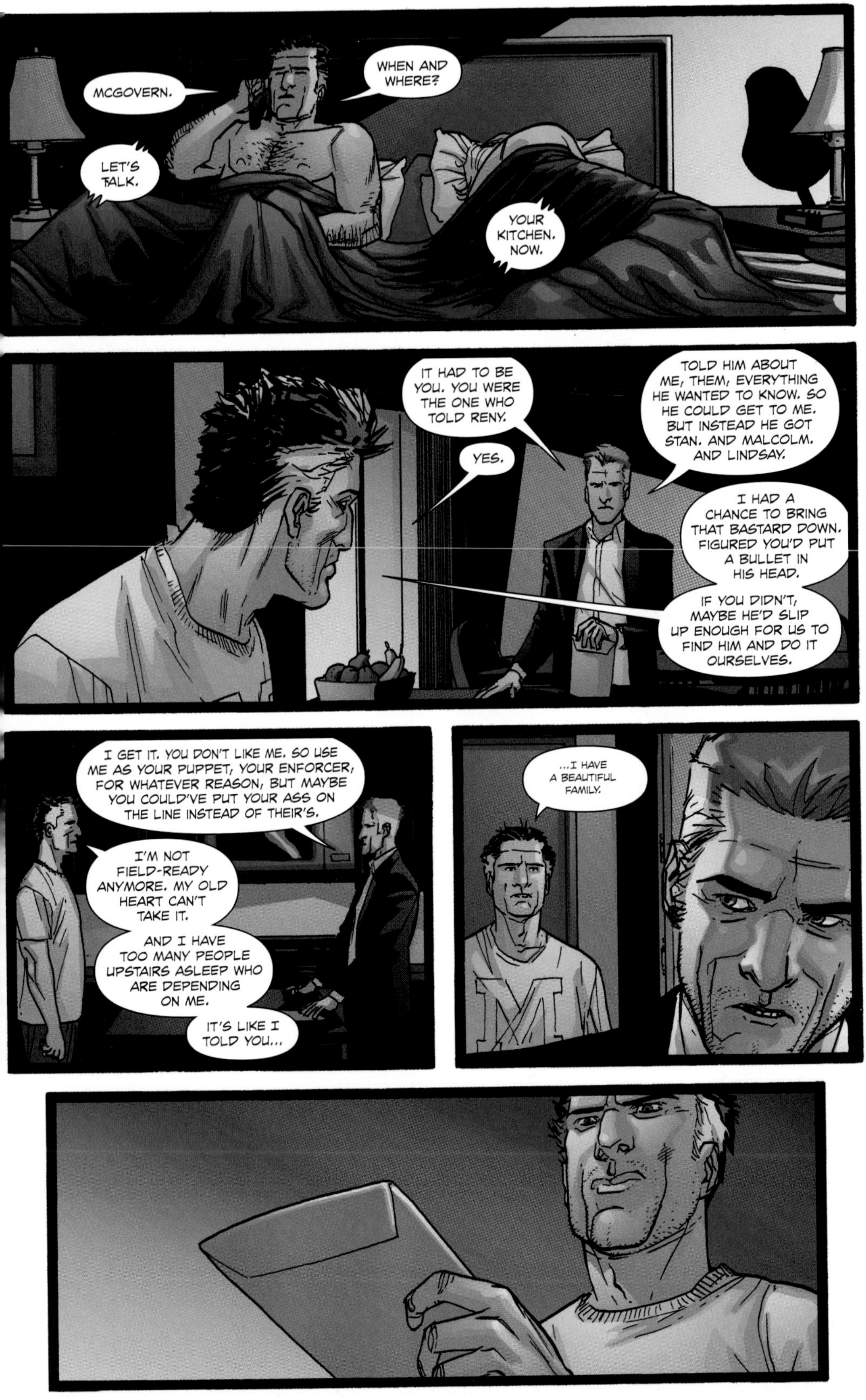
MCGOVERN.
WHEN AND WHERE?
LET'S TALK.
YOUR KITCHEN. NOW.
IT HAD TO BE YOU. YOU WERE THE ONE WHO TOLD RENY.
YES.
TOLD HIM ABOUT ME, THEM, EVERYTHING HE WANTED TO KNOW. SO HE COULD GET TO ME. BUT INSTEAD HE GOT STAN. AND MALCOLM. AND LINDSAY.
I HAD A CHANCE TO BRING THAT BASTARD DOWN. FIGURED YOU'D PUT A BULLET IN HIS HEAD.
IF YOU DIDN'T, MAYBE HE'D SLIP UP ENOUGH FOR US TO FIND HIM AND DO IT OURSELVES.
I GET IT. YOU DON'T LIKE ME. SO USE ME AS YOUR PUPPET, YOUR ENFORCER, FOR WHATEVER REASON, BUT MAYBE YOU COULD'VE PUT YOUR ASS ON THE LINE INSTEAD OF THEIR'S.
I'M NOT FIELD-READY ANYMORE. MY OLD HEART CAN'T TAKE IT.
AND I HAVE TOO MANY PEOPLE UPSTAIRS ASLEEP WHO ARE DEPENDING ON ME.
IT'S LIKE I TOLD YOU...
...I HAVE A BEAUTIFUL FAMILY.

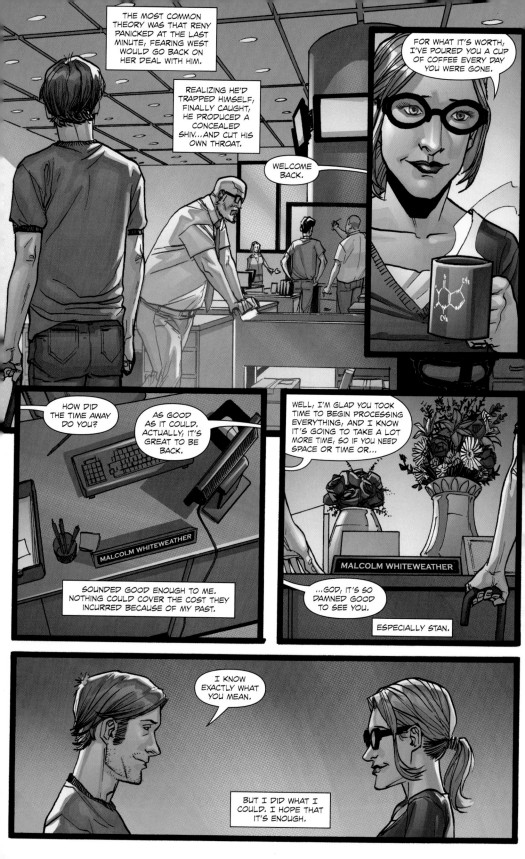

THE MOST COMMON THEORY WAS THAT RENY PANICKED AT THE LAST MINUTE, FEARING WEST WOULD GO BACK ON HER DEAL WITH HIM.

REALIZING HE'D TRAPPED HIMSELF, FINALLY CAUGHT, HE PRODUCED A CONCEALED SHIV...AND CUT HIS OWN THROAT.

WELCOME BACK.

FOR WHAT IT'S WORTH, I'VE POURED YOU A CUP OF COFFEE EVERY DAY YOU WERE GONE.

HOW DID THE TIME AWAY DO YOU?

AS GOOD AS IT COULD. ACTUALLY, IT'S GREAT TO BE BACK.

WELL, I'M GLAD YOU TOOK TIME TO BEGIN PROCESSING EVERYTHING, AND I KNOW IT'S GOING TO TAKE A LOT MORE TIME, SO IF YOU NEED SPACE OR TIME OR...

MALCOLM WHITEWEATHER

SOUNDED GOOD ENOUGH TO ME. NOTHING COULD COVER THE COST THEY INCURRED BECAUSE OF MY PAST.

MALCOLM WHITEWEATHER

...GOD, IT'S SO DAMNED GOOD TO SEE YOU.

ESPECIALLY STAN.

I KNOW EXACTLY WHAT YOU MEAN.

BUT I DID WHAT I COULD. I HOPE THAT IT'S ENOUGH.

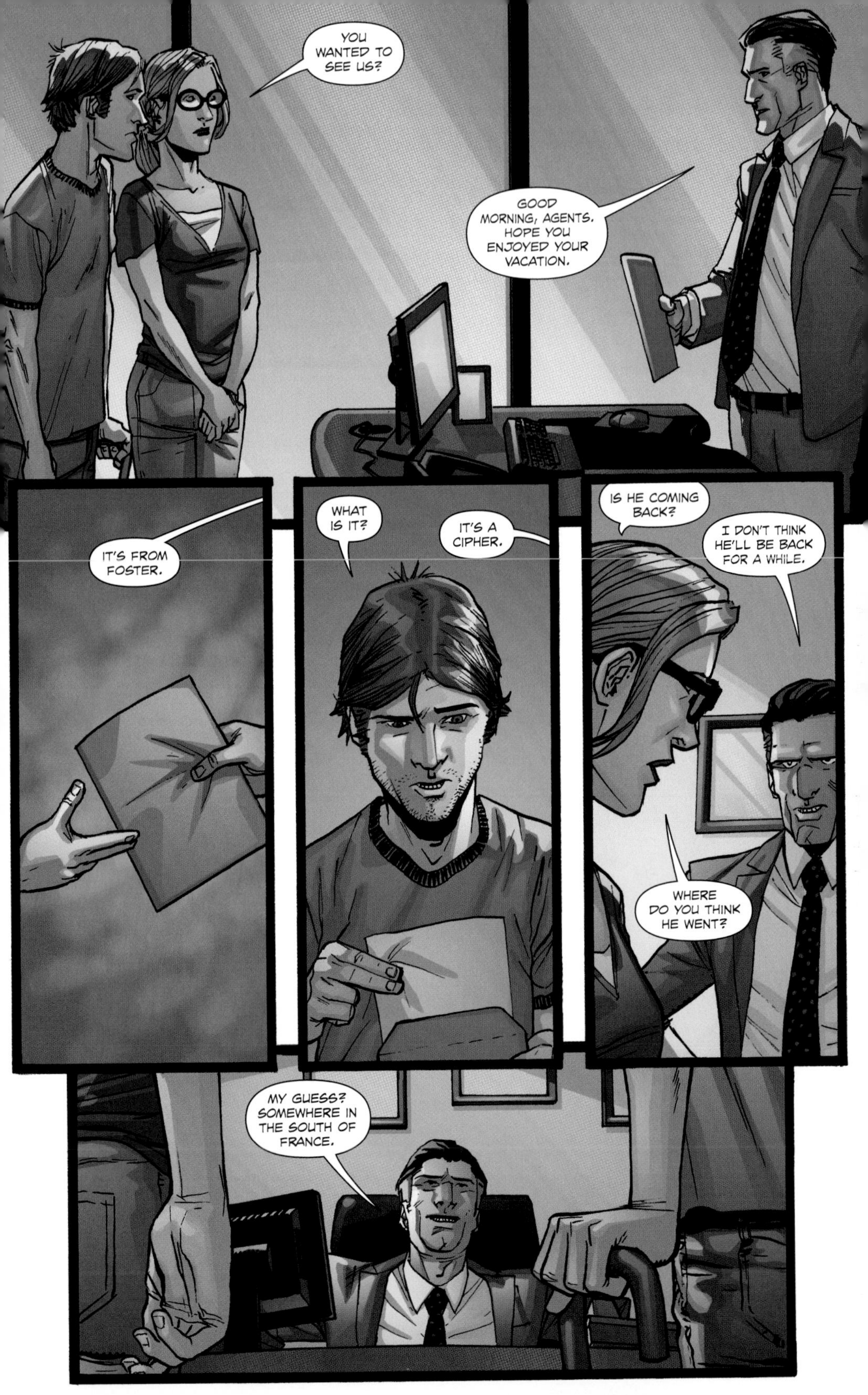
YOU WANTED TO SEE US?
GOOD MORNING, AGENTS. HOPE YOU ENJOYED YOUR VACATION.
IT'S FROM FOSTER.
WHAT IS IT?
IT'S A CIPHER.
IS HE COMING BACK?
I DON'T THINK HE'LL BE BACK FOR A WHILE.
WHERE DO YOU THINK HE WENT?
MY GUESS? SOMEWHERE IN THE SOUTH OF FRANCE.

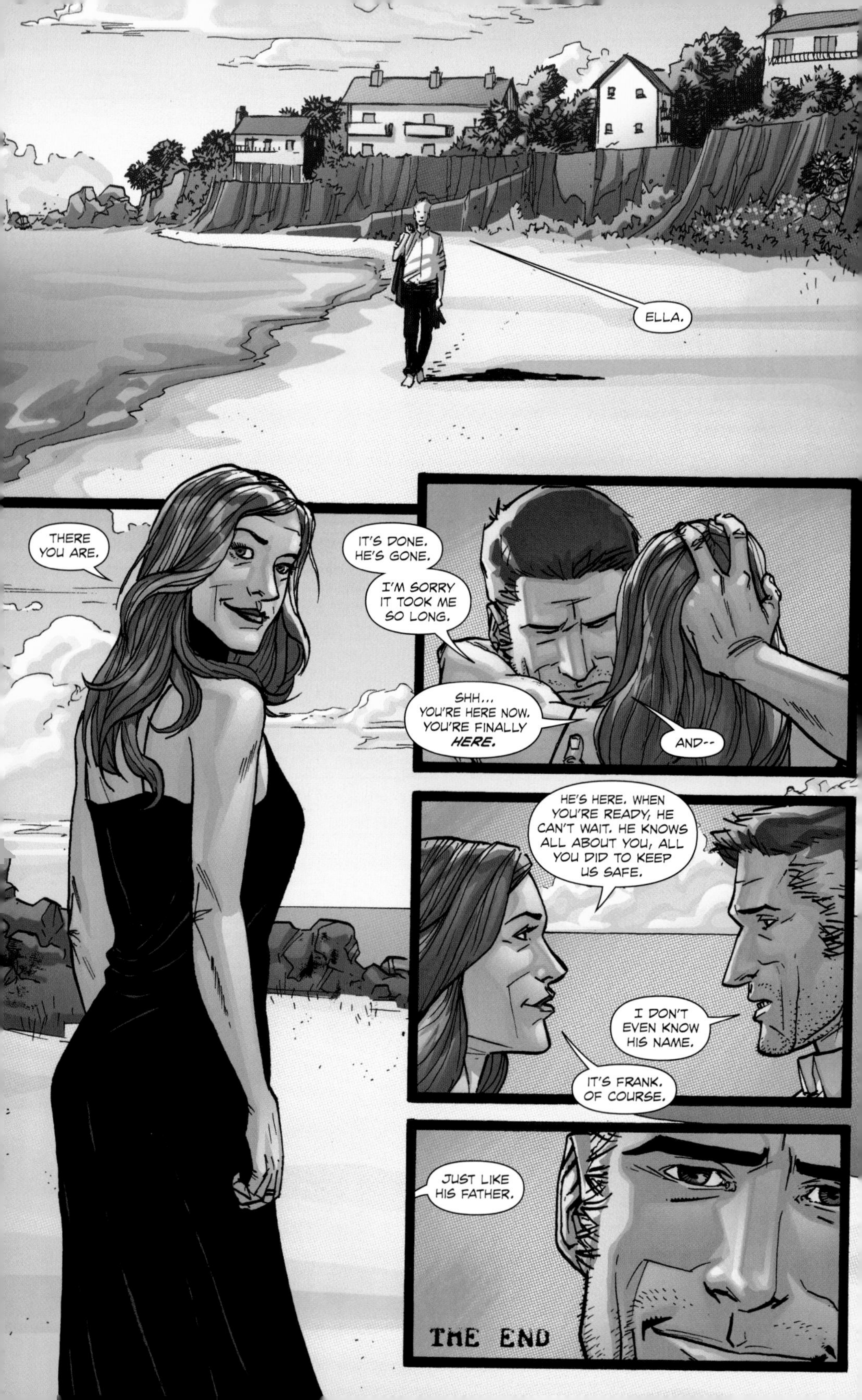
ELLA.
THERE YOU ARE.
IT'S DONE. HE'S GONE.
I'M SORRY IT TOOK ME SO LONG.
SHH... YOU'RE HERE NOW. YOU'RE FINALLY *HERE.*
AND--
HE'S HERE. WHEN YOU'RE READY, HE CAN'T WAIT. HE KNOWS ALL ABOUT YOU, ALL YOU DID TO KEEP US SAFE.
I DON'T EVEN KNOW HIS NAME.
IT'S FRANK. OF COURSE.
JUST LIKE HIS FATHER.
THE END

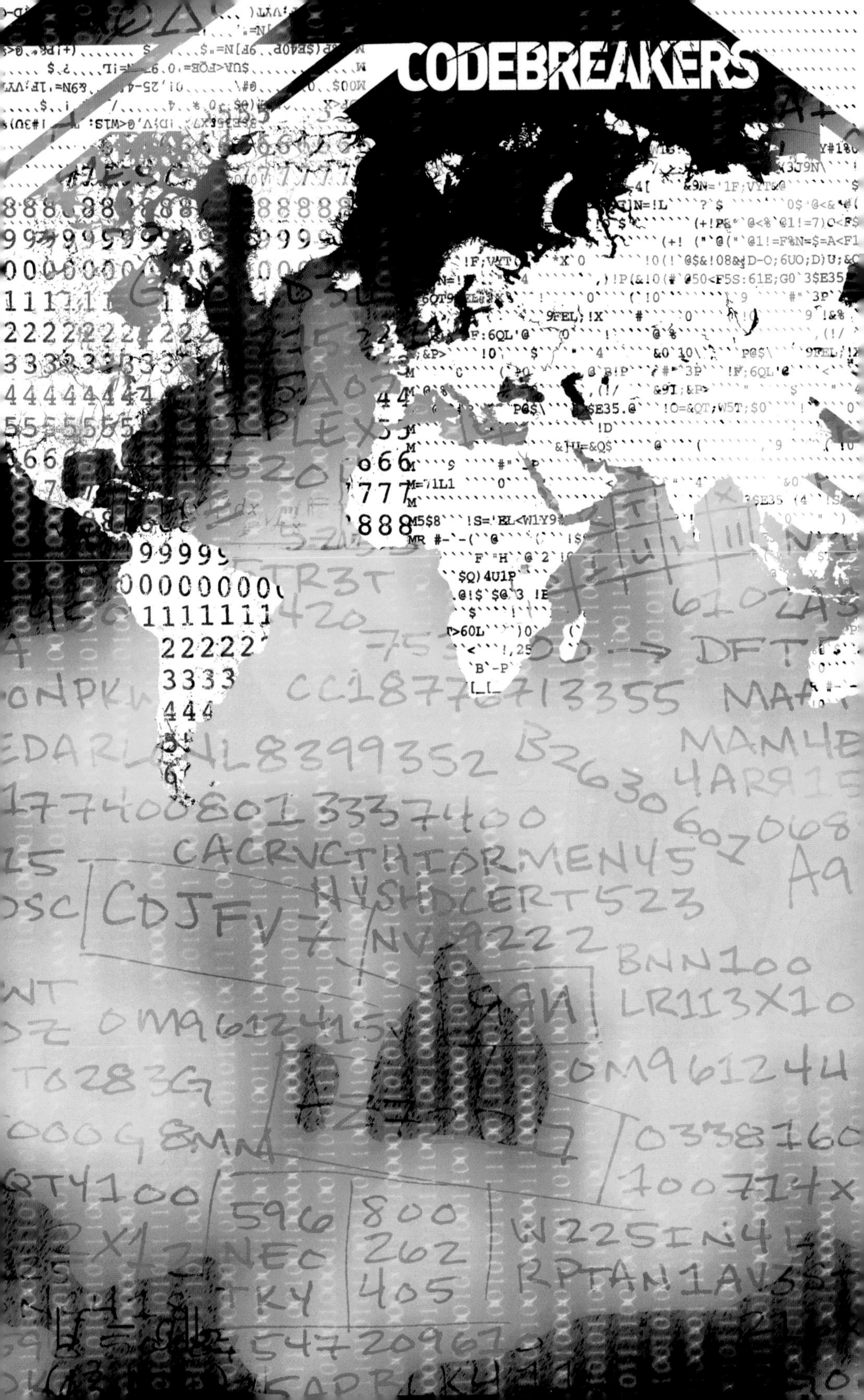
CODEBREAKERS

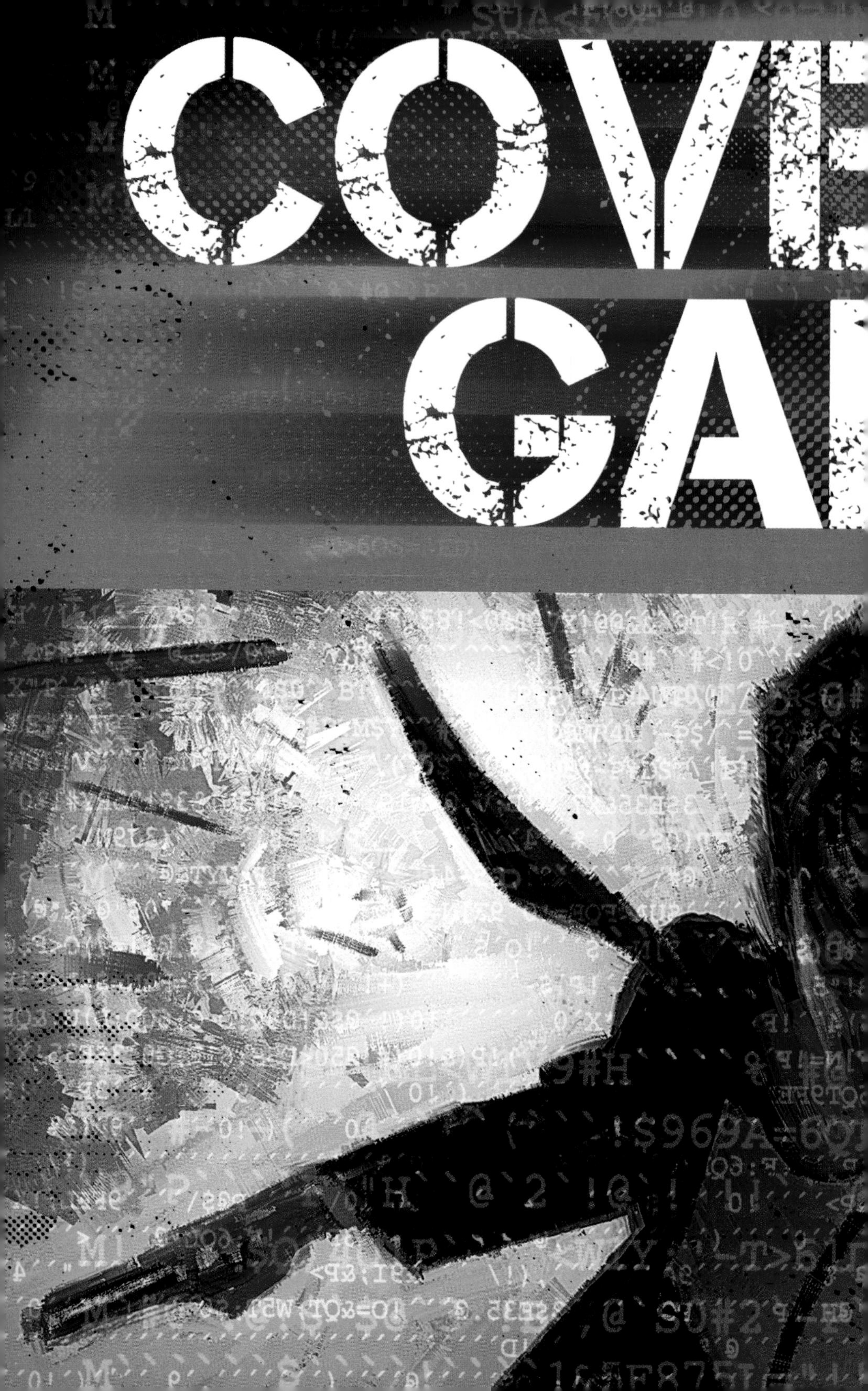
COV
GA

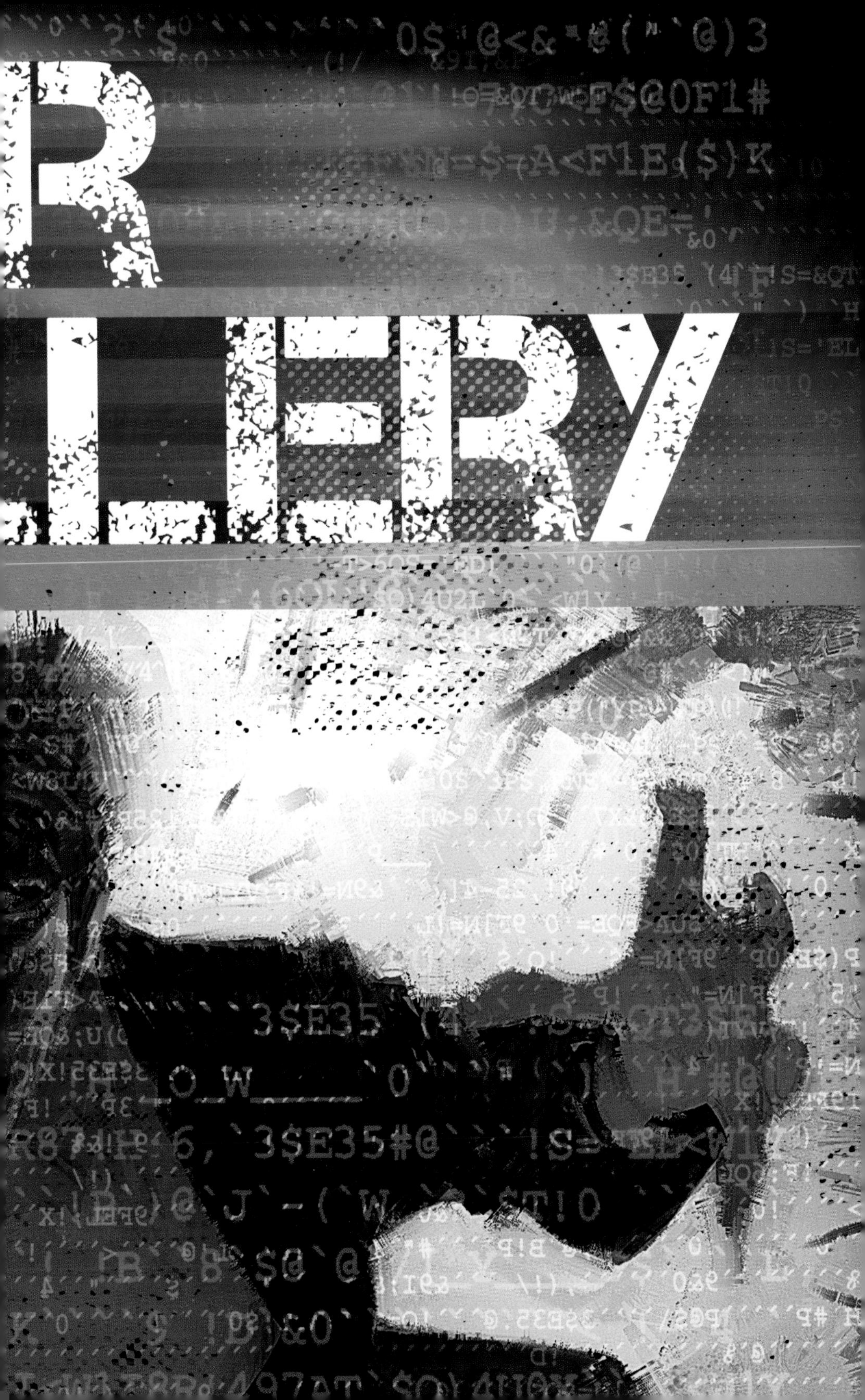
R
LERY

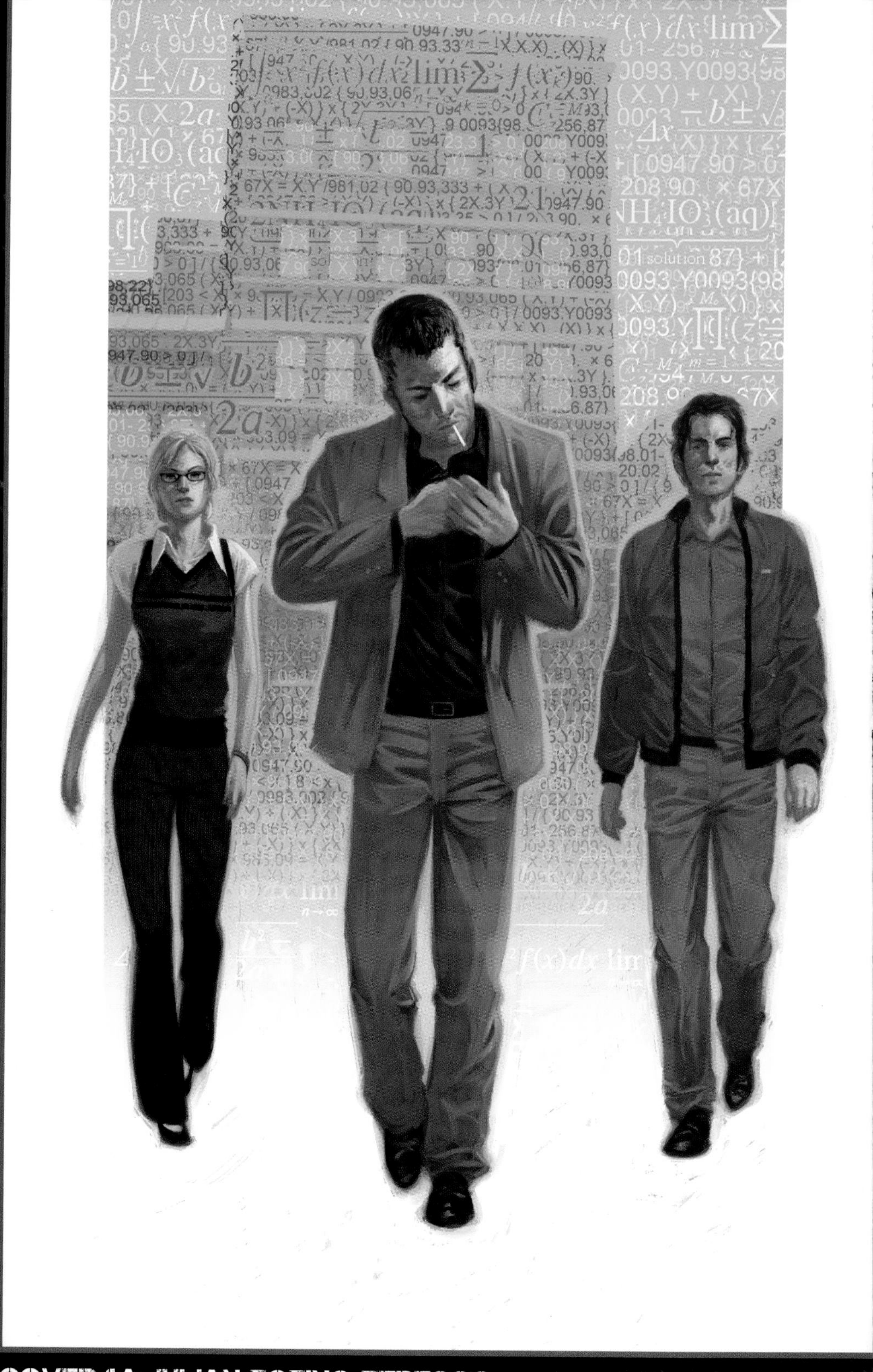

COVER 1A: JULIAN TOTINO TEDESCO

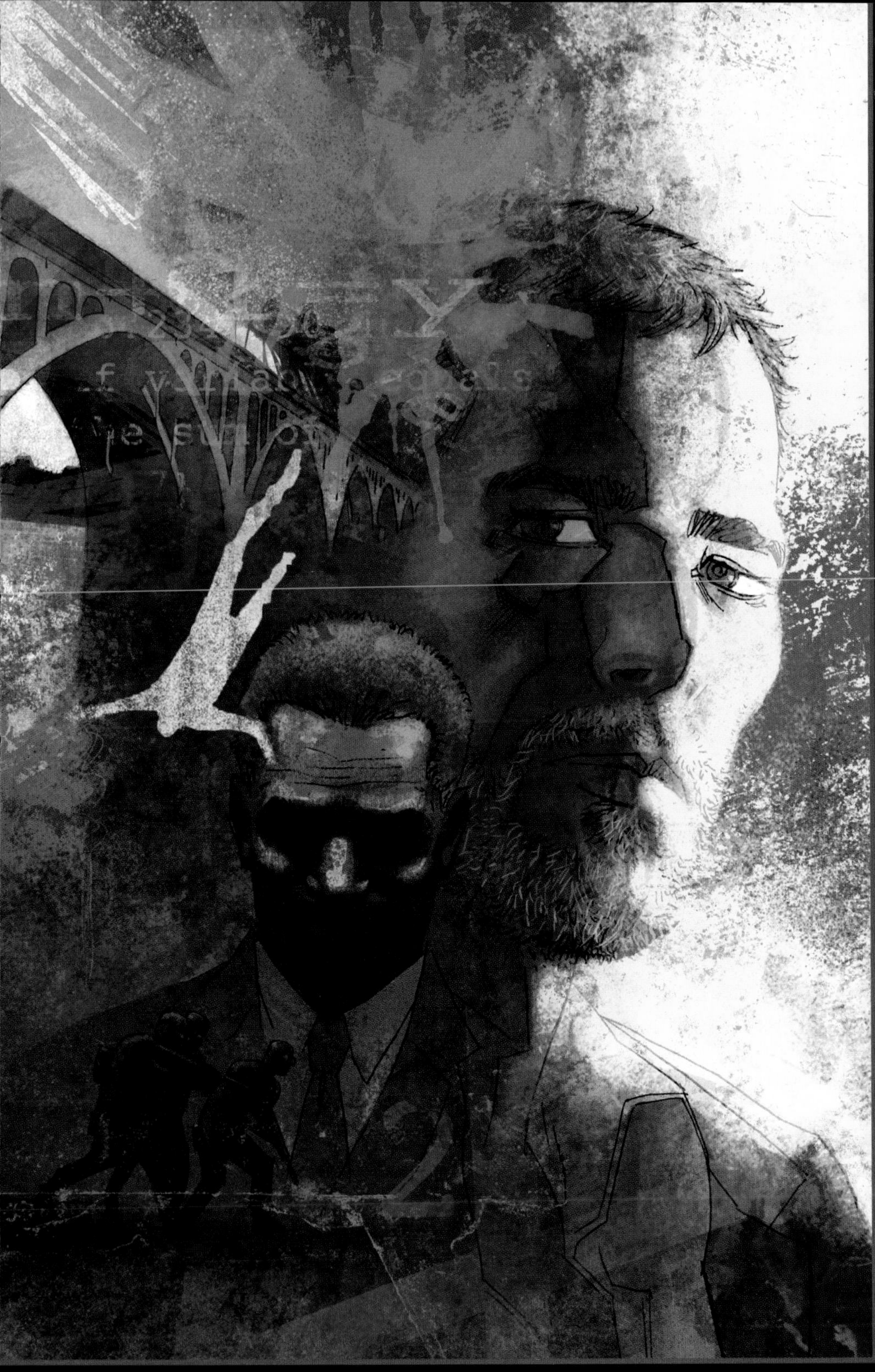

COVER 1B: BRETT WELDELE

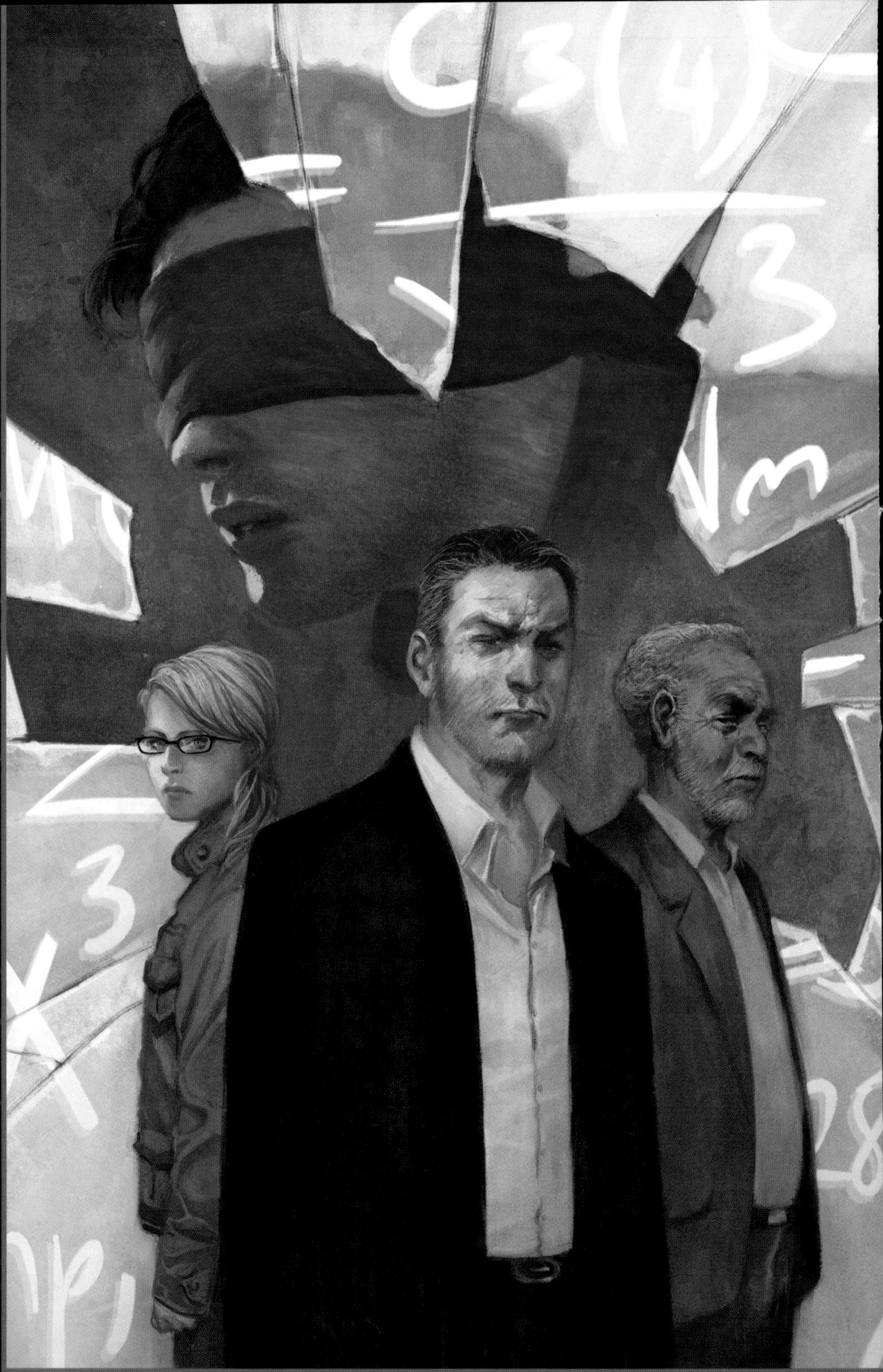

COVER 2A: JULIAN TOTINO TEDESCO

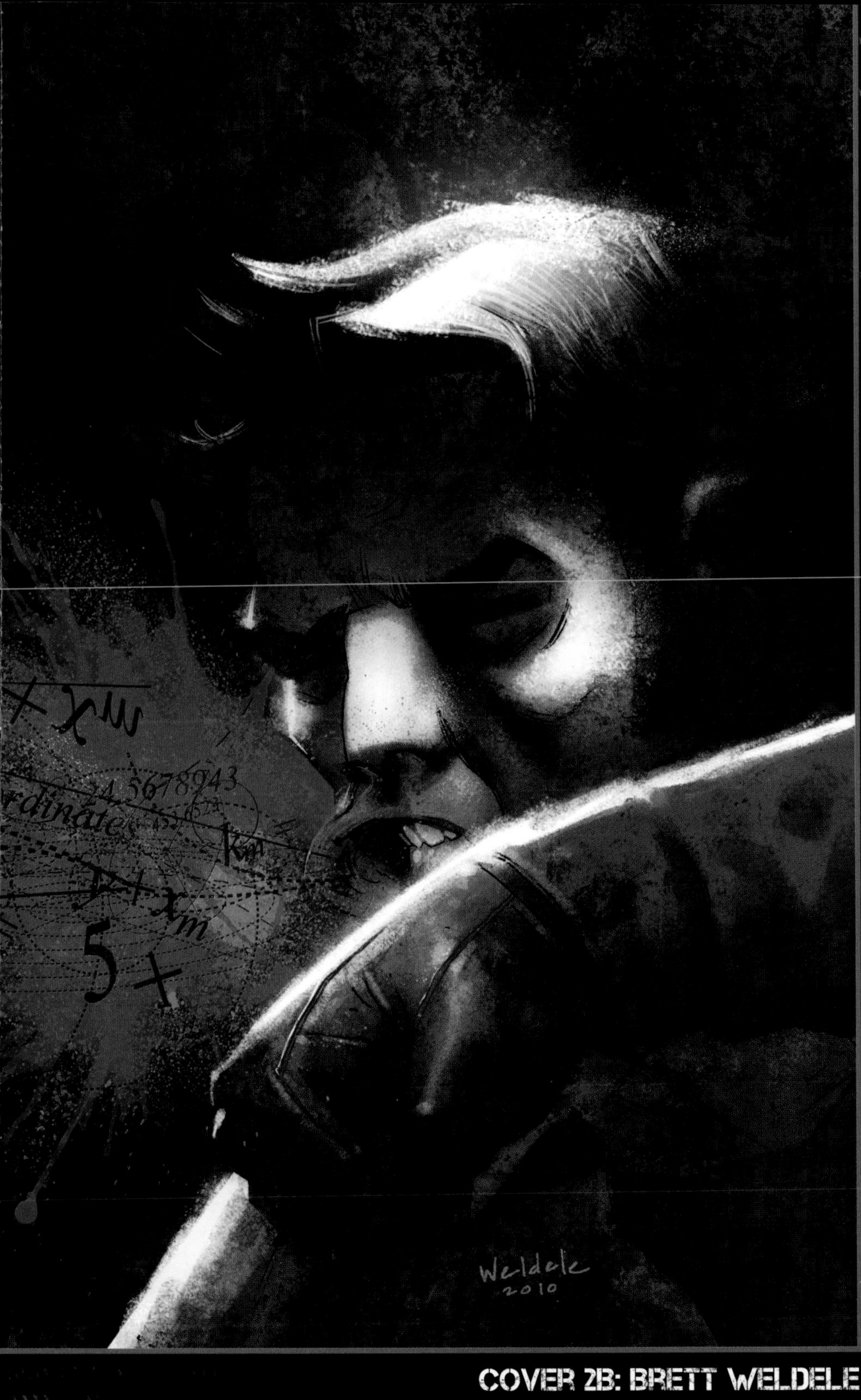

xm
24 5678943
rdinates
km
xm
5
Weldele
2010

COVER 2B: BRETT WELDELE

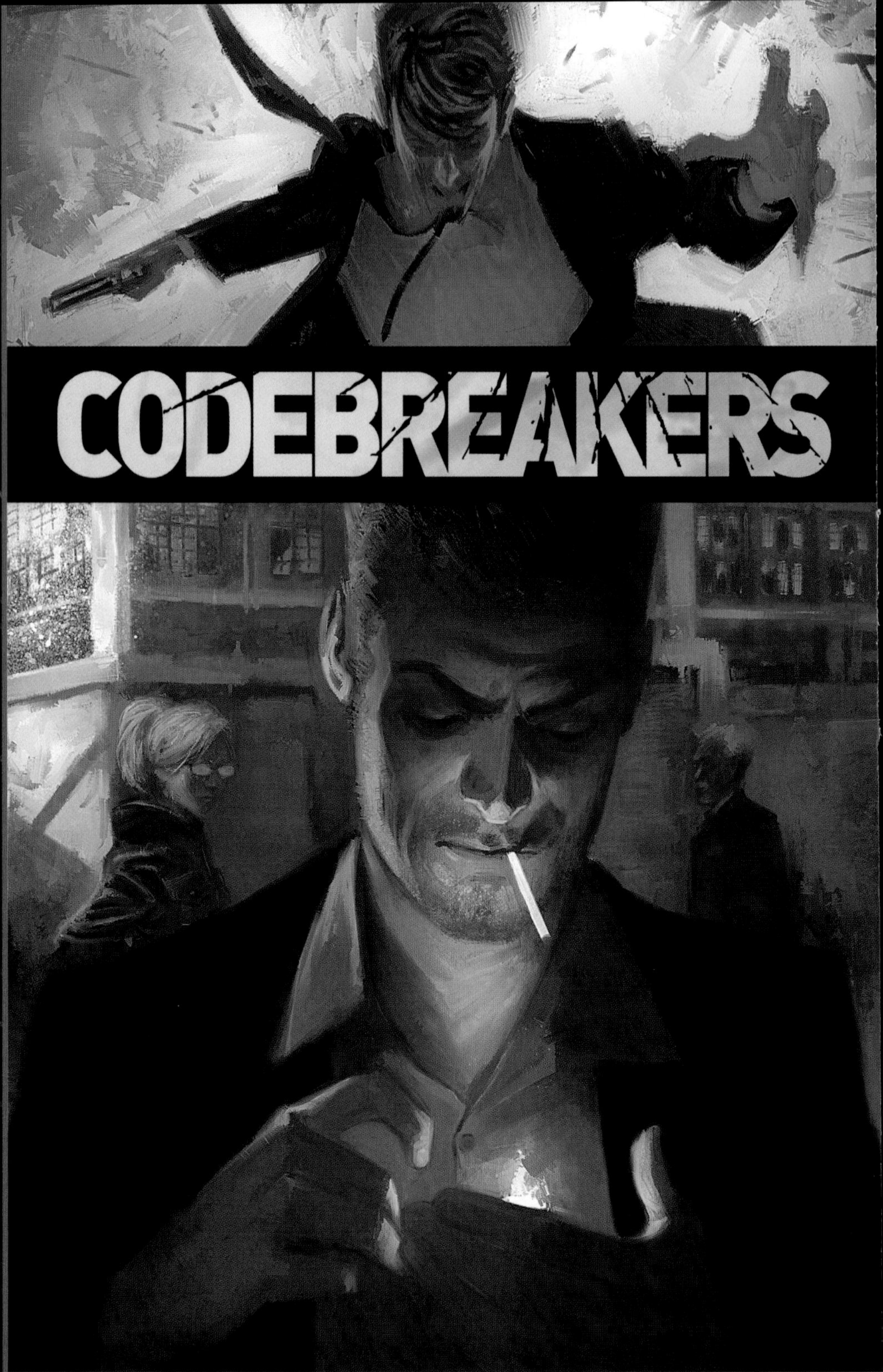
CODEBREAKERS
COVER 3A: JULIAN TOTINO TEDESCO

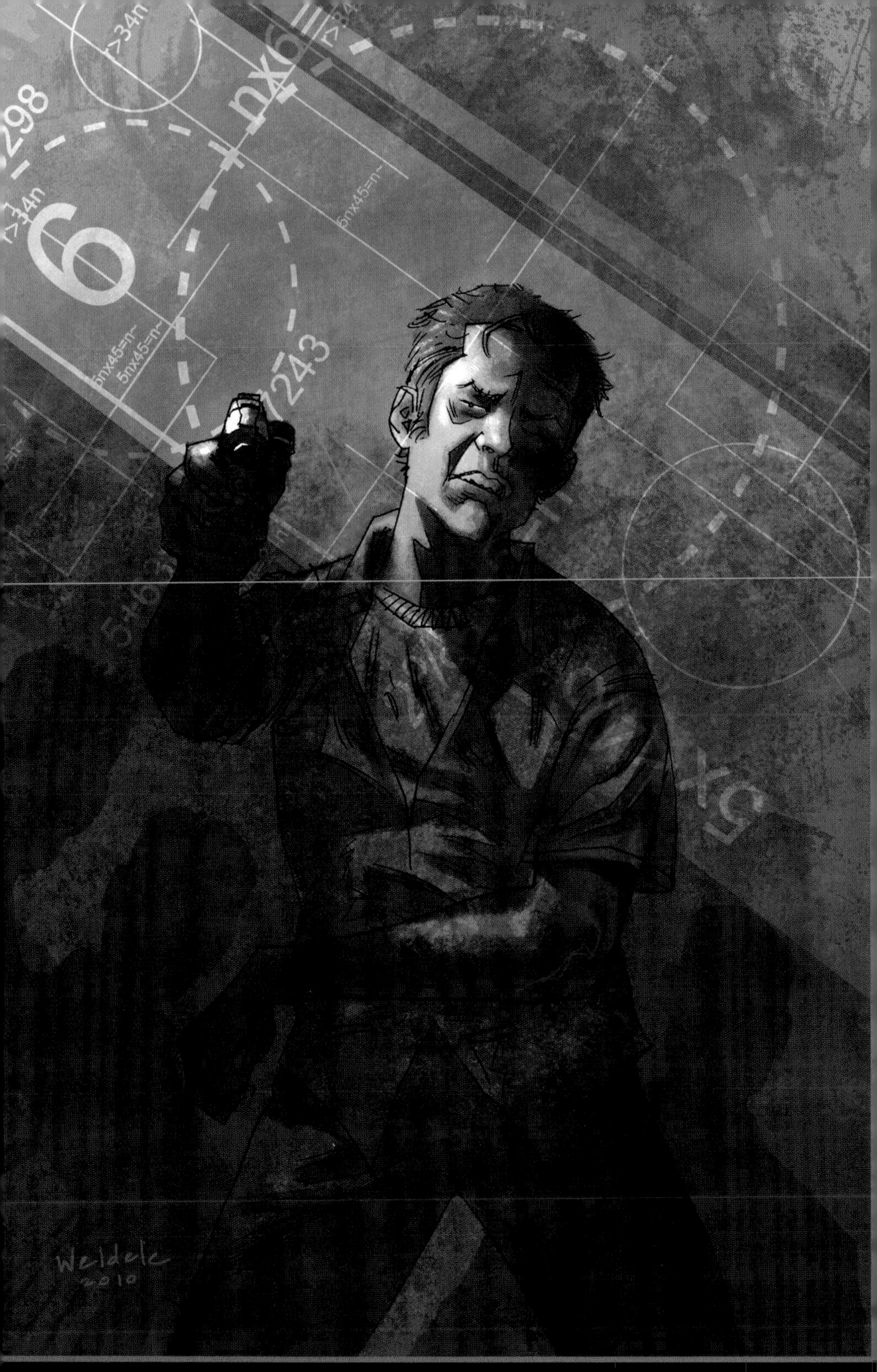
Weldele
2010

3: BRETT WELDELE

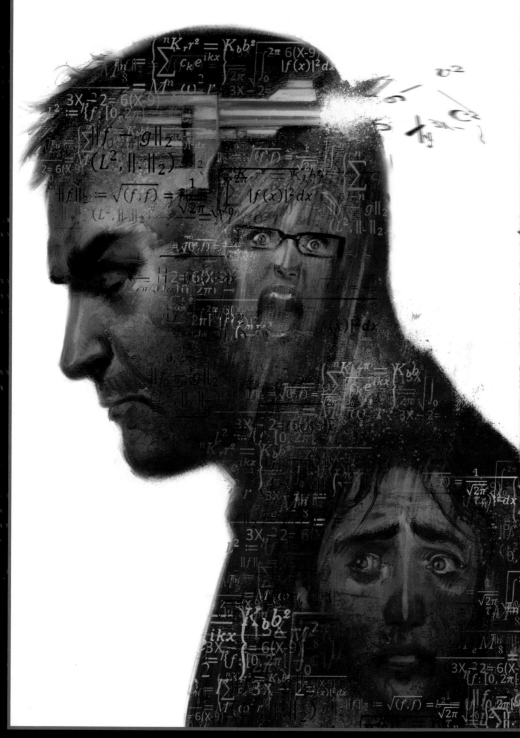

COVER 4A: JULIAN TOTINO TEDESCO

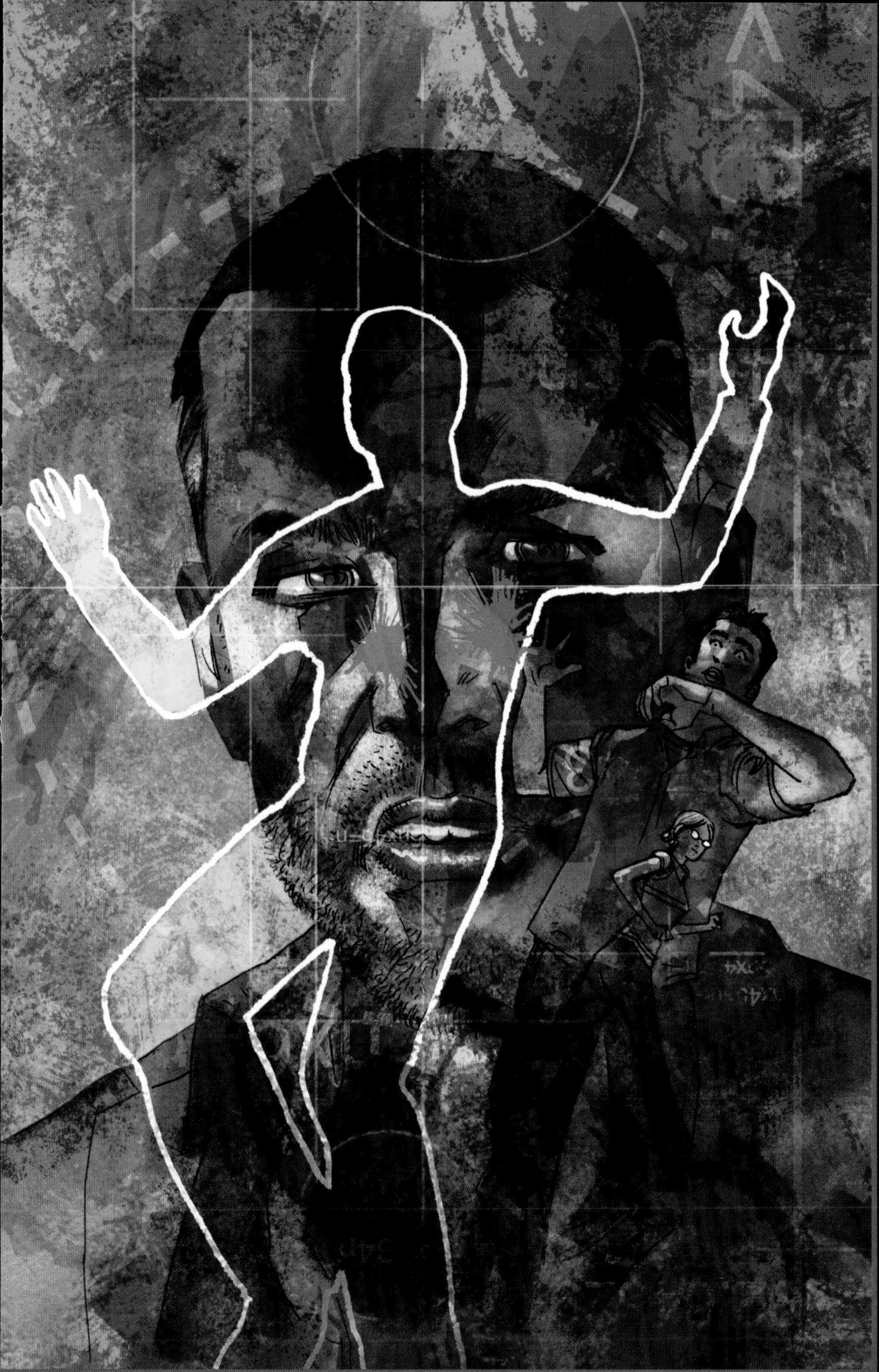

COVER 4B: BRETT WELDELE

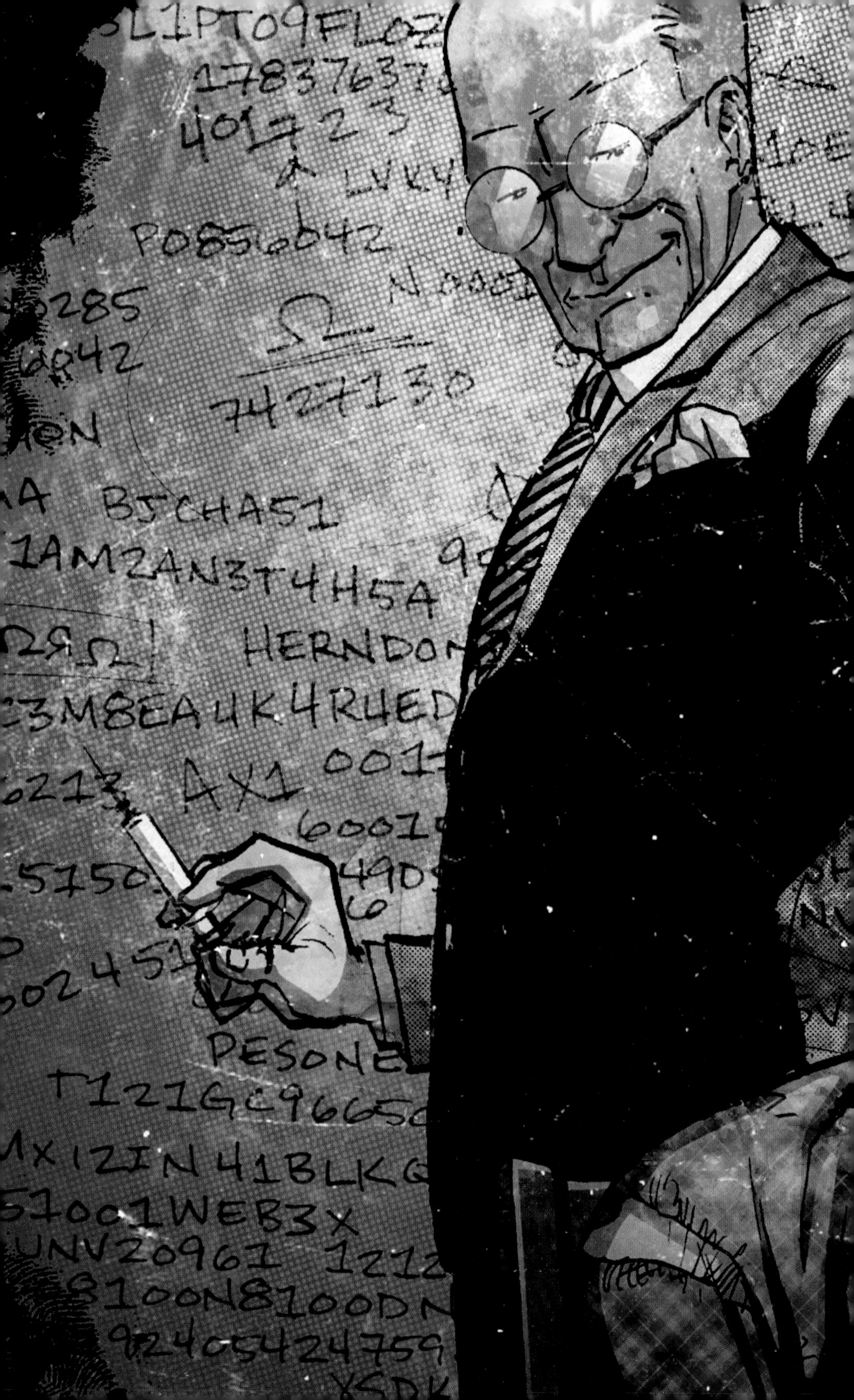